Primary Sources
of Liturgical Theology

Dwight W. Vogel, *Editor*

Primary Sources
of Liturgical Theology

A Reader

A PUEBLO BOOK

The Liturgical Press Collegeville, Minnesota

A Pueblo Book published by The Liturgical Press

Design by Frank Kacmarcik, Obl.S.B.
Cover illustration by Clemens Schmidt

Library of Congress Cataloging-in-Publication Data

Primary sources of liturgical theology : a reader / Dwight W. Vogel, editor.
    p. cm.
    "A Pueblo book."
    Includes bibliographical references and indexes.
    ISBN 0-8146-6178-5 (alk. paper)
    1. Liturgics. I. Vogel, Dwight.
BV176.P75 2000
264—dc21

00-057478

Contents

Preface

Teaching graduate seminars in liturgical theology constantly confronts me with a vast treasury of resources. While I want my students to "dig deep" in their reading, I also want them to develop a sense of the broad range of writings available to them through firsthand encounter with primary sources. In this book, I seek to meet that need.

Several apologies are in order. The first is to my colleagues in the field. None of us will be satisfied with what is here. All of us will identify crucial omissions of seminal contributors to liturgical theology, among them Lambert Beauduin, Louis Bouyer, John Burkhart, Jean Daniélou, Peter Fink, A. G. Hebert, Catherine Mowry LaCugna, and Cyrian Vagaggini. And that does not include the work of persons such as Paul Bradshaw, Nathan Mitchell, Josef Jungmann, and James White, whose contributions to liturgical studies have important implications for liturgical theology. The limitation of length, gently but firmly enforced by the publisher in order to keep this book economically accessible for students, has been a real struggle.

The result may be thought of as a "tasting party" of resources, which brings me to my second apology, this time to the writers (living and dead) whose work is included here. These excerpts are often taken out of their total context (although the introductions seek to provide some sense of that context), and there are parts of the text that have been deleted (although I have sought to maintain the integrity of each entry in the process). Readers should note the omissions signaled by an ellipsis (. . .) in the case of material omitted within a paragraph or asterisks (* * *) in the case of the omission of a paragraph or more. What is left will, I hope, provide a glimpse of the profound contributions made by each writer. The serious student will find the suggestions "for further reading" indispensable, and anyone undertaking an in-depth study of the scholar's work will need to read the original work in its entirety.

A third apology concerns the lack of inclusive or expansive language in some of these articles. For those of us who have a deep commitment to the use of such language, the preponderance of male nouns, pronouns, and images for humanity and for God is deeply disturbing. Yet this reader includes material from early in the century when there was little sensitivity in this area, as well as material from writers who are insistent about the use of traditional trinitarian language. The reader will note that all the material written directly for this volume reflects my commitment to inclusive and expansive language. Readers are encouraged to have compassion for earlier writers and mentally translate the language used so they can appropriate the meaning beyond and behind the language.

These apologies are balanced by expressions of gratitude. First and foremost, I give thanks to God for my colleagues in the liturgical theology seminar of the North American Academy of Liturgy, whose wisdom, support, and friendship are grace to me. I have sought to do this work on your behalf. Without your direct contributions to it, it could not have been birthed. There is a sense of collegiality in the seminar that treats presentations of graduate students and junior scholars with as much respect and affirmation as those made by "giants" in the field, whose presence as peers is a source of joy. My thanks to all those who have written the introduction/commentaries, which are an essential part of this reader: graduate students, junior scholars, and senior mentors in the field. Often this work is across "confessional" lines, a mark of the ecumenical nature of the dialogue in liturgical theology.

I have arranged the articles around nine seminal questions that students of liturgical theology need to engage, an approach suggested to me by my students at Garrett-Evangelical Theological Seminary. However, I expect that my colleagues will rearrange these entries in ways that meet their own pedagogical approaches. To aid in that process, three indices are provided: an alphabetical list of major contributors, a chronological list of major entries by date of original publication, and an index of selected themes.

This work would not have been possible without the support of Garrett-Evangelical Theological Seminary, its president Neal Fisher, and academic dean Jack Seymour. That support has made possible the participation of three outstanding editorial assistants: Barbara

Javore (who coordinated correspondence related to contributions and permissions), Jennifer Dust-Cottrill (who entered the text according to the editorial specifications of the publisher), and Kimberly Anne Willis (who oversaw the preparation of the final manuscript). My friend and colleague, David Himrod, reference librarian for the seminary, provided answers to many questions along the way. The support of Mark Twomey, managing editor of The Liturgical Press, has been invaluable throughout the process. I continue to rejoice in the stimulating collaboration of my colleagues in the liturgical studies doctoral program at Garrett-Evangelical Theological Seminary.

And finally, I say "thank you" to Linda, my life partner for more than forty years, whose love of liturgy and life and me is a continuing sacrament of God's grace.

Dwight W. Vogel

List of Contributors

Lorraine S. Brugh, Evangelical Lutheran Church in America, Valparaiso University

Peter Brunner, German Lutheran Church, University of Heidelberg

Andrew Cameron-Mowat, S.J., Roman Catholic, Hethrop College, London

Odo Casel, O.S.B., Roman Catholic, Abbey of Maria Laach

Louis-Marie Chauvet, Roman Catholic, Priest of the Diocese of Pontoise, France, Institut Catholique de Paris

Anscar J. Chupungco, O.S.B., Roman Catholic, Pontifical Liturgical Institute, Rome

Mary Collins, O.S.B., Roman Catholic, prioress of the Benedictine community, Atchison, Kansas

Jill Y. Crainshaw, Presbyterian, Wake Forest University Divinity School, Winston-Salem, North Carolina

Irénée Henri Dalmais, O.P., Institut Supérieur de Liturgie and Institut Catholique de Paris

Arlo D. Duba, Presbyterian (U.S.A.), University of Dubuque Theological Seminary

Ruth C. Duck, United Church of Christ, Garrett-Evangelical Theological Seminary, Evanston, Illinois

David W. Fagerberg, Roman Catholic, Concordia College, Moorhead, Minnesota

Justo L. González, United Methodist, Hispanic Theological Initiative, Asociación para la Educación Teológica Hispana

Romano Guardini, Roman Catholic, University of Munich

Angelus A. Häussling, O.S.B., Roman Catholic, Salesian's Theological Institute, Benedictbeuern

J. Frank Henderson, Roman Catholic, Edmonton, Alberta, Canada

Mary Catherine Hilkert, O.P., Roman Catholic, Notre Dame University

Lawrence A. Hoffman, Jewish, Hebrew Union College, Jewish Institute of Religion, New York

Paul Waitman Hoon, United Methodist, Union Theological Seminary, New York

Tércio Bretanha Junker, Brazilian Methodist, Faculdade de Teologia da Igreja Metodista do Brasil

Aidan Kavanagh, O.S.B., Roman Catholic, St. Meinrad's Archabbey, Yale Divinity School

Edward J. Kilmartin, S.J., Roman Catholic, Pontifical Oriental Institute, Rome

Gordon W. Lathrop, Evangelical Lutheran Church in America, The Lutheran Theological Seminary, Philadelphia, Pennsylvania

John D. Laurance, S.J., Roman Catholic, Marquette University, Milwaukee, Wisconsin

Ruth A. Meyers, Episcopal Church, Seabury-Western Theological Seminary, Evanston, Illinois

Bruce T. Morrill, S.J., Roman Catholic, Boston College

Gilbert Ostdiek, O.F.M., Roman Catholic, Catholic Theological Union, Chicago

L. Edward Phillips, United Methodist, Garrett-Evangelical Theological Seminary, Evanston, Illinois

David N. Power, O.M.I., Roman Catholic, The Catholic University of America, Washington, D.C.

Gail Ramshaw, Evangelical Lutheran Church in America, La Salle University, Philadelphia

Thomas A. Rand, O.S.L., United Methodist, Summerside United Methodist Church, Cincinnati, Ohio

Roy A. Reed, United Methodist, Methodist Theological School in Ohio

Don E. Saliers, O.S.L., United Methodist, Candler School of Theology, Emory University

Philip James Sandstrom, Roman Catholic, Priest of the Archdiocese of New York, Cathedral Parish of Archdiocese of Malines-Bruxelles, Belgium

Alexander Schmemann, Russian Orthodox, St. Vladimir's Orthodox Theological Seminary

Thomas J. Scirghi, S.J., Roman Catholic, Fordham University

R. Kevin Seasoltz, O.S.B., Roman Catholic, Saint John's Abbey, Collegeville, Minnesota

Laurence Hull Stookey, United Methodist, Wesley Theological Seminary

Byron David Stuhlman, Episcopal Church, Rector, Grace Church, Waterville, New York

Robert F. Taft, S.J., Roman Catholic, Byzantine-Slavonic Rite, Pontifico Istituto Orientale, Rome

Harold Dean Trulear, New York Theological Seminary, Zion Baptist Church & St. Mary's Episcopal Church, Ardmore, Pennsylvania

Evelyn Underhill, Church of England, King's College, London

Dwight W. Vogel, O.S.L., United Methodist, Garrett-Evangelical Theological Seminary, Evanston, Illinois

Jean Jacques von Allmen, Eglise Reformé de Suisse, Protestant Faculty of Theology, Neuchâtel, Switzerland

Geoffrey Wainwright, British Methodist, Duke University, Durham, North Carolina

Robin Knowles Wallace, O.S.L., United Methodist, Methodist Theological School in Ohio

Fritz West, United Church of Christ, United Theological Seminary, New Brighton, Minnesota

Kimberly Anne Willis, O.S.L., United Methodist, Institute for Ecumenical and Cultural Research, Collegeville, Minnesota

Susan K. Wood, S.C.L., Roman Catholic, St. John's University, Collegeville, Minnesota

Joyce Ann Zimmerman, C.PP.S., Roman Catholic, Institute for Liturgical Ministry, Dayton, Ohio

What Is Liturgical Theology?

In the following article I seek to clarify why the chapters in this reader cover the ground they do. Some of my colleagues (who may in fact be teaching—or taking—the course in which you find yourself) are likely to say: "This (or that) chapter is interesting, to be sure, and certainly has something to say about liturgical studies, but it hardly qualifies as liturgical theology."

If they do, listen very carefully: the emphasis they use will be an important clue to the position they are taking. They might be saying: "this isn't *liturgical* theology," meaning "it's theology, all right, but it doesn't really qualify as liturgical theology; rather it's systematic theology, or dogmatic theology, or biblical theology, or something else." Then again, they might be saying: "this isn't liturgical *theology*," meaning "it's about liturgy, all right, but it certainly doesn't qualify as theology." Behind that assertion is an understanding of theology as involving a certain methodology and/or subject matter.

In either case, a concern for careful definition is at stake, and my advice is that you ask some clear and penetrating questions that will help you understand the definitions inherent in their perspective. Not only will you then know more clearly what they are talking about and why they talk the way they do, but it will help you sharpen up your own definitional skills—a valuable and indispensable part of the educational process.

Some of my colleagues (both professors and students) will agree that it is helpful to cast as wide a net as possible, including as much territory as can legitimately be a part of our study. For those of us who share that perspective, however, the challenge of defining "liturgy" and "theology" and "liturgical theology" remains. So sharpen your pencil (or turn on your computer) and have a go at it. What do you think those words mean?

Dwight W. Vogel

Liturgical Theology: A Conceptual Geography

WHAT IS LITURGICAL THEOLOGY?
 Truth is always a quarry hard to hunt,
 and therefore we must look everywhere for its tracks.
 Basil of Caesarea[1]

   In that search, Basil asserts, "the beginning of teaching is speech"
and "words are parts of speech."[2] What then do we mean by the
words "liturgical theology"? That noted philosopher of language,
Humpty Dumpty (of *Alice in Wonderland* fame), contends that words
can mean whatever we want them to mean, so long as we "pay them
enough."[3] The payment, in this instance, is the discipline of careful
exploration, using enough ordinary language so that meaningful
communication can take place. For the words "liturgical theology," it
turns out that "paying them enough" is no simple task. Kevin W.
Irwin observes that neither in the past nor in the present is there an
"agreed-upon meaning" for liturgical theology.[4]

---

   [1]"The Treatise De Spiritu Sancto" (On the Holy Spirit), ch. 1, sec. 3, American edition of *St. Basil: Letters and Select Works,* The Nicene and Post-Nicene
Fathers: second series, vol. 8, originally published in the United States by the
Christian Literature Publishing Company, 1895; rpt ed. (Peabody, Mass.: Hen-
drickson Publishers, Inc., 1994).
   [2]Ibid.
   [3]Lewis Caroll, *Through the Looking Glass* (first published in Great Britain in
1872), ch. 6. The word under discussion is "glory," although the definition of
it as "a nice knock-down argument" is not particularly helpful to our discussion, even if liturgical theologians sometimes engage in them!
   [4]Kevin W. Irwin, "Liturgical Theology," *The New Dictionary of Sacramental
Worship,* ed. Peter Fink (Collegeville, Minn.: The Liturgical Press, 1990) 722.

Yet we persist in using "liturgical theology" as a way to identify books, articles, classes, and seminars. We might say that liturgical theology is what liturgical theologians do. However, that ignores the fact that liturgical theologians do (and talk about) subjects other than liturgical theology and do not always say: "Now I am doing liturgical theology" and "Now I am not." With apologies to Bishop Butler: the words "liturgical theology" should mean what they mean and not another thing. That is not as simple as it sounds.

What is called "liturgical theology" can be examined as a geography of the landscape of a certain kind of human activity. Some liturgical theologians focus their attention on one part of the landscape, some on another. Some use particular filters to make parts of that landscape more apparent, while different filters are used by others. Liturgical theologians will differ in the tools and methods they employ in their work. Rather than looking at one part of the landscape and ignoring the rest, I will seek to identify prominent provinces, noting features that appear across the whole landscape. Mapping the terrain of liturgical theology may enable us to travel into new areas as well as to locate our own "home" in relation to a larger context.

Building on the work of Kevin Irwin,[5] Maxwell Johnson,[6] David Fagerberg,[7] and the discussions of the liturgical theology seminar of the North American Academy of Liturgy, the provinces I want to include on the map are

theology of worship,
liturgy as theology,
theology of liturgy,
theology in liturgy,
theology because liturgy, and
liturgy and life.

Finally, I will return to the question of what ought to be included and what ought to be excluded from the terrain I am mapping.

---

[5]In addition to the previously cited article, see Irwin's *Context and Text: Method in Liturgical Theology* (Collegeville, Minn.: The Liturgical Press, 1994).

[6]Maxwell Johnson, "Liturgy and Theology," *Liturgy in Dialogue: Essays in Memory of Ronald Jasper,* ed. Paul Bradshaw and Bryan Spinks (Collegeville, Minn.: The Liturgical Press, 1995) 203–27.

[7]David W. Fagerberg, *What Is Liturgical Theology?: A Study in Methodology* (Collegeville, Minn.: The Liturgical Press, 1992).

For some liturgical theologians, worship is the continent underlying all other features. But we are immediately confronted with Mr. Dumpty's dictum that we can have a word mean what we want it to mean only if we pay it enough. I want to distinguish between the meaning of the word "worship" and the word "liturgy" because I believe the task of mapping this terrain demands it. However, I must acknowledge that sometimes the words are used interchangeably and that the distinction between them is not self-evident.

Peter Brunner is able to use the German word *Gottesdienst*, reflecting what he calls the "duality" of worship: God's service to humans and humans' service to God.[8] Paul W. Hoon speaks of Christian worship as including both revelation and response.[9] For Hoon and Brunner, God is operative in both dimensions.

For me, the word "worship" implies human response to that which is worshiped, including such elements as prayer and praise, lament and thanksgiving, confession and commitment. These elements may be manifested through ritual expressions, but they are not restricted to those expressions. Praise of God is worship whether or not it is embodied in ritual.

Alexander Schmemann asserts that the capacity for worship is the distinctive mark of our humanity in this classic passage:

"So the only *natural* (and not 'supernatural') reaction of [humanity], to whom God gave this blessed and sanctified world, is to bless God in return, to thank [God], to see the world as God sees it and—in this act of gratitude and adoration—to know, name and possess the world. All rational, spiritual and other qualities of [humanity], distinguishing [us] from other creatures, have their focus and ultimate fulfillment in this capacity to bless God, to know, so to speak, the meaning of the thirst and hunger that constitutes [our lives]. '*Homo sapiens*,' '*homo faber*' . . . yes, but, first of all, '*homo adorans*.' The first, the basic definition of [human beings] is that [we are] priest[s]. [We] stand in the center of the world and unif[y] it in [t]his act of blessing God, of both receiving the world from God and offering it to God—and by filling the world with this eucharist, [we] transform [our] life, the one that [we] receive from the world, into life in God, into communion

[8]See the article by Peter Brunner on pp. 204–12.
[9]Paul W. Hoon, *The Integrity of Christian Worship* (Nashville: Abingdon Press, 1971) 77.

with [God]. The world was created as the 'matter,' the material of one all-embracing eucharist, and [human beings were] created as the priest[s] of this cosmic sacrament."[10]

Worship as a human activity appears in both individual and social expressions. It does not have to be corporate in nature. Liturgy is corporate by definition; worship is not. Liturgy involves ritual action; worship may or may not. Why then include this province in the conceptual geography of liturgical theology?[11] I include it because theologies of worship may recognize that ritual liturgical action is a basic way of "doing" worship.[12] The innate capacity of human beings for worship can be coupled with insights from such fields of study as anthropology, ritual studies, and biogenetic structuralism, which give evidence of the deep human need to express this capacity through ritual. I. H. Dalmais begins his "Theology of the Liturgical Celebration" with a treatment of "the liturgy as social act."[13]

The concept of worship is not restricted to the Christian context and can be open to cross-cultural and inter-religious studies. However, it is possible to do a theology of worship in light of the Christian context. It can be argued that communal response is essential to Christian worship.[14] For those who place liturgy within the conceptual landscape of worship, a theology of worship is a necessary component in understanding liturgical theology.

Few, if any, examples of a strict "theology of worship" approach can be found.[15] The work of Brunner, Hoon, Saliers, Underhill, and

[10]Alexander Schmemann, *For the Life of the World* (New York: St. Vladimir's Seminary Press, 1973) 15. Quoted and adapted for inclusive language by permission.

[11]Fagerberg contends that liturgical rite *per se* is "insignificant to the project" for theology of worship and that theology of worship should not be included in the terrain of liturgical theology. See Fagerberg, *What Is Liturgical Theology?*, 12).

[12]See the discussion in Don Saliers, *Worship as Theology* (Nashville: Abingdon Press, 1994).

[13]See the excerpt from Dalmais on pages 18–20, following.

[14]Note the discussion of corporate worship in Evelyn Underhill, *Worship* (New York: Harper & Brothers, 1937), ch. 5. See excerpt below, pp. 48–50. In her teaching, my colleague Ruth Duck identifies five emphases in theology of worship: ritual, revelation, response, relationship, and rehearsal.

[15]Fagerberg points to Regin Prenter's *Creation and Redemption* (Philadelphia: Fortress Press, 1968) and Vilmos Vajta's *Luther on Worship* (Philadelphia: Muhlenberg Press, 1958). While both books include theology of worship, they include other dimensions of liturgical theology as well.

Schmemann, however, includes explicit treatments of a theology of worship as part of their liturgical theology. Theology of worship may not be so much a "province" on the liturgical theology terrain as an underlying "continent," out of which some expressions of it arise.

LITURGY AS THEOLOGY[16]

The meaning of "liturgy" will be explored in many ways in the articles that follow. Frequently we point to its etymology as "the work of the people," or "work on behalf of the people." Dalmais will speak of liturgy as "worship actually offered in the name of the community, which acknowledges it as its own."[17] One province on the terrain of liturgical theology contends that since the liturgy is a theological act, the celebration of the liturgy is itself liturgical theology.

The term "theology" is sometimes restricted to systematic or dogmatic reflections on the content of belief. When asked what the generative source and basic expression of belief is, however, we may be pointed to the liturgy, the Church's "sustained summons home to God in Christ."[18] The liturgy is our *theologia prima*, our primary theology. Aidan Kavanagh notes that what we usually think of as theology

"is not the very first result of an assembly's being brought by the liturgical experience to the edge of chaos. Rather, it seems that what results in the first instance from such an experience is deep change in the very lives of those who participate in the liturgical act. . . . It is the *adjustment* which is theological in all this. I hold that it is theology being born, theology in the first instance. It is what tradition has called *theologia prima*."[19]

The immediacy of the liturgy as theological act often escapes our notice. It is the nature of primary experience not to be concerned with naming or labeling itself. Yet we are aware that in our corporate worship we are speaking to and about God. We are engaging in sign-acts that manifest and embody the presence of God and transform us.

The nature of this theological act is not restricted to the words we use (whether the language of Scripture, liturgical texts, or congregational

[16]Cf. Robert Taft, "Liturgy as Theology," *Worship* 56 no. 2.
[17]For the complete passage, see page 18, below.
[18]Aidan Kavanagh, *Elements of Rite* (New York: Pueblo Publishing Co., 1982) 47.
[19]Aidan Kavanagh, *On Liturgical Theology* (New York: Pueblo Publishing Co., 1984) 74–5.

song), or the actions we perform, although it is embodied in both of them. Rather, it is the transforming incorporation into the paschal mystery of Christ that we experience.[20] We also reflect upon that experience and its implications, but without the primary experience, the secondary reflections are hollow. The liturgy both manifests and engenders the faith of the Church. It speaks both to us and for us.

Recovery of a sense of liturgy as theology is an important part of the landscape for contemporary liturgical theology. However, I do not believe it should be the only feature on that landscape. Once one begins to talk about primary theology, it becomes secondary theology. These paragraphs are a case in point. The primary experience itself can be enriched and enlivened through reflection and analysis.

Participation in the liturgy involves us in a hermeneutical circle, whether we are aware of it, or name it that, or not. After engaging in the liturgy, we may talk with one another about it. We may read about it. We remember something about it. Indeed, to the extent we were incorporated into its transforming mystery, we are changed by it. All this means that the next time we gather for a liturgy, we are different than we were the last time. Our anticipation, our expectations, our memories, make us different, individually and corporately. All this becomes part of our primary theology, too. Our reflection on and articulation of this dynamic matrix are important for liturgical theology.

It is important to note that such reflections are not to be equated with the liturgical act itself. The description of a work of art such as a painting or musical composition is not that work of art, just as reading the recipe is not a culinary experience. Liturgy as theology reminds us of the aquifer that provides water and nourishment for the various provinces of liturgical theology. It is essential to the quality of life on the terrain, but to restrict liturgical theology to this perspective alone would ignore the features it feeds.[21]

THEOLOGY OF LITURGY

The province of liturgical theology that focuses on theology of liturgy seeks to engage in a theological reflection on "the Church's

[20]See the articles by Odo Casel and Joyce Ann Zimmerman that follow.

[21]My position here is contra that of Fagerberg. See *What Is Liturgical Theology?* p. 12 for the summary of his position and ch. 5 for a fuller articulation of its implications.

act of worship." For Irwin, the focus of this task is expressed specifically as a reflection on "the theological meaning of the liturgy as the actualization of the paschal mystery through an act of proclaiming and hearing the word and/or celebrating the sacramental rituals."[22]

The intended beneficiaries of this reflection vary. (1) Sometimes it is addressed to systematic theology, for which the question "what is the theological significance of the liturgy?" may be explored under its study of ecclesiology. (2) Sometimes it is appropriated by the Church as a basic resource for both catechesis and mystagogy. (3) Sometimes theology of the liturgy is part of the dynamic conversation of liturgical studies, a multi-disciplinary field in its own right. When the liturgy is seen as an inherently sacramental action, it lives in the village of sacramental theology. When sacramental theology is seen as primarily addressing the sacraments, and liturgy as including but not being restricted to the sacraments, sacramental theology lives in the village of liturgical theology. Whatever the village, sacramental and liturgical theology are neighbors.

Theologies of liturgy also vary in scope and focus. (1) They may focus on the theological significance of the liturgy as a whole (for example, the liturgy as transforming incorporation into the paschal mystery as in the articles by Dalmais, Casel, and Zimmerman). (2) They may focus on theological implications inherent in certain parts of the liturgy (as in the articles by Hilkert and Trulear). (3) Theological reflection on dynamics underlying the liturgy may be explored (as in the articles by Lathrop, Ramshaw, and Saliers).

Theology of liturgy also includes a critical component, for in theological reflection on the liturgy, certain aspects of the liturgical event may stand in creative tension or even judgment over others. The liberation themes that now seem so evident in the Magnificat were prayed and sung for centuries before being explicitly identified and appropriated. Once the formation inherent in that prayer is recognized, the implications must be critically explored. This critical exploration is undertaken by Collins, Duck, and, in a different way, by Häussling.

Most of the articles included in this book involve theology of the liturgy in one way or another. The development of liturgical theology in the Euro-North American context has been concentrated in this part of the landscape.

[22]Irwin, "Liturgical Theology," 722.

Another province understands liturgical theology as using liturgy as a source for systematic theology. The liturgical theology seminar of the North American Academy of Liturgy speaks of this approach as "theology informed by liturgy." Just how this should take place depends upon the theologian's interpretation and appropriation of *lex orandi, lex credendi*. In this abbreviated form, its literal meaning is "law of prayer, law of belief."[23] The comma between the two terms does not specify the relationship between the two, and therein lies the challenge for this province of liturgical theology.

The full form of the statement (which can be dated 435–42 C.E.), attributed to Prosper of Aquitane, is *ut legem credendi lex statuat supplicandi* ("the law of prayer grounds the law of belief"). Irwin notes that the original context implies that "the liturgy manifests the Church's faith" and can be "a theological source to the degree that it is founded on Scripture and is the expression of a praying Church." He points out that it is "the fact of the Church's engagement in rites, not just texts only, [that] grounds the articulation of the Church's belief."[24]

Thus, it is much too simplistic to contend that the statement means that the words of the liturgical texts should determine and judge statements of belief. Prosper's point is that the intercessions that are a part of the Good Friday event clearly presume the theological primacy of grace rather than works (contra the Pelagians). Yves Congar asserts that

"the lex orandi is not the liturgy but the evangelical and apostolic precept of praying without ceasing and for all necessities; this entails a belief in the necessity also of grace, which is the lex credendi. Nevertheless, it is true that we can get to know what we are to believe by starting from an order on how to act, but this advantage is something much greater than a mere dogmatic precision; it contains a more interior element. We come to understand many things through prayer and as a result of prayer: such is the case, for example, with God's attributes, by which we invoke him and in doing so enter into a communion with him. A large part of the Church's belief has become known to it through the holy living-out of its faith, hope and love. Thus the liturgy is the privileged locus of Tradition, not only

[23]For a clear and comprehensive analysis, see Kevin Irwin, *Context and Text: Method in Liturgical Theology,* 3–6.

[24]Ibid., 5–6.

from the point of view of conservation and preservation, but also from that of progress and development."[25]

We are left with three possible relationships between theology and liturgy:[26] (1) Liturgy is a source for theological assertions and has priority over them (the patristic period provides examples of this approach). For example, Schmemann sees the theological task as a process that seeks "to grasp the 'theology' as revealed in and through liturgy."[27] (2) Theology has priority over liturgy and should judge the adequacy of liturgical formulations (examples can be found in reformation perspectives and feminist critiques).[28] (3) Liturgy and theology affect and ground each other and exist in a creative and symbiotic relationship.

What is distinctive about this province of liturgical theology is its understanding of theology as systematic or dogmatic in nature. All three approaches seek to identify theological assertions or dynamics present in the liturgy. The categories explored are those of systematic theology. Articulation of the Church's belief is the crucial concern. Aspects of the liturgical theology of Brunner, von Allmen, and Wainright reflect this perspective, and Taft's article is related to it.

THEOLOGY BECAUSE LITURGY: DOXOLOGICAL THEOLOGY

This province is closely identified with the one I have called "theology in liturgy." Some call that province "theology from liturgy" with justification.[29] I have resisted using that terminology, since the province of "theology *because* liturgy" (or "doxological theology," as it is often called) is also "theology *from* liturgy," but in a different sense.

Doxological theology recognizes and articulates the conviction that "the very nature of theology ought to be oriented to praise and the acknowledgment of God in prayer and reflection."[30] Thus, liturgy in

[25]Yves M.-J. Congar, *Tradition and Traditions* (London: Burns & Oates, 1966) 429.

[26]Developed on the basis of the alternatives noted by Irwin, *Context and Text*, 1, and Maxwell Johnson, "Liturgy and Theology."

[27]Alexander Schmemann, "Liturgical Theology, Theology of Liturgy, and Liturgical Reform," *St. Vladimir's Theological Quarterly* (1969) 218. See the analysis of this position by Maxwell Johnson, "Liturgy and Theology," 205–10.

[28]Cf. Maxwell Johnson's analysis of Wainwright's position in "Liturgy and Theology," 210–8. I find Wainwright closer to the third position.

[29]Fagerberg, *What Is Liturgical Theology?*, ch. 3, and Irwin, "Liturgical Theology," 724.

[30]Irwin, "Liturgical Theology," 725.

its broadest and deepest meaning is seen as the generative dynamic for theology. Prosper's claim that "the law of prayer grounds the law of belief" is understood here ontologically. Doxological theology may be grounded in theology of worship, but when the generative dynamic is seen as focused in the liturgy of the Church, it can be understood as a form of liturgical theology.

We noted that in the province of theology in liturgy, specific categories and dynamics from systematic and dogmatic theology are identified, analyzed, and interpreted. In doxological theology, on the other hand, *the entire theological enterprise* is understood to be generated by and reflective of liturgy. Hence, theological activity can take place "because of" liturgy. The liturgical theology of Wainwright illustrates this part of the landscape, and aspects of the theology of Kavanagh, Kilmartin, and Saliers exemplify it.[31]

Citizens of this province hold dual citizenship in systematic theology and liturgical theology. Doxological theology requires that theologizing not only recognize the liturgy as the generative source for theology but also understand liturgy to be the dominant dynamic within it.

LITURGY AND LIFE

The final feature to note in our geography of the continent of liturgical theology is theological reflection on the relationship between liturgy and our lived experience. Irwin points to this by adding *lex agendi* to *lex orandi* and *lex credendi* as dominant concerns for contemporary liturgical theology. He includes reflections on "what is experienced in actual liturgical rites."[32] Questions and concerns from pastoral liturgical theology is part of the work of liturgical theologians.[33]

But liturgical theology is also related to spirituality (see Zimmerman's concluding article in this volume) and ethics (as for Saliers, Phillips, Collins, and Powers). Liturgical theology should finally be not for its own sake (although there is value there, to be sure). Liturgy is an event of the Church, which, as Schmemann teaches us, is "for the life of the world."[34] Not to include it in our geography would be a serious omission.

---

[31]See the treatment of Kavanagh in Maxwell Johnson, "Liturgy and Theology," 218–24.

[32]Irwin, "Liturgical Theology," 725.

[33]For example, see pt. 3 of Gordon Lathrop's *Holy Things: A Liturgical Theology* (Minneapolis: Fortress Press, 1993).

[34]Schmemann, *For the Life of the World.*

BORDER PATROLS AND BORDER CROSSINGS

We cannot escape the question of what ought to be included and what ought to be excluded from the geography I have proposed. There are *"liturgical theologians of the strict observance"* who believe that the borders should be clearly marked and carefully patrolled. For example, if only the province of liturgy-as-theology qualifies as liturgical theology,[35] then other theological activities, however valid in and of themselves, do not qualify. These theologians remind us of the need for careful definition, disciplined methodology, and rigorous reflection.

Others of us are *"liturgical theologians of an evangelical apostolate."* We live in a multi-cultural world and have only begun to realize what that can mean for liturgical theology (see the articles by Chupungco, Trulear, and González). We recognize that this book only includes representatives from a subcontinent of liturgical theology and that further exploration and conversation is needed with the wider community. Even within those limits, we participate in the commerce and communication between a variety of provinces with varying perspectives on the work of liturgical theology. For us, the conceptual geography of the region is ever-expanding and a source of continuing delight and thanksgiving as our own perspectives are enriched. Furthermore, while some of us have a principal residence in one of the provinces, we travel and work in several of them, and our sojourns there enrich our principal perspective.

However, if liturgical theology is what it is and not another thing, what are its borders? I propose that those borders should be confined to two distinguishing characteristics, characteristics that are inherent in the term itself. Liturgical theology must deal with the liturgy and it must be theological in nature. To say more, or to attempt to define terms too precisely, would be to impoverish our geography. At this point, and for the purposes of exploring the geography of liturgical theology, I am content to say: that is all we know, and all we need to know.[36]

FOR FURTHER READING

David W. Fagerberg, *What Is Liturgical Theology?: A Study in Methodology.* Collegeville, Minn.: The Liturgical Press, 1992; Thomas Fisch, ed. *Liturgy and Tradition: Theological Reflections of Alexander Schmemann.* Crestwood, N.Y.: St.

[35]This is the position of David Fagerberg.
[36]Paraphrased from lines 49 and 50 of John Keats (1795–1821), " Ode on a Grecian Urn."

Vladimir's Seminary Press, 1990; Kevin W. Irwin, "Liturgical Theology." *The New Dictionary of Sacramental Worship.* ed. Peter Fink. Collegeville, Minn.: The Liturgical Press, 1990; Kevin W. Irwin. *Context and Text: Method in Liturgical Theology.* Collegeville, Minn.: The Liturgical Press, 1994; Maxwell Johnson. "Liturgy and Theology." *Liturgy in Dialogue: Essays in Memory of Ronald Jasper.* ed. Paul Bradshaw and Bryan Spinks. 203–27. Collegeville, Minn.: The Liturgical Press, 1995; Nathan Mitchell, "Liturgical Theology, Ritual as Reading." *Source and Summit: Commemorating Josef A. Jungmann, S.J.,* ed. Joanne M. Pierce and Michael Downey. Collegeville, Minn.: The Liturgical Press, 1999; Geoffrey Wainwright. *Doxology: The Praise of God in Worship, Doctrine, and Life.* New York: Oxford Univ. Press, 1980.

2

What Is Liturgy?

We could continue our study by asking any of a number of basic questions: what is theology? what is worship? from whose perspective are we asking our questions? whose voices will we be hearing? whose voices are we likely not to hear? All of those questions are important to raise, and you and your colleagues may want to explore them together.

I have chosen to focus our attention on the nature of liturgy. However, we are not asking that question in the way an anthropologist or a historian might ask it (although their answers will be helpful to us). We are asking a *theological* question and are seeking theological perspectives that will help us answer it. By now, it will not surprise you that my definition of theology is a broad one. I want to include language that we speak *to* God (as in prayer and the liturgy) and *about* God (including hymns, teaching and preaching, creeds and "official" church statements, as well as more extended theological reflections). However, I also want to include thinking and speaking that is characterized by *God-consciousness*—to borrow a concept from Frederich Schliermacher. This larger context, out of which the reflections which follow grow, is what makes these writings "liturgical theology."

After an "overview" provided by Dalmais, we turn to three early voices of liturgical theology in the twentieth century who have helped shape the way we think about liturgy. In the brief excerpts from Casel, Guardini, and Underhill we will discover insights that still "speak" to the nature of the worshiping assembly today. We will also catch some "time-bound" ways of speaking and thinking that will remind us that liturgical theology does not stand still.

Philip James Sandstrom

Irénée Henri Dalmais: Encyclopedic Synthesizer

Irénée-Henri Dalmais was born in Vienne, in the department of Isère, in France in 1914. He did his university studies at Lyons, where he obtained a Licence et D.E.S. Lettres—Philosophie. After teaching philosophy in Lebanon from 1935 to 1937, Dalmais joined the Dominicans in their Province of France during the Second World War, making his profession on March 7, 1942, the feast of Saint Thomas Aquinas. Ordained to the priesthood in 1945, after further theological studies at the Saulchoir (where he obtained a doctorate in theology), Dalmais solidified his abiding interest in the worship of the Church in the East as well as the West. He also is Diplômé École Practique des Hautes-Études, Sciences Religieuses.

He produced two volumes at the end of the 1950s that were translated into English: *Initiation à la liturgie* (Desclée De Brouwer, 1958), and *Les liturgies d'Orient* (ed. Fayard, 1959). A revised version of this last book is still in print and used as a general source in French.

From 1956 on he engaged in teaching oriental liturgies and other liturgical subjects at the Institut Supérieur de Liturgie (Institut Catholique de Paris). He is now an emeritus professor at the same institute. In 1966, after the Second Vatican Council, he was appointed as a consultor to the Concilium.

During many years Dalmais spent much time visiting and working in the Middle East (Syria, Lebanon, Egypt, Iran) and in North Africa as well as in India. He is a corresponding member of the Institut Dominicain d'Études Orientales at Cairo, Egypt, and of the Centres de recherches de la Théologie de la Mission. He is also a member of the Comité mixte Catholique-Orthodox en France.

Although Dalmais has not written a great number of books or promoted a new theoretical view of liturgy, he has contributed many articles over the years to journals, reviews, and scholarly collections in several languages. The list of back issues of *La Maison-Dieu*, *La vie spirituelle*, and *Worship*, for example, list numerous contributions and articles. An insatiable reader, he also prepares book reviews, mainly on liturgical and Eastern spirituality topics, for many different magazines.

Dalmais is a man who has set out to know the "Tradition and the traditions" as fully as possible and then to make them known. Knowing well all the various usages of the varied liturgies of the Church, he has an openness to match his synthetic gifts for presentation to his readers. Aside from his active life, he is a living link and contact with all of the great workers for liturgical reform at the end of the nineteenth and during the twentieth centuries. He lives, as he has for most of his Dominican life, at the Convent de St. Jacques, Paris, France.

FOR FURTHER READING

"Divinisation," "Liturgie et la vie spirituelle," "Maxime le Confesseur," "Mission et Missions," "Pâques," and "Sacrements." *Dictionaire de spiritualité*. Paris: Beaushesne, 1933–95; *Eastern Liturgies*. Trans. D. Attwater. *Twentieth Century Encyclopedia of Catholicism*. New York: Hawthorne Books, 1960; "Image, icône, symbole, mystère (aprés la commémoration séculaire de Nicée II)." *La Maison-Dieu* no. 176, 37–53; *Introduction to the Liturgy*. Trans. D. Attwater. *Twentieth Century Encyclopedia of Catholicism*. New York: Hawthorne Books, 1960; "The Liturgy in the First Four Centuries," "The Eastern Liturgical Families," and "Theology of the Liturgical Celebration." *The Church at Prayer*, ed. A. G. Martimort. Trans. Matthew J. O'Connell. Collegeville, Minn.: The Liturgical Press, 1987; "Le mystère de la foi dans l'anaphore de saint Basile." *La Maison-Dieu* no. 191, 45–59.

Irénée Henri Dalmais

The Liturgy as Celebration[1]

1. THE LITURGICAL FACT

The Liturgy as Social Act

Whatever the reasons that led to the universal use of the word
"liturgy," the choice seems especially appropriate as a name for the
complex of actions often called "cultic." As used originally in the
Greek cities, "liturgy" could mean any "public service," but especially services that were costly and were accepted as done in the
name of the city because they were linked to its most vital interests.
In a culture permeated by religious values (as most of the traditional
cultures were), "liturgy" thus understood was predicated first and
foremost of actions expressing the city's relations to the world of divine powers on which it acknowledged itself to be dependent.
"Liturgy" referred, therefore, not to cultic actions of individuals or
private groups but only to those of the organized community, that is,
the entire people, who realized that they shared a single destiny and
a collective memory. In other words, liturgy belonged to what has
sometimes been called a "perfect (or: complete) society." This is why
the name can and even ought to be reserved (as it is in official documents) for the exercise of a worship that is public in the fullest sense,
that is, a worship actually offered in the name of the community,
which acknowledges it as its own.

[1]Excerpted from Irénée Henri Dalmais, "The Liturgy as Celebration," ch. 1,
sec. 3, "Theology of the Liturgical Celebration," *The Church at Prayer*, ed. A. G.
Martimort, trans. Matthew J. O'Connell, vol. 1, "Principles of the Liturgy"
(Collegeville, Minn.: The Liturgical Press, 1987) 233–43.

This situation should make us more aware of the risks involved when the collective psyche is brought into play. In such situations the sense of human companionship reaches a depth rarely achieved elsewhere, for here community can become communion, that is, it can reach a level of intimacy and exchange in which the dialoguing "I" and "thou" become a "we" that is one in heart and mind. At this point there is a great danger that communion may be replaced by a social monolithism or an affective and even sensual rapture, both of which are equally destructive of the inalienable values of the person. It would be presumptuous to think that Christian liturgy is completely free of this danger, but it is doubtless more able than others to overcome it when it remains true to its own nature.

The history of religions—and I am not speaking only of Christianity—displays a doubtless unavoidable tension between the socially organized expression of spiritual values and the call to interiorization and silence that these same values bring with them to an intense degree. These are irreducible components of a genuinely human attitude, and every liturgy must respect them. This is why "liturgy" cannot be viewed solely in terms of "ceremonies." It must be the vehicle of values, it must convey meaning; this implies diversification of the liturgy according to cultural milieu as well as fidelity in expressing the foundational actions that have been handed down in the tradition.

It is through and in gestures that human beings interact with their fellows, and it is through and in gestures that they express their relations with a world that the senses cannot directly grasp. It follows that liturgy, as a complete expression of the involvement of all dimensions of the human being, must be chiefly gestural; it must make discriminating use of the various human gestures in order to bring out their deepest meaning and ritualize them so that once purified of any infrahuman elements still remaining in their secular use, they may become the sensible signs of spiritual realities. This is why all liturgy prefers to use the most basic—one might almost say the most biological—gestures, those in which human beings reveal the deepest needs of their nature and disclose the innermost dynamic of their calling. The first and foremost of these basic gestures is the communal meal. Is it possible to think of a more appropriate sign of the communion attainable by a human group and of the communion that can unite it to the invisible powers, than eating of one and the same food in which the divinity is somehow also given a share? The same can be said of the bath, the first act by which a newborn child is welcomed into the human community, the life-giving immersion in which human beings intuitively realize, long before they can reflectively know it, the extent to which all life on earth has its origin in the womb of the waters. The fact that all Christian liturgies have accepted these two actions as coming from Christ and actualizing his saving work gives these liturgies roots that strike deep into the soil of humanity.

The Liturgy as Symbolic Action

The gestures that the liturgy ritualizes derive their value less from what they are than from what they suggest. Into the field of the visible and sensible they bring realities or values that in themselves are alien to that field. In other words, the liturgy, being the action of a community that draws upon all its available means of expression, constantly makes use of the symbolic character of those means, be they gestures or words. It can be said that in a sense the liturgy functions as play. In play human beings look beyond the immediate, utilitarian purposes of their actions and pass to a level at which actions that in everyday life are simply means acquire a coherence of their own and yield a meaning that delights not only their authors but those who identify with the game as they watch and listen.[2]

The twofold danger of play is that the departure from the conditions of everyday existence that play makes possible may turn into an escape or into a form of self-absorption. The liturgy avoids these two dangers to the extent that it clearly expresses its reference to situations that completely transcend the present limits of the human condition. The gestures and words of the liturgy carry a meaning and an energy that become present and operative every time that the liturgical action is repeated. There is in fact no liturgy that does not more or less explicitly claim to effect what it signifies. This is precisely what distinguishes liturgical action from every other kind of representation. But for that very reason the liturgy is also always in danger of degenerating into magic if it loses sight of its reference to a transcendent reality that human action by itself cannot apprehend. The properly liturgical value of a rite or text is a function of the echoes that the celebration as a whole is able to awaken in the assembly; in other words, it depends on a recognition of the symbolic meaning of the gestures or words.

[2]J. Huizinga, *Homo ludens. A Study of the Play-Element in Culture*, trans. R. F. C. Hull (London: Routledge & Kegan Paul, 1949).

The reason is that symbol cannot be reduced to sign, as people too often tend to think. An object, word, or gesture is a symbol only to the extent that it can be immediately understood as vehicle of a meaning that is greater than its own reality or, more accurately, as being something more and other than it appears to be. It is this material density, this concrete value attached to a thing, that gives symbols their realism and ensures their validity; they also become more capable of conveying the realities of a spiritual world that extends beyond them and transcends them. It is therefore important to preserve the material density of the elements used in the liturgy: baptism is a washing or, better, an immersion in life-giving water; in an anointing the oil ought to penetrate what it touches; the Eucharistic meal implies that the participants eat real bread and that, unless there is some serious obstacle, they drink from the cup.

In addition, symbols are multivalent because the sensible reality used is necessarily deficient in relation to the transcendent reality it symbolizes; in many instances there is even ambiguity. Reason finds satisfaction only in clear and distinct ideas; symbolic thinking, on the other hand, is captivated by the constant fluidity of the themes it evokes. Words alone make it possible to bring into focus the meaning intended, but without eliminating the multivalence proper to symbols, for then symbol would be reduced to allegory; an intuitive, comprehensive grasp of meaning would be replaced by an analysis that makes use only of the processes of logical thought. In the course of its history the Christian liturgy has only too often been the victim of this misunderstanding. Far from bringing simplification or the discard of practices whose meaning is no longer grasped, allegorization most often leads to complication and a concentration on secondary details that multiply and proliferate like suckers and end up choking the essential elements that are the vehicles of the richest symbolic values. But it also can happen, at times, that a symbolism initially not perceived can in this way become coherent and recognizable.

The Liturgy as Sacral Action

Because of its Christian use (which is based on the Septuagint translation of the Bible), the word "liturgy" now has inescapable religious and sacral overtones. It has become a specifically cultic term and retains this cast even when it is used for activities in which any religious reference is deliberately excluded.

"Sacred" is one of those words that all and sundry think they under-stand, but whose content, when an attempt is made to pin it down, proves to be multiform and may even vanish like mist. According to the classic analysis of R. Otto, the sacred is initially experienced as an attitude compounded of fright and attraction *(horrendum et fascinosum)*. It is an ambiguous attitude in that it can be aroused by very different causes and that it tells us nothing in advance about the nature and ob-jective value of these causes. As a result, it is open to very serious aber-rations and very dangerous deviations; recourse to drugs, hypnosis, and all kinds of pseudo-ecstasies has been and continues to be all too common. The sacred therefore requires rectification; it is a basically subjective attitude that arises spontaneously in the human depths prior to any intervention of reason or will.

The "religious," on the contrary, requires human beings to exercise their higher powers in recognition of their dependence on realities that transcend them. Acknowledgment of an objectively transcendent being and its unlimited moral perfection implies a new characteristic of the object, namely, *holiness*. This value was gradually made known through biblical revelation; it emerges with special clarity in Isaiah's inaugural vision of God (Isaiah 6). But it is only the full revelation of the mystery of divine holiness in the person of Christ that enables us to recognize its ultimate effects in human behavior.

At the start, the revelation of divine holiness came through a mani-festation of power in a cultic context. It began in the dazzling vision of the burning bush on Horeb and reached its climax in the theo-phany at Sinai. The sense of the sacred that it elicited was such that death seemed inevitable. At the same time, however, the community found itself turned into a "holy people," empowered now to deal with the holy God and transcend the limitations of secular existence. In this first covenantal liturgy we can see the essential characteristics every liturgy must have if it is not to betray its mission. When Isaiah once again experiences that inaugural theophany, but this time in the explicitly liturgical setting of the sanctuary, he discovers its real meaning: the God to whom all worship in the temple is directed and who is to be the dynamic source of the whole life of the "holy people" is not only an all-powerful being who manifests himself in an explosion of the most fearsome energies of the cosmos; he is also a being of utterly spotless purity and perfection and one who jealously demands uprightness. He requires that the community which is his offer him the total gift of itself, one that excludes any and all self-seeking. The liturgy cannot be reduced to a meticulous observance of rites and a respect for cultic prohibitions; it must have its origin in purified hearts that are completely given to God. Here we have the basis for the personalist requirements of a sacrality that does not betray the vocation proper to human beings.

These requirements were to be made known fully when Christ came and replaced the symbolic presence of God *(Shekinah)* in the secrecy of the Holy of Holies with his actual presence in the incarnation of the divine one who is fully human. At that moment, Christ began the true spiritual worship that consisted in the offering of his own body, which is the new and definitive temple in which the holy God dwells in all his fullness. Christ seemed to be abolishing the sacred by removing the hitherto uncrossable boundary separating creatures—which are profane in themselves—from a divine Beyond. In fact, however, he was bringing the sacred to fulfillment; he was setting human beings free to follow their call to a sacrality consisting of the holiness that alone can provide a solid basis for the dignity of the person. This is why Christians, to the extent that they live in accordance with their dignity as members of the ecclesial body of Christ, must in every act and aspect of their lives offer in Christ the spiritual sacrifice which was foretold by the prophets (Mal 1:11) and to which the Fathers of the Church constantly refer[3] in keeping with the directives of St. Paul (Rom 12:1). Within Christianity a liturgical celebration properly understood can only be the ritualized expression of this spiritual worship in its ecclesial manifestation. All this represents a real revolution of outlook in comparison with normal religious behavior.

It is a revolution because human beings and human groups cannot find in themselves, and express by means completely their own, the final word about their being and destiny. Would it be possible for them to project themselves, hypostasize themselves, in an ideal "I" which they could then worship and in which they would learn to transform themselves by contemplating and imitating it? Any such attempt could only be idolatrous, the idol in this case being the ghostly counterpart that human beings set up for themselves; this counterpart is most often nothing but their own "shadow side" and therefore deserves the anathemas that echo throughout the biblical tradition. The risk of this kind of idolatrous religion is always

---

[3]M. Jourjon, *Les sacrements de la liberté chrétienne selon l'Eglise ancienne* (Rites et symboles 12; Paris: Cerf, 1981) ch. 1.

present, given the concrete condition of human beings, for this is characterized by a self-sufficient turning in on the self that the Christian tradition has always interpreted as the manifestation of a refusal to be open to transcendence.

The danger is especially marked in our time as a result of a deliberate and at times brutal confrontation between, on the one hand, purely human liturgies of the state or of social groups claiming to be the predestined community of the future and, on the other, religious liturgies that find their justification in a living communion with God and in the consciousness of being the expression of a community whose destiny transcends the limitations of history. This opposition is new in the brutal forms that we see it taking in so many places. It could not have come about if two millennia of Christianity had not slowly brought to light the repercussions of the distinction between two levels of reality: the human level with its coherent secular dimensions, and the level proper to holiness of a personal God who is clearly untouched by all the ambiguities inherent in the "sacred," but who also, without losing anything of his transcendence, calls the human race to share his very own life. In this light we are better able to appreciate the multivalence and ambiguities of "natural" liturgies, as well as the confusions in which they have always been to a greater or lesser extent involved and of which even Christian cult has not managed to remain free in every case.

The Liturgical Assembly as Celebration and Feast

The word "celebration" has increasingly come to be seen as the most suitable description of the liturgical action. The development has not been an arbitrary one, for the word has surprisingly rich overtones in the Latin religious language in which it originated. We can see there

"a combination of three factors or circumstances, one or the other of which, however, may be lacking in exceptional cases. The point of departure or occasion for a celebration is usually an important or sensational event *(festivitas, solemnitas)*. The event, whether present or commemorated, then leads to the calling of an assembly, a more or less large and solemn gathering *(conventus, coetus, frequentia)*. This, finally, leads to the festal action *(actio, effectio)*, which is the third constitutive element in a typical celebration. As a rule, the action is communal, comprising the combined activities of many or even of an entire populace and involving the life of society, the family, or the state in one or other manner. Sometimes this action is the reason for the assembly, but in every case it constitutes the celebration in the strict sense. For to celebrate is primarily to do something in common and in a solemn, religious way. This rather complex idea of celebration originates in Latin conceptions but the reality is found among all ancient peoples, Jews as well as Greeks (though the technical language may be missing at times).[4] Everywhere, moreover, in pagan and above all in Jewish thought, the religious element is always an almost inseparable part of all real celebrations, however secular these may appear to be. . . . In Christianity, with its essentially religious and even eschatological outlook, a celebration is always cultic."[5]

The same remarks apply to the feast, which was originally inseparable from a celebration. The word itself suggests a break in the continuity of everyday life. As a result, it has quite natural ties with the idea of the sacred, for the attitude conveyed by the word "sacred" attests that a Beyond has broken into the ordinary life of the human race and into its secular universe, though the Beyond is marked by an ambiguity that will be removed only through the revelation of Holiness. This revelation alone, therefore, will make it possible for the feast to become fully what it strives to be. For if the ordinary passage of time is suspended, the purpose is not to give way to chaos and open the door to every kind of excess. The reason is rather that a Presence has shown itself to human beings. This manifestation calls for their response and also makes the response possible, because it is a gift and a favor. It is in the idea and reality of the festive celebration that the liturgy finds its authentic meaning.

2. THE LITURGY AS ACT OF THE CHURCH

The specific nature of Christian cult depends on that of the assembly that practices it. The Church of Christ sees itself as the people of God in its messianic fulfillment, as a manifestation on earth of the mystery of God the Savior (1 Tim 3:16), and as a community participating in the definitive covenant by which it has pleased God to bind himself to a people he has freely chosen to benefit from the economy of salvation and bear witness to it among the nations.[6] The Church's

[4]The Greek word was *heortē*; the corresponding Latin words were *feria* and *festus*.

[5]J. Hild, "Notion et structure classique d'une célébracion," *La Maison-Dieu. Revue de pastorale liturgique (LMD)* no. 20 (1949) 114–5.

[6]See Vatican Council II, *Lumen gentium* (Dogmatic Constitution on the Church) ch. 2.

liturgy has for its function, then, not only to offer God the worship due to him but also to make this mystery of salvation (the characteristics of which remain to be determined) present and active among human beings.

* * *

It follows from all this that the liturgy has a twofold function in the Church: to constitute the Church and to express the Church. The first is the work chiefly of the sacramental liturgy; the second, that of the liturgy of praise, which follows the rhythms of time. The eucharistic liturgy is par excellence the sacrament of the ecclesial mystery: "a sign and instrument, that is, of communion with God and of unity among all men."[7] In liturgical action human beings exercise fully the power given to them through baptism, namely, to be active members of a community in which the reign of God is proclaimed and begun. Consequently, the Christian liturgy has no place for passive spectators.[8] As soon as the liturgical function begins, all who take part in it are in the official service of God as persons who have been regenerated in the innermost depths of their being and have been led as by a new act of creation into the divine world of which they are now citizens.

[7]*Lumen gentium,* 1.

[8]Vatican Council II, *Sacrosanctum concilium* (The Constitution on the Sacred Liturgy) Latin text: *(VSC)* 11, 14, etc., *Documents on the Liturgy 1963–1979. Conciliar, Papal, and Curial Texts,* ed. International Commission on English in the Liturgy (Collegeville, Minn.: The Liturgical Press, 1982).

Kimberly Anne Willis

Odo Casel: Reclaiming the Mystery in Liturgy

Odo Casel (1886–1948), a pivotal figure in the modern liturgical movement, was born in Germany. While studying classics at Bonn, he met Benedictine Ildefons Herwegen. Under his influence Casel entered the Abbey of Maria Laach and was professed in 1907. Casel wrote his thesis on the eucharistic teaching of Justin Martyr and earned a doctorate from Bonn in 1913. In 1919, after further study at Maria Laach and Rome, he earned a second doctorate in philosophy from Bonn, writing on the mystical silence of the Greek philosophers. In 1921 Casel joined A. Baumstark and R. Guardini as an editor for the *Jahrbuch für Liturgiewissenschaft*. The following year Casel left Maria Laach to serve as the spiritual director of a Benedictine convent at Herstelle. This cloistered setting provided him the opportunity for further study and reflection on mystery theology. After carrying the paschal candle into the darkened sanctuary at Herstelle during the Easter Vigil of 1948, Casel collapsed just prior to chanting the *Exultet*. He died early Easter morning.

His primary contribution to liturgical theology is his development of "mystery theology." Mystery for Casel does not refer to what is innately inaccessible to humanity but rather to that which is *only* accessible through participation in sacred actions within the community of faith. Making reference to Scripture, patristic writings, and ancient liturgies, Casel develops this mystery theology around three foci: (1) God as "infinitely holy, distant, and unapproachable," (2) Jesus Christ, who comes to us through grace as the invisible Godhead-made-flesh, and (3) the sacred actions, especially the Eucharist, that render present the redemptive acts of Jesus Christ.

Within this framework we find three of Casel's major contributions to liturgical theology. First, the redemptive acts of Jesus Christ are made present in the sacraments. The sacraments do not merely convey grace but rather contain the redemptive acts from which grace emerges. Second, liturgy involves action on the part of believers. Since the sacraments convey the redemptive acts of Christ, Casel strongly advocates that believers actively encounter Christ through their participation. Inward transformation emerges as a result of participation in the liturgy. Third, liturgy innately involves the corporate community. This emphasis was designed by Casel specifically to address the rise of individual pietism, which leads to a spirituality of "rugged individualism."

Prior to the excerpt that follows, Casel proposes that the mystery of Christ we enter through liturgy is the central foundation of Christianity. This depends upon reclaiming the ancient understanding of the liturgy as truly *leitourgia*. Rather than being passive bystanders we are active participants ripe for inward transformation. He then surveys the dual functions of symbols that both point to and hide the mystery of Jesus Christ. When we participate in the liturgy of the Church, the veil of symbols is lifted and the mystery of Christ is made a present reality.

FOR FURTHER READING

The Mystery of Christian Worship. Ed. Burkhard Neuneuhser, with an introduction by Aidan Kavanagh. New York: Crossroad Publishing Co., 1999; *Die Liturgie als Mysterienfeier.* Freiburg: Herder, 1922; *Mysterium der Ekklesia: Von der Gemeinshaft aller Erlösten in Christus Jesus.* Mainz: Grünewald, 1961; *Das christliche Opfermysterium: Zur Morphologie and Theologie des eucharistischen Hochgebetes.* Graz: Verlag Styria, 1968; *Jarbuch für Liturgiewissenschaft.* Munster, 1921–41.

Odo Casel

Mystery and Liturgy[1]

Christ's mystery in God's revelation in the saving action of his incarnate Son and the redemption and healing of the Church . . . continues after the glorified God-man has returned to his Father, until the full number of the Church's members is complete; the mystery of Christ is carried on and made actual in the mystery of worship. Here Christ performs his saving work, invisible, but present in Spirit and acting upon all men of goodwill.[2] It is the Lord himself who acts this mystery; not as he did the primeval mystery of the Cross, alone, but with his bride, which he won there, his Church;[3] to her he has now given all his treasures; she is to hand them on to the children she has got of him. Whoever has God for his father must, since the incarnation, have the Church for his mother.[4] As the woman was formed in paradise from the side of the first Adam, to be a helpmate, like to him,[5] the Church is formed from the side of Christ fallen asleep on

---

[1]Excerpted from Odo Casel, "Mystery and Liturgy," part iii, ch. 2, "The Mystery of Worship in the Christian Cosmos," in part 1, "The Christian Mystery," *The Mystery of Christian Worship and Other Writings,* ed. Burkhard Neunhauser (London: Darton, Longman & Todd, 1962; Regensburg: Verlag Friedrich Pustet, 1932). See the Crossroad's edition of 1999, 38–47.

[2]Luke 2:14.

[3]Eph 5:14ff.

[4]Cf. Cyprian, *de Unitate Ecclesiae,* 5f. "We are born of the Church, drink her milk, are enlivened by her Spirit. . . . She keeps us for God, leads those she had born to his kingdom. The man who cuts himself off from the Church and joins an adulteress is separated from the Church's promise. He will not attain Christ's reward, if he deserts Christ's Church. He is a stranger, an uninitiate, a foreigner. No one can have God for his father who does not have the Church for his mother."

[5]Gen 2:18.

29

the cross to be his companion and helper in the work of redemption. At the same time, the fathers teach us[6] the mysteries flow in water and blood from the Lord's side; the Church was born from Christ's death-blood and the mystery with it; Church and mystery are inseparable. This is the last ground for the fact that the mystery of worship becomes liturgy.

The Greek word for Liturgy[7] originally meant the act of an individual in the service of the city; for example fitting up a ship for war, or sponsoring a choir for the tragedies in honor of Dionysus; service generally, and in particular the service of God in public worship. In this sense it is used by Old and New Testament. Thus, Zacharias, the father of John the Baptist, performed his liturgy in the temple.[8] St. Clement of Rome speaks in his letter to the Corinthians (40 ff.) of the liturgy of the Old Testament which he puts before them as the model for the service of the New. And if in the New Testament the whole of life is sacred and a service of God, the fathers' directions have particular application to the common worship of the Christian community. . . . Christ's sacrifice is not a liturgy in the old, ritual sense, but plain and noble reality, the ultimate and greatest fulfillment of what the old covenant had given in type. But when the Church carries out the mystery of Christ in her own mystery of worship, in ritual, forms and expressions of the old covenant find a new and higher kind of reality, and fulfillment in the new rites. Here a liturgy arises which is first of all an exterior form, but does not carry "a foreshadowing of things to come";[9] rather it is the grace-filled reality, the redemption itself.

[6]As one of many we present Augustine's *Tractatus in Joannem* 120.2: "It is a pregnant word the evangelist has used; he does not say the soldier thrust into his side, or wounded him in his side, or anything else, but that he opened his side. Thus, so to speak, the doors of life were to be opened through which the Church's mysteries proceed, without which no one goes into the life which is true life. This blood was poured out for the remission of sins, this water was preparation for salvation's cup; it made the cleaning water and the good drink. An image of it was the door which Noah made in the side of the ark; through it the animals were to enter, which were not to die in the flood: they signified the Church. Therefore the first woman was made from the side of a sleeping man and called life, and mother of the living. She signified a great good thing, before the great woe of sin. And the second Adam fell asleep here on the Cross, with head bowed, so that his spouse might be formed from what flowed out of his side . . . ."

[7]Λειτουργία—old Attic ληϊτουργία: λάος, ἔργον: public work, public service.
[8]Luke 1:23.
[9]Heb 10:1.

When we place the words "mystery" and "liturgy" side by side, and take mystery as mystery of worship, they will mean the same thing considered from two different points of view. Mystery means the heart of the action, that is to say, the redeeming work of the risen Lord, through the sacred actions he has appointed; liturgy, corresponding to its original sense of "people's work," "service," means rather the action of the church in conjunction with this saving action of Christ's. We saw above, that Christ and the church work together inseparably in the mystery; but we can nonetheless characterize mystery as more the act of the bridegroom, and liturgy the act of the bride, without thereby making too great a division. For when the Church performs her exterior rites, Christ is inwardly at work in them; thus what the church does is truly mystery. Yet it is still proper to use the term liturgy in a special fashion for the Church's ritual action. And this gives rise to the question, how has the mystery of the new covenant become liturgy?

The deepest ground for it lies in the fact we have already mentioned, that Christ has given the mysteries to his Church. . . . The content, and so the essential form of the mysteries have been instituted and commanded by our Lord himself; he has entrusted their performance to the Church, but not laid down to the last detail what is necessary or desirable for a communal celebration. By leaving the Spirit to his Church, he has given her the ability as well, to mint inexhaustible treasure from the mystery entrusted to her, to develop it and to display it to her children in ever new words and gestures. Her bridegroom's love moves her to make of his gifts a praise to his love; her motherly goodness leads her to explain it to her children with all care, so that they may make it their own. So the liturgy, born of her fullness of the Spirit, and love, becomes a work of beauty and wisdom.

It would be worthwhile to make clear this development of mystery into liturgy, with examples. But we must be content to point out some of the main lines of development. The Lord demanded a rebirth for entry into his kingdom; the natural man cannot reach God unless he first be changed. The old man must die, the new man, begotten out of God, must rise. "If a man be not begotten of water and *pneuma*, he cannot enter heaven."[10] *Pneuma* is the breath of God, from which supernatural life flows; it is God himself,[11] and his life dwelling in the

[10]John 3:5.
[11]John 4:24.

31

new man. This word shows clearly that it is not a change of will that makes the Christian, but a completely new being, a "sharing in God's being"[12] as St. Peter says: we are then in the pure realm of grace and the invisible life of God. But the Lord says that the new man must be born again of water; thus the mystery of worship arises; for in the realm of God's supernatural action this birth from water can only be the exterior and visible expression of the inward, real birth from *pneuma*. It has therefore no natural worth of its own, but only symbolic value; this symbolic value is what the Lord says is absolutely necessary. For without this exterior act we could not recognize God's act. The plain, objective, sensible, tangible act of plunging into water is the pledge for the reality of God's new begetting; at the same time the community gives the necessary witness that a new member has been added to it. It would be an error to think that it was enough to have a dumb dipping into water to form a picture of God's grace: water, matter from below, has no capacity for that. It must be complemented by something higher, formed and fashioned by it: the Spirit which comes from above. But what is better suited to express Spirit than the lightness and refinement of the Word, as the Lord speaks of it in the third chapter of St. John's Gospel? It gives motion to what thought would express; the ancients called it *Logos*, spirit-shaped, and thence it was so connected with *pneuma* that the two words are often interchanged. The element of sense and tangibility which the word indicated is clear. The fullness of the mystery comes from both:

"take away the word, and what is water except mere water. Word comes to the water, and the *mysterium* is there, itself like a word to be seen. Where does water have so great a power that when it touches the body, it should wash the heart? All of that from the mere word."[13]

The Lord called for a rebirth: the death of the old man. He himself showed us how it was to be done by dying on the cross and rising for God. Christians must be plunged into this death and resurrection, so that Christ's life, the life of the Trinity, revealed through him in the new alliance, might dwell in them. Therefore the candidate is

[12] 2 Pet 1:4.

[13] Augustine, *Tractatus in Joann*, 80.3, cf. 15.4. The translation "Word" does not give the full sense of λόγος; in later times this sentence of Augustine's was misused to make the sacrament a mere kind of sermon. This would have been impossible if there had been a proper understanding of λόγος—*verbum*.

stripped bare, as God made the first man, and as the second Adam hung on the cross.[14] The old man is to die and a wholly new one to come out of the waters. The name of the Trinity is spoken over him; according to ancient Christian faith this meant that the whole power of the present Godhead came down upon this man and fashioned him anew by grace to God's own likeness. This plunging into Christ's death, and resurrection with him to God's life, as the words of Christ in St. John's Gospel (chapter 2) describe it, is approved by St. Paul as the meaning of baptism in his deep discourse in Romans (6). An extraordinarily rich store of meaning is contained in the simple words which Matthew uses to tell of baptismal institution: "go out, then, and teach all peoples to be disciples, baptizing them in the name of the Father and the Son and the Holy Spirit, teaching them to observe all things which I have entrusted to you."[15] How simply this command is to be carried out is related in the story of the chamberlain's baptism by Philip.[16] They came to water, and the eunuch said, "What is to keep me from baptism?" Both go into the water, the eunuch is put under, and made a Christian. Here we see the mystery in its simplest form, as it had to be under the circumstances.

With deep understanding and love the Church has gradually expanded this simple rite and formed it into a rich service, without neglecting the mystery-center. All the variety of texts, rites, and objects only serve to express the one content and do God honor, to bring it as close as possible to all the faithful.

* * *

The proper content of the mystery is given by the actions and words which the Lord has himself laid down. Still, he did not intend to create something completely new, to teach or fashion a new salvation. He used the age-old forms mankind had always known, changing them and improving them. The idea and even the form of some kind of baptism is a live thing among most of mankind, when purification from sin and passage into a new and holier life is to be expressed and realized. In particular the exterior rites and the objects used, because they are bound up with the natural movements of life and the things nature makes, are already, to a high degree, settled;

[14]Cyril of Jerusalem, *Mystagogical Catechesis*, 2.2.
[15]Matt 28:19.
[16]Acts 8:26.

water is water, whether it is used for natural rites of cleansing or highly elaborate rituals. The word is freer and more mobile; but it, too, is bound up with a language as it has grown to be. For his revelation God uses the word of human speech; it is thus that men are to understand him. The liturgy, too, uses human expressions and human formulae to make the mystery of God known. For the texts of its celebrations there is an extraordinary pattern in the Word of God in Scripture; here the Holy Spirit itself proclaims the gospel in the tongues of men, but with the power of God. Much has passed unchanged from the Scripture into the liturgy, taking on a new form, a new dimension; from mere writing it has gone back to its first life.[17]

* * *

The "plenitude of time"[18] when Christianity came into the world was peculiarly well-suited to give form to the liturgy. It was the mark of the entire ancient world that it had shaped the indwelling symbolism of the natural world into an elaborate yet simple language; this was particularly true of religious forms, and the mysteries we have just been speaking of. It was a custom in antiquity to anoint oneself after a bath with fragrant oil, for strength and beauty. The church has made this custom a rite of the new life by anointing the baptized, for an image of the sweet odor of the Spirit. Another custom was for a newborn child to take milk, mixed with honey. In many mysteries the "newborn" received a cup of sweet milk: in just the same way, the Christians give their newly-begotten in Christ a drink of milk and honey; St. Peter tells the young Christians, that like newborn children, they are to feel longing for the Spirit's milk, so that they may grow in salvation.[19] It was similar with clothing. In the Greco-Roman world, clothing was not a casual or indifferent matter; with a new garment went a new manhood. In the mysteries a garment or a sign of the God was put on, and the initiate became that god. In connection with these customs, Paul cries out, "all of you who have been baptized in Christ, have put on Christ";[20] in Easter week the church sings this of the baptized who stand about the altar in their white clothing. This last example shows us once more that some customs

[17]Cf. Ildefons Herwegen in *Lit. Zeitschrift* 3 (1930–31) 8ff.
[18]Gal 4:4; Eph 1:10.
[19]1 Pet 2:2.
[20]Gal 3:27.

which signify a mystical uniting with the godhead, were particularly well-appointed to serve the Christ-mysticism of the liturgy. Thus the age-old idea of representing the embodiment of divine strength with food and drink is brought up to its highest pitch of reality by the Eucharist: a real meal with God, representing our deepest union with the god-man and rendering it fact, as the Lord himself says of it in John 6.

In these ways the whole of mankind, the whole creation has "done service to the mysteries" as the blessing of the water in the Roman Ritual says of it.[21] Similarly different elements make their own contributions, as do different peoples, races, and ages. Christendom, then, is Catholic, common to mankind; despite all unity in faith and moral teaching, it can and must express itself in a variety of ways. The liturgical forms of the sober, serious, lapidary Roman is one thing; the mystical depth and warmth of the orientals, the agile-minded, poetical Gauls, the dreamy and passionate Celts, or the cloudy, emotional Germans quite other things—to name only a few currents. Every people has expressed its peculiarities in the liturgy, and made of them a sacrifice to God.[22]

But even within the one Church different conditions have taken changing roles in the development of the liturgy. The clergy's part was a leading one, but laymen, too, have contributed with poetry, music, and the other arts; the liturgy of the seculars was not that of the monks, and the liturgy of cathedrals not that of village churches.

The whole church, therefore, and all conditions of men in her have worked together, and shaped the liturgical ornaments of the mystery, each man in his way, each according to his own *charisma*, all on the ground of their inner sharing in the mysteries.

[21]*Creatura tua mysteriis tuis serviens.*
[22]A. Baumstark, *The Growth of the Liturgy* (Mowbray, 1957).

Andrew Cameron-Mowat

Romano Guardini: Faith, Wisdom and Experience for Tomorrow's Church

Romano Guardini, one of the most important Roman Catholic theologians of this century and an inspiration to many in the modern liturgical movement, was born in 1885 in Verona, Italy, and grew up in Mainz, Germany, from 1886. Following education in other fields he studied theology at the University of Tübingen. Several years later he entered the seminary in Mainz and was ordained in 1910. A Ph.D. in theology followed (1915). After further study Guardini taught in Berlin from 1923 until 1939 and then at the University of Munich from 1948 until his death in 1968 in a specially created position, one to which Karl Rahner was subsequently appointed.

Guardini's courses were famous for their profundity and breadth of knowledge. During his life he spent much of his time when not in the classroom undertaking various forms of pastoral work with a special regard for preaching. His reputation as an orator, teacher, preacher, man of spiritual wisdom and prayer was legendary.

Out of the enormous number of books (over seventy) and articles (over one hundred) published by Guardini, his importance is perhaps most clearly shown by two of these: *The Spirit of the Liturgy* and *The Lord,* reprinted numerous times and in several languages. Present at the inaugural German Liturgical Conference in 1950, he also worked with the preparatory commission on the liturgy for the Second Vatican Council. He was held in high regard by most theologians and bishops at the time.

Guardini is justifiably famous for several aspects of his liturgical theology. By employing insights from his study of anthropology, he is able to place the spirituality of worship at the center of what it means to be fully human. His contribution to liturgical theology lies in his ability to incorporate a deep spiritual and pastoral awareness of the achievements of the human condition along with its stresses and subsequent failures, from which he shows the importance of liturgy, through which come celebration, reconciliation, and restoration. One who is filled with God's Spirit can respond to the call of grace and to the fruit of prayer in action.

For anyone seeking theological enlightenment in preparation for the postmodern era, the writings of Guardini are an excellent starting point. *The Spirit of the Liturgy* was published in 1918 as the first in the series of liturgical works, *Ecclesia Orans*, at the request of the abbot of Maria Laach, Ildefons Herwegen. Through this and other writings, including *Meditations Before Mass*, *The Church and the Catholic*, and *Sacred Signs*, Guardini proclaims the importance of liturgy as the primary place at which people come together to pray. His ideas were to be followed and expanded by other theologians, including Congar, Kavanagh, Saliers, and Lathrop. Vatican II's stress on the importance of full participation in liturgy finds its origin (at least in part) in his work.

At the present time there are indications of a tendency to reassess the legacy of Guardini's thought and to oversimplify his achievement. He does not emphasize the glory of mystery at the expense of the needs and experiences of the world. Quite the reverse. "The Playfulness of the Liturgy," from *The Spirit of the Liturgy*, reminds us that the most effective celebration takes place within the context of the human condition in all its frailty, humanity, and true sense of joy; we come before the Lord with the innocence of the child loved by God.

FOR FURTHER READING
The Spirit of the Liturgy. New York: Crossroad, 1998; *The Essential Guardini*. Ed. Heinz R. Kuehn. Chicago: Liturgy Training Publications, 1997; *The Art of Praying: The Principles and Methods of Christian Prayer*. Sophia Institute Press, 1995; *The Lord*. Chicago: Regnery Publishing Inc., 1996.

Romano Guardini

The Playfulness of the Liturgy[1]

Grave and earnest people, who make the knowledge of truth their whole aim, see moral problems in everything, and seek for a definite purpose everywhere, tend to experience a particular difficulty where the liturgy is concerned.[2] They incline to regard it as being to a certain extent aimless, as superfluous pageantry of a needlessly complicated and artificial character. . . . The liturgy tends to strike people of this turn of mind as—to use the words which are really most appropriate—trifling and theatrical.

The question is a serious one. It does not occur to everyone, but in the people whom it does affect it is a sign of the mental attitude which concentrates on and pursues that which is essential. It appears to be principally connected with the question of purpose.

That which we call purpose is, in the true sense of the word, the distributive, organizing principle which subordinates actions or objects to other actions or objects, so that the one is directed towards the other, and one exists for the sake of the other. That which is subordinate, the means, is only significant insofar as it is capable of serving that which is superior, the end. The purpose does not infuse a spiritual value into its medium; it uses it as a passage to something

[1]Excerpted from Romano Guardini, "The Playfulness of the Liturgy," *The Spirit of the Liturgy* (London: Sheed & Ward, 1930). Originally published as *Vom Geisst der Liturgie* in 1918.
[2]In what follows the writer must beg the reader not to weigh isolated words and phrases. The matter under consideration is vague and intangible, and not easy to put into words. The writer can only be sure of not being misunderstood if the reader considers the chapter and the general train of thought as a whole.

else, a thoroughfare merely; aim and fulcrum alike reside in the former. From this point of view, every instrument has to prove in the first place whether, and in the second to what extent, it is fitted to accomplish the purpose for which it is employed. This proof will primarily be headed by the endeavor to eliminate from the instrument all the nonessential, unimportant, and superfluous elements. It is a scientific principle that an end should be attained with the minimum expenditure of energy, time, and material. A certain restless energy, an indifference to the cost involved, and accuracy in going to the point, characterize the corresponding turn of mind.

* * *

If we want to do justice to the whole question, we must shift our angle of vision. The conception of purpose regards an object's center of gravity as existing outside that object, seeing it lie instead in the transition to further movement, i.e., that towards the goal which the object provides. But every object is to a certain extent, and many are entirely, self-sufficient and an end in itself—if, that is, the conception can be applied at all in this extensive sense. The conception of meaning is more adaptable. Objects which have no purpose in the strict sense of the term have a meaning. This meaning is not realized by their extraneous effect or by the contribution which they make to the stability or the modification of another object, but their significance consists in their being what they are. Measured by the strict sense of the word, they are purposeless, but still full of meaning.

Purpose and meaning are the two aspects of the fact that an existent principle possesses the motive for, and the right to, its own essence and existence. An object regarded from the point of view of purpose can be seen to dovetail into an order of things which comprehends both it and more beyond it; from the standpoint of meaning, it is seen to be based upon itself.

* * *

When life lacks the austere guidance of the sense of purpose it degenerates into pseudo-aestheticism. But when it is forced into the rigid framework that is the purely purposeful conception of the world, it droops and perishes. The two conceptions are interdependent. Purpose is the goal of all effort, labor and organization; meaning is the essence of existence, of flourishing, ripening life. Purpose and meaning, effort and growth, activity and production, organization and creation—these are the two poles of existence.

The life of the Universal Church is also organized on these lines. In the first place, there is the whole tremendous system of purposes incorporated in the Canon Law, and in the constitution and government of the Church. Here we find every means directed to the one end, that of keeping in motion the great machinery of ecclesiastical government. The first-mentioned point of view will decide whether adjustment or modification best serves the collective purpose, and whether the latter is attained with the least possible expenditure of time and energy.[3] The scheme of labor must be arranged and controlled by a strictly practical spirit.

The Church, however, has another side. It embraces a sphere which is in a special sense free from purpose. And that is the liturgy. The latter certainly comprehends a whole system of aims and purposes, as well as the instruments to accomplish them. It is the business of the Sacraments to act as the channels of certain graces. This mediation, however, is easily and quickly accomplished when the necessary conditions are present. The administration of the Sacraments is an example of a liturgical action which is strictly confined to the one object. Of course, it can be said of the liturgy, as of every action and every prayer which it contains, that it is directed towards the providing of spiritual instruction. This is perfectly true. But the liturgy has no thought-out, deliberate, detailed plan of instruction. In order to sense the difference it is sufficient to compare a week of the ecclesiastical year with the Spiritual Exercises of St. Ignatius. In the latter every element is determined by deliberate choice, everything is directed towards the production of a certain spiritual and didactic result; each exercise, each prayer, even the way in which the hours of repose are passed, all aim at the one thing, the conversion of the will. It is not so with the liturgy. The fact that the latter has no place in the Spiritual Exercises is a proof of this.[4] The liturgy wishes to teach, but not by means of an artificial system of aim-conscious educational influences; it simply creates an entire spiritual world in which the soul can live according to the requirements of its nature. The difference resembles that which exists between a gymnasium, in which every

[3]Even when the Church is considered from its other aspect, that of a Divine work of art. Yet the former conception is bound to recur in this connection.

[4]The Benedictines give it one, but do so in an obviously different system of spiritual exercises to that conceived by St. Ignatius.

detail of the apparatus and every exercise aims at a calculated effect, and the open woods and fields. In the first everything is consciously directed towards discipline and development, in the second life is lived with Nature, and internal growth takes place in her. The liturgy creates a universe brimming with fruitful spiritual life, and allows the soul to wander about in it at will and to develop itself there. The abundance of prayers, ideas, and actions, and the whole arrangement of the calendar are incomprehensible when they are measured by the objective standard of strict suitability for a purpose. The liturgy has no purpose, or, at least, it cannot be considered from the standpoint of purpose. It is not a means which is adapted to attain a certain end—it is an end in itself. This fact is important, because if we overlook it, we labor to find all kinds of didactic purposes in the liturgy which may certainly be stowed away somewhere, but are not actually evident.

When the liturgy is rightly regarded, it cannot be said to have a purpose, because it does not exist for the sake of humanity, but for the sake of God. In the liturgy, man is no longer concerned with himself; his gaze is directed towards God. In man it is not so much intended to edify himself as to contemplate God's majesty. The liturgy means that the soul exists in God's presence, originates in Him, lives in a world of divine realities, truths, mysteries and symbols, and really lives its true, characteristic and fruitful life.[5]

* * *

In the earthly sphere there are two phenomena which tend in the same direction: the play of the child and the creation of the artist.

The child, when it plays, does not aim at anything. It has no purpose. It does not want to do anything but to exercise its youthful powers, pour forth its life in an aimless series of movements, words and actions, and by this to develop and to realize itself more fully; all of which is purposeless, but full of meaning nevertheless, the significance lying in the unchecked revelation of this youthful life in thoughts and words and movements and actions, in the capture and expression of its nature, and in the fact of its existence. And because

[5]The fact that the liturgy moralizes so little is consistent with this conception. In the liturgy the soul forms itself, not by means of deliberate teaching and the exercise of virtue, but by the fact that it exists in the light of eternal Truth, and is naturally and supernaturally robust.

it does not aim at anything in particular, because it streams unbroken and spontaneously forth, its utterance will be harmonious, its form clear and fine; its expression will of itself become picture and dance, rhyme, melody, and song. That is what play means; it is life, pouring itself forth without an aim, seizing upon riches from its own abundant store, significant through the fact of its existence. It will be beautiful, too, if it is left to itself, and if no futile advice and pedagogic attempts at enlightenment foist upon it a host of aims and purposes, thus denaturizing it.

Yet, as life progresses, conflicts ensue, and it appears to grow ugly and discordant. Man sets before himself what he wants to do and what he should do, and tries to realize this in his life. But in the course of these endeavors he learns that many obstacles stand in his way, and he perceives that it is very seldom that he can attain his ideal.

It is in a different order, in the imaginary sphere of representation, that man tries to reconcile the contradiction between that which he wishes to be and that which he is. In art he tries to harmonize the ideal and actuality, that which he ought to be and that which he is, the soul within and nature without, the body and the soul. Such are the visions of art. It has no didactic aims, then; it is not intended to inculcate certain truths and virtues. A true artist has never had such an end in view. In art, he desires to do nothing but to overcome the discord to which we have referred, and to express in the sphere of representation the higher life of which he stands in need, and to which in actuality he has only approximately attained. The artist merely wants to give life to his being and its longings, to give external form to the inner truth. And people who contemplate a work of art should not expect anything of it but that they should be able to linger before it, moving freely, becoming conscious of their own better nature, and sensing the fulfillment of their most intimate longings. But they should not reason and chop logic, or look for instruction and good advice from it.

The liturgy offers something higher. In it man, with the aid of grace, is given the opportunity of realizing his fundamental essence, of really becoming that which according to his divine destiny he should be and longs to be, a child of God. In the liturgy he is to go "unto God, Who giveth joy to his youth."[6] All this is, of course, on the supernatural plane, but at the same time it corresponds to the

---

[6]Entrance prayer of the Mass.

same degree to the inner needs of man's nature. Because the life of the liturgy is higher than that to which customary reality gives both the opportunity and form of expression, it adopts suitable forms and methods from that sphere in which alone they are to be found, that is to say, from art. It speaks measuredly and melodiously; it employs formal, rhythmic gestures; it is clothed in colors and garments foreign to everyday life; it is carried out in places and at hours which have been coordinated and systematized according to sublimer laws than ours. It is in the highest sense the life of a child, in which everything is picture, melody and song.

Such is the wonderful fact which the liturgy demonstrates; it unites art and reality in a supernatural childhood before God. That which formerly existed in the world of unreality only, and was rendered in art as the expression of mature human life, has here become reality. These forms are the vital expression of real and frankly supernatural life. But this has one thing in common with the play of the child and the life of art—it has no purpose, but is full of profound meaning. It is not work, but play. To be at play or to fashion a work of art in God's sight—not to create, but to exist—such is the essence of the liturgy. From this is derived its sublime mingling of profound earnestness and divine joyfulness. The fact that the liturgy gives a thousand strict and careful directions on the quality of the language, gestures, colors, garments and instruments which it employs, can only be understood by those who are able to take art and play seriously. Have you ever noticed how gravely children draw up the rules of their games, on the form of the melody, the position of the hands, the meaning of this stick and that tree? It is for the sake of the silly people who may not grasp their meaning and will persist in seeing the justification of an action or object only in its obvious purpose. Have you ever read of or even experienced the deadly earnestness with which the artist-vassal labors for art, his lord? Of his sufferings on the score of language? Or of what an overweening mistress form is? And all this for something that has no aim or purpose! No, art does not bother about aims. Does anyone honestly believe that the artist would take upon himself the thousand anxieties and feverish perplexities incident to creation if he intended to do nothing with his work but to teach the spectator a lesson, which he could just as well express in a couple of facile phrases, or one or two historical examples, or a few well-taken photographs? The only answer to this can be an emphatic negative. Being an artist means wrestling with the expression of the hidden life of man, avowedly in order that it may be given existence; nothing more. It is the image of the Divine creation, of which it is said that it has made things *"ut sint."*

The liturgy does the same thing. It, too, with endless care, with all the seriousness of the child and the strict conscientiousness of the great artist, has toiled to express in a thousand forms the sacred, God-given life of the soul to no other purpose than that the soul may therein have its existence and live its life. The liturgy has laid down the serious rules of the sacred game which the soul plays before God. And, if we are desirous of touching bottom in this mystery, it is the Spirit of fire and of holy discipline "Who has knowledge of the world"[7]—the Holy Ghost—Who has ordained the game which the Eternal Wisdom plays before the Heavenly Father in the Church, Its kingdom on earth. And "Its delight" is in this way "to be with the children of men."

Only those who are not scandalized by this understand what the liturgy means. From the very first every type of rationalism has turned against it. The practice of liturgy means that by the help of grace, under the guidance of the Church, we grow into living works of art before God, with no other aim or purpose than that of living and existing in His sight; it means fulfilling God's Word and "becoming as little children"; it means foregoing maturity with all its purposefulness, and confining oneself to play, as David did when he danced before the Ark. It may, of course, happen that those extremely clever people, who merely from being grown-up have lost all spiritual youth and spontaneity, will misunderstand this and jibe at it. David probably had to face the derision of Michal.

It is in this very aspect of the liturgy that its didactic aim is to be found, that of teaching the soul not to see purposes everywhere, not to be too conscious of the end it wishes to attain, not to be desirous of being over clever and grown-up, but to understand simplicity in life. The soul must learn to abandon, at least in prayer, the restlessness of purposeful activity; it must learn to waste time for the sake of God, and to be prepared for the sacred game with sayings and thoughts and gestures, without always immediately asking "why?" and "wherefore?" It must learn not to be continually yearning to do something, to attack something, to accomplish something, but to play the divinely ordained game of the liturgy in liberty and beauty and holy joy before God.

[7]Responsory at Terce, Pentecost.

In the end, eternal life will be its fulfillment. Will the people who do not understand the liturgy be pleased to find that the heavenly consummation is an eternal song of praise? Will they not rather associate themselves with those other industrious people who consider that such an eternity will be both boring and unprofitable?

Ruth A. Meyers

Evelyn Underhill: The Mystical Body and Diversity

Evelyn Underhill (1875–1941), an Anglican laywoman who became a popular lecturer, retreat leader, and spiritual director, was born in England in 1875. In 1893 she began her studies in the newly opened "ladies' department" at King's College, London, where she studied history, languages, and philosophy. Although baptized and confirmed in the Church of England, Underhill grew up with little Christian formation. As her faith began to awaken during her young adult years, she was attracted to the Roman Catholic Church, but in 1907 she stopped short of being received into that communion. Much later, in 1921, she made a public commitment to the Church of England.

Underhill's first major book, *Mysticism,* describing the experience of being grasped and transformed by divine love, was published in 1911 and catapulted her into prominence. Numerous other books followed, many of them arising from her lectures or retreats. *Worship* was undertaken during the last decade of her life.

Like *Mysticism, Worship* is divided into two sections, the first discussing fundamental characteristics and the second exploring different dimensions of the experience. Throughout, Underhill approaches her subject from the perspective of a believer engaged in the experience of worship.

For Underhill the starting point of worship is God: "worship . . . is the response of the creature to the Eternal." Worship thus draws human beings beyond themselves to encounter the transcendent reality of God. Yet the creaturely limits of humanity require that worship be given concrete expression, the principal means available for this expression being ritual, symbol, sacrament, and sacrifice. Among these elements, sacrifice summarizes all worship. It is not something given up, but rather the free self-offering of the individual to God.

The first chapters of Underhill's work take a broad theocentric approach, describing the human phenomenon of worship using examples as diverse as Jewish and Buddhist practice and the cave paintings of prehistoric worshipers. Only after this wide-ranging discussion does she explain that the distinctive character of Christian worship lies in adoration of Christ, who is the single revelation in time and space of the essential nature of God. Christian worship has many different expressions, each a response to the reality that is God.

Underhill devotes the second half of *Worship* to description and analysis of the riches offered by specific traditions. Drawing upon her own experiences of worship, she boldly offers an ecumenical perspective, appreciating rather than denigrating the various emphases of these different expressions of worship.

The excerpt that follows comes from part 1 of *Worship*. The preceding chapter, introducing the distinctiveness of Christian worship, concludes with the assertion that Christian worship is never a solitary undertaking. Not only does a Christian worship as part of the communion of saints, but in Christian worship one is drawn beyond oneself to participate in the self-offering of the Church to God. At a time when the corporate aspect of worship was not widely comprehended in the Church, Underhill emphasizes the necessity of the corporate.

FOR FURTHER READING

Eucharistic Prayers from the Ancient Liturgies. Chosen and arranged by E. Underhill. London: Longmans, Green, 1939; *The Golden Sequence: A Four-Fold Study of the Spiritual Life.* London: Methuen, 1932; *The Life of the Spirit and the Life of Today.* New York: E. P. Dutton, 1922; San Francisco: Harper & Row, 1986; *The Mystery of Sacrifice: A Meditation on the Liturgy* and *The School of Charity.* London: Longmans, Green, 1954; *Mysticism: A Study in the Nature and Development of Man's Spiritual Consciousness.* London, Methuen & Co., 1962; *Worship.* [New York:] Harper and Brothers, 1937; New York: Crossroad, 1985.

Evelyn Underhill

The Principles of Corporate Worship[1]

The corporate life of worship has . . . an importance far exceeding
the personal salvation or blessedness of the individual worshipers, or
the devotional opportunity which it gives to them. It stands for the
total orientation of life towards God; expressed both through stylized
liturgical action, and spontaneous common praise. Moreover, the personal relation to God of the individual—his inner life—is guaranteed
and kept in health by his social relation to the organism, the spiritual
society, the Church. What is best for the All, as Plato says, turns out
best for him too. It checks religious egotism, breaks down devotional
barriers, obliges the spiritual highbrow to join in the worship of the
simple and ignorant, and in general confers all the supporting and
disciplinary benefits of family life. Therefore, corporate and personal
worship, though in practice one commonly tends to take precedence
[over] the other, should complete, reinforce, and check each other.
Only where this happens, indeed, do we find in its perfection the
normal and balanced life of full Christian devotion; with its vast
metaphysical reference, its noble historic framework, its deep tender-
ness, its ordered beauty, its daily and seasonal rhythm, its sacred inti-
macies and willing activities, its self-oblivious spirit of oblation
before God and generous fellowship with men, its sanctifying power.
No one soul—not even the greatest saint—can fully apprehend all
this has to reveal and demand of us, or perfectly achieve this balanced richness of response. That response must be the work of the
whole Church; within which souls in their infinite variety each play a
part, and give that part to the total life of the Body.

[1]Excerpted from Evelyn Underhill, "The Principles of Corporate Worship,"
ch. 5 of *Worship* (Harper & Brothers, 1937) 84–7.

The Christian liturgy—taking this word now in its most general sense—is the artistic embodiment of this social yet personal life. Here we are not concerned with its historic origins, its doctrinal implications, or the chief forms it has assumed in the course of its development; but simply with its here-and-now existence, value, and meaning as the ordered framework of the Church's corporate worship, the classic medium by which the ceaseless adoring action of the Bride of Christ is given visible and audible expression. It is plain that the living experience of this whole Church, visible and invisible, past and present, stretched out in history and yet poised on God, must set the scene for Christian worship; not the poor little scrap of which any one soul, or any sectional group, is capable. Thus there must be a traditional worshiping act of the Church, a great liturgical life, of which the sectional worship of its various groups and branches will form a part, and to which the many-leveled action of its isolated members with all their varying moods and insights contributes; an act which includes and harmonizes all apparent differences, looking ever more and more towards that perfected heavenly life of adoration where these differences vanish in the single movement of all loving souls toward "the Abiding, the Prevenient, the Beginning and the End and Crown of light and life and love."[2] This total liturgical life of the *Corpus Christi* is not merely a collection of services, offices, and sacraments. Deeply considered, it is the sacrificial life of Christ Himself; the Word indwelling his Church, gathering in his eternal priestly action the small Godward movements, sacrifices, and aspirations of "all the broken and the meek,"[3] and acting through those ordered signs and sacraments by means of these his members on earth. Whether this Church be given hard and fast juridical boundaries, as in Roman Catholicism, or is seen as a group of autonomous families, as by Anglicans and Orthodox, or felt to be independent of visible expression, as by Quakers and other Independents, the principle is the same: the eternal self-offering of Christ to God in and through this mystical body. Hence the corporate worship of the Church is not simply that of an assembly of individuals who believe the same things, and therefore unite in doing the same things. It is real in its own right; an action transcending and embracing all the separate souls taking part in it. The individual as such dies to his separate selfhood—even his spiritual selfhood—on entering the Divine Society: is "buried in

[2]F. von Hügel, *The Reality of God*, 18.
[3]F. von Hügel, *Letters to a Niece*, 25.

baptism" and reborn as a living cell of the Mystical Body of Christ. St. Paul insists again and again on this transfer of status as the essential point about Christianity.[4] Therefore the response to God of this whole Body, this supernatural organism, in life and in worshiping acts, is of cardinal importance; and since this response is to take place on earth as in heaven, it must have its here-and-now embodiment— inadequate as this must always be to the supernatural situation it shows forth. Nor should we expect simplicity, clarity, uniformity, to be the marks of this action as seen from our point of view; but rather great diversity of level and function within that one great organism of which no man knows the limits but God alone.[5]

---

[4]Cf. Eph 1:22, 23; 2:19-22; Col 2:10, 13; 3:1-3, etc.
[5]1 Corinthians 12.

3

How Can We "Do" Liturgical Theology?

Logically, it seems to me, one ought to be able to talk about how one is going to go about doing something before one begins the task. However, my attempts to begin introductory classes with an extended treatment of the methodological options involved have been quite unsatisfactory. It seems that reflection on methodology presumes experience with the task at hand. Only when we know something about what we are doing can we step back and ask how to do it well. Of course, doing the task at all involves some "method," some way of going about it. But methodology, a reflective consideration relating well-designed process and appropriate procedures to recognized intentions and clearly articulated goals, involves knowing a lot both about what we are doing and how we are doing it.

I am assuming that you have some knowledge and experience with both theology and liturgy, or else you would not be taking a course in liturgical theology or—the very possibility gives me joy!—would never have plucked this volume from the library or bookstore shelf! That should give you some basic experiences upon which to reflect.

We turn to three scholars representing three different traditions—Orthodox, Roman Catholic, and Jewish—for help in answering this question. They propose three different approaches to the task of doing liturgical theology, approaches that overlap at some points and diverge at others. Each of them contributes important insights to contemporary studies in liturgical theology.

Suppose you wanted to encourage a group of laity interested in Christian worship to "do" liturgical theology. You don't want to use jargon that would "get in the way," but you respect their insight, wisdom, and experience. How would you proceed?

Bruce T. Morrill and Don E. Saliers

Alexander Schmemann: Liturgy as Life for the World

As a small child in the early 1920s, Alexander Schmemann emigrated with his family from Estonia to the Russian enclave in Paris, where he grew up and studied, becoming a presbyter in the Russian Orthodox Church. While his intellectual love was church history, his deepest passion proved to be contemporary ecclesiology. For Schmemann the content and practice of liturgy constituted the Church's very life. While the inspiration for that conviction came from the Orthodox scholar Nicholas Afanassiev at St. Sergius, it was from the great figures of the Roman Catholic theological and liturgical revival in Paris during the forties and fifties that Schmemann learned the principles of liturgical theology, especially its philosophy of time and concept of the paschal mystery. Schmemann found these principles to have been best preserved in the Orthodox Church's liturgy, despite problematic developments that clouded the light of genuine tradition.

Schmemann identified tradition with the liturgical practices of the earliest Christian centuries and the writings of the Church Fathers. He dedicated his theological work to the recovery of what inspired the Fathers to be witnesses of the Church. Schmemann did not, as he is often misunderstood, advocate a sort of patristic fundamentalism. On the contrary, he constantly berated the inordinate conservative desire of many Orthodox to recover and adhere to rituals and customs presumed essential to or characteristic of the liturgies of the early Church but which Schmemann argued were merely the external forms of the Church's life. Neither did Schmemann support a simple, literalist interpretation of Prosper of Aquitaine's phrase *lex orandi statuat lex credendi* in the sense of a rigid, unidirectional relationship from the Church's ritual to the content of theology.

The heart of Schmemann's liturgical theology is the principle that Christian faith and truth are made incarnate and manifested in the liturgy. The genuine experience of the Church is the liturgy, the "rule of faith" experienced within the "rule of prayer." Schmemann's is a functional definition of liturgy, for the function of worship is to give Christians a practical knowledge of the integral connection between religion and life. The liturgy's power to judge, transform, and change believers and their world lies in what Schmemann identifies to be the basis and content of Christian worship. The basis of liturgy, the doctrine of the incarnation, expounds a world that was created to be a means of communion, or participation in life, which is God-the-Logos, Jesus the Christ. This life is hidden in the world due to sin. Thus the content of worship is the revelation of life in the risen Christ as the kingdom of God, realized presently in the Church through the eucharistic liturgy and anticipated amidst a world wherein time is yet to be fulfilled. Schmemann thereby regularly summarizes genuine Christian liturgy as cosmological (the world as sacramental), eschatological (the kingdom that is to come), and ecclesiological (the Church as manifestation of the kingdom in this world). Liturgy's transformative potential for the Church and Christians in society lies therein.

In the passage that follows, Schmemann identifies the task of liturgical theology in relation to the primary theological action of the Church, the prayerful engagement of believers in the liturgy. A method appropriate to this task requires that historical studies and scholastic theories find their proper role in service to the structures of the Church's actual liturgical practice.

FOR FURTHER READING

The Eucharist: Sacrament of the Kingdom of God. Trans. Paul Kachur. Crestwood, N.Y.: St. Vladimir's Seminary Press, 1987; *For the Life of the World: Sacraments and Orthodoxy,* 2nd ed. Crestwood, N.Y.: St. Vladimir's Seminary Press, 1973; *Introduction to Liturgical Theology.* Trans. Asheleigh E. Moorhouse. Crestwood, N.Y.: St. Vladimir's Seminary Press, 1966, 1986; *Liturgy and Tradition: Theological Reflections of Alexander Schmemann.* Ed. Thomas Fisch. Crestwood, N.Y.: St. Vladimir's Seminary Press, 1990.

Alexander Schmemann

The Task and Method of Liturgical Theology[1]

TOWARDS A DEFINITION OF LITURGICAL THEOLOGY

As its name indicates, liturgical theology is the elucidation of the meaning of worship. Of course liturgics has always had as its goal the explanation of worship, but . . . this explanation was very often content with an elementary and in many ways superficial and arbitrary symbolism. Even the concept of symbolism was taken in its simplest and most popular sense: as the "representation" of something. The Little Entrance of the Liturgy was seen as the symbolic representation of Christ going out to preach, the Great Entrance as the representation of his burial, and so on. But in all this it was forgotten that before using this symbolic explanation it is necessary to define the nature and essence of the liturgical symbol and its place in worship. There is also another concept which liturgics has frequently used without clarifying its theological content: liturgical commemoration. It is not hard to say that such and such a ceremony "symbolizes" something, or that on such and such a day we celebrate the commemoration of something. But in popular usage both these concepts are so vague that their precise meaning must be clarified prior to their use in any explanation of worship.

The examples mentioned are enough to show what the explanation of worship ought to be: it ought to be the elucidation of its theological meaning. Theology is above all explanation, "the search for words appropriate to the nature of God" (θεοπρεπεῖς λογοι), i.e., for a sys-

[1]Excerpted from Alexander Schmemann, parts 3 and 4 of "The Task and Method of Liturgical Theology," *Introduction to Liturgical Theology*, trans. Asheleigh E. Moorhouse (Crestwood, N.Y.: St. Vladimir's Seminary Press, 1986) 16–27. Reprinted by permission.

tem of concepts corresponding as much as possible to the faith and experience of the Church. Therefore the task of liturgical theology consists in giving a theological basis to the explanation of worship and the whole liturgical tradition of the Church. This means, first, to find and define the concepts and categories which are capable of expressing as fully as possible the essential nature of the liturgical experience of the Church; second, to connect these ideas with that system of concepts which theology uses to expound the faith and doctrine of the Church; and third, to present the separate data of liturgical experience as a connected whole, as, in the last analysis, the "rule of prayer" dwelling within the Church and determining her "rule of faith."

If liturgical theology stems from an understanding of worship as the public act of the Church, then its final goal will be to clarify and explain the connection between this act and the Church; i.e., to explain how the Church expresses and fulfills herself in this act.

The accepted doctrine of the Church sees in "the tradition of sacraments and sacred rites"[2] an inviolable element of Tradition, and thus also one of the sources which theology must utilize if it seeks to expound fully the faith and life of the Church. The neglect of this source in scholastic theology is explained by a narrowing down of the concepts both of Tradition and of the Church.[3] But the early Church firmly confessed the principle: *lex orandi lex est credendi.* Therefore the science of liturgics cannot fail to be a theological science by its very character and purpose; and theology as a whole cannot do without the science of liturgics.

All that has been said thus far points to the place liturgical theology must occupy in the system of theological disciplines. Of course each of the classifications is conditioned by its own nature.[4] In the

[2]"The term 'Sacred Tradition' refers to the fact that those who truly believe in and honor God transmit by word and deed, to one another and as ancestors to descendants, the doctrine of faith, the law of God, the sacraments and sacred rites" (*Catechism:* "Concerning Sacred Tradition").

[3]Thus, for example, the author of the well-known Catholic survey of Orthodox theology, M. Jugle, hardly mentions worship in his definition of Tradition according to Russian and Greek theologians; cf. *Theologia Dogmatica Christianorum ab Ecclesia Catholica Dissidentium,* vol. 1 (Paris, 1926), vol. 2 (Paris, 1933); cf. also F. Gavin, *Some Aspects of Contemporary Greek Orthodox Thought* (Milwaukee: Morehouse, 1923) 27ff.

[4]Cf. Y. M. Congar, "Théologie," *Dictionaire de Théol. Cath.,* 15, col. 492ff., and J. M. Dalmais, "Théologie et Liturgie," *Initiation Théologique,* vol. 1 (Paris: Editions du Cerf, 1952) 102ff.

last analysis they all have the same goal: the setting forth and explanation of the doctrine of the Church. But some division is necessary, since the one truth preserved by the Church is discovered from different angles and, what is most important, if it is to be discovered at all various methods or means of apprehension are required. In the accepted classification dogmatic theology is the discipline which unites the conclusions of all the others and brings them together into a balanced and convincing whole. But that it may be a crowning synthesis there must be an independent "order" for each of the disciplines which lead into it. If Holy Tradition and Holy Scripture are the sources of dogmatics, neither can be drawn simply from "texts" and "proofs"—whether biblical, liturgical, patristic, etc. By using its sources in such an oversimplified way dogmatics frequently overlooks the essential part of the Word of God and Tradition and falls into the error of one-sidedness. In order to use them properly, dogmatics must accept the evidence of Scripture and Tradition not in the form of "texts," but in the fullness and interrelatedness of their theological significance. Thus, between Scripture as a "text" and its use in dogmatics there stands biblical theology, and between worship as a fact and its use in dogmatics there stands liturgical theology. In order to be "useful" to dogmatics, liturgics must first of all be the independent and complete setting forth of the liturgical tradition. We say "complete," because under the old concept of liturgics, its relationship with dogmatics suffered one major weakness: liturgics had to do with worship, while dogmatics used only liturgical texts or separate rites. In the meantime, as has been said above, worship simply cannot be equated either with texts or with forms of worship. It is a whole, within which everything, the words of prayer, lections, chanting, ceremonies, the relationship of all these things in a "sequence" or "order" and, finally, what can be defined as the "liturgical coefficient" of each of these elements (i.e., that significance which, apart from its own immediate content, each acquires as a result of its place in the general sequence or order of worship), only all this together defines the meaning of the whole and is therefore the proper subject of study and theological evaluation. To the extent that this study must have its own method, in many respects different from the method of other theological disciplines, it is only right that liturgical theology should occupy a special, independent place in the general system of theological disciplines. For without an appropriate theological systematization and interpretation, the liturgical tradition does not "arrive" at dogmatic consciousness, and there is a danger either of its complete neglect, or of its haphazard and improper use.

Liturgical theology is therefore an independent theological discipline, with its own special subject—the liturgical tradition of the Church, and requiring its own corresponding and special method distinct from the methods of other theological disciplines. Without liturgical theology our understanding of the Church's faith and doctrine is bound to be incomplete.

TOWARDS A METHODOLOGY OF LITURGICAL THEOLOGY

The question of the method of liturgical theology deserves special attention because the lack of clear methodological principles opens the door to arbitrariness in the theological use of liturgical material. Not a few examples of such arbitrariness could be cited. First of all, we might ask if everything in the immense liturgical tradition which has come down to us is of equal value. Does it all have the same significance? Can it all be equated with "Tradition" in this theological sense of the word? We know of course that worship has passed through a long and complicated development, and that the contemporary uniformity of liturgical norms in Orthodoxy is a comparatively late phenomenon. The Church has never believed that complete conformity in ceremonies and prayers is an obligatory condition of her unity, nor has she ever identified her *lex orandi* with any particular "historical" type of worship. Even now, in spite of the virtual monopoly of the Byzantine type of worship, there exists between the various Orthodox Churches a quite significant variation in rubrics and liturgical practice. And it is characteristic of the Church's view that the *Typicon,* the basic rule book for her worship, is in its two basic variants (the Greek and the Slavonic) not called the "Typicon of the Orthodox Church," but is referred to in terms of its place of origin: *The Ordo of Saint Savva Monastery,* or *The Ordo of the Great Church of Constantinople.* Liturgical life has developed, it has changed its forms. It would not be difficult to show that it is changing still. The absence of development would be the sign of a fatal sclerosis. But then it is very important to know, first, whether all these changes express the Church's "rule of prayer" in equal measure, and second, whether it is possible to find in liturgical development itself some law, something which in fact makes it a development of the age-old and immutable *lex orandi* and not just a series of more or less accidental metamorphoses. It is evident that liturgical theology must begin with the historical study of worship.

* * *

In contrast to the old historical liturgics which we have been speaking about, the history of worship no longer appears as an end in itself. It is precisely the theory of worship of the Church that remains as the ultimate problem to resolve. History is needed only to the extent that this theory has from the very beginning expressed itself in facts, has become concrete and has revealed itself in facts, and also in these facts has been exploded or distorted. In our liturgical practice there are things which to many people seem to be the age-old tradition of the Church, but which in fact distort this tradition. It is impossible to discern them outside their historical perspective, without comparing facts, just as it is impossible to define the basic path of liturgical development and its general meaning outside a similar perspective. But after historical analysis there must come a theological synthesis—and this is the second and major part of liturgical theology. The theological synthesis is the elucidation of the rule of prayer as the rule of faith, it is the theological interpretation of the rule of prayer. Here the work of the liturgiologist is extremely varied, and it is impossible to give in advance a detailed definition of its approach. However it should be emphasized once again that both historically and theologically the liturgiologist is above all dealing with the basic structures of worship. These structures can be defined as worship as a whole, i.e., the interrelatedness of all the individual services and of each liturgical unit in particular. So then the liturgical cycle of the week could develop, become more complex and find ever newer expressions in hymnody and ceremony, but its basic kernel—the rhythm of the "Lord's Day" as the day of the Eucharistic commemoration of the death and resurrection of Christ—is integral to the liturgical tradition itself, and in this sense appears as its original and basic structure. The same also with the order of the Eucharist; no matter how it has developed and changed its form in history, it has from the beginning been defined by a certain basic structure ("shape" in the words of G. Dix) and it is precisely this shape which appears as the starting point for the discovery of the meaning of the Eucharist and its development. The concept of "structure" must be applied also to the offices of the daily and yearly cycles, to the rites of other sacraments, and so on. Historical liturgics establishes the structures and their development, liturgical theology discovers their meaning: such is the general methodological principle of the task. The significance of these basic structures is that only in them is there any full expression of the general design of worship, both as a whole, and taken in its separate elements. They fix the "liturgical coefficient" of each element and point to its significance in the whole, giving to worship a consistent theological interpretation and freeing it from arbitrarily symbolic interpretations. Thus when we compare rubrics which have been long accepted as mere "rubrical details" and establish their position in their respective liturgical structures, they sometimes reveal their theological meaning and the tradition is as it were "decoded." In the light of the discernible general "structure" of liturgical action the "details" of the Ordo can reveal something which was at one time expressed by the Church in the language of worship but which we have forgotten how to apprehend directly. . . . From the establishment and interpretation of the basic structures of worship to an explanation of every possible element, and then to an orderly theological synthesis of this data—such is the method which liturgical theology uses to carry out its task, to translate what is expressed by the language of worship—its structures, its ceremonies, its texts and its whole "spirit"—into the language of theology, to make the liturgical experience of the Church again one of the life-giving sources of the knowledge of God. What is needed more than anything else is an entrance into the life of worship, into life in the rhythm of worship. What is needed is not so much the intellectual apprehension of worship as its apprehension through experience and prayer.

The question of the plan and subdivisions of liturgical theology would not present any special interest if there were not already signs of the inadequacy and evil effects of scholastic theology. Under its influence, for example, a distinction has arisen in the minds of believers between "corporate" worship and "private" worship designed to meet some need. The sacraments of baptism, chrismation, marriage, not to speak of requiems, funeral services, etc., have fallen into the category of requested ceremonies or "private" offices.[5] In the meantime this distinction between "corporate" and "private" worship is a contradiction of the basic and ancient concept of Christian worship as the public act of the Church, in which there is nothing private at all,

[5]Cf. K. Nikolsky, *Posobie k izucheniu ustava* [An Aid to the Study of the *Typicon*] (St. Petersburg: Synodal Typograph, 1907) 6, 656. Also L. Mirkovich, *Pravoslavnaya liturgika* [Orthodox Liturgics] (Skremski Karlovtzy, 1918) 22–23.

nor can there be, since this would destroy the very nature of the Church. Under this same scholastic influence, liturgics began to regard the Eucharist as just one among a number of offices or sacraments of the Church, in this way distorting the whole perspective of the liturgical tradition, which has always regarded the Eucharist as the center and source of the whole life of the Church. Old fashioned liturgics was unable to view critically that realm of the Church's life in which worship had long since in fact been accepted on the one hand as a "meeting of needs" governed by the "demands" of believers. The venom poisoning our ecclesiastical life was as it were "legitimized" by liturgics which, instead of having as its goal the theological comprehension of worship, thought of itself first of all as an applied science, called only to meet "practical needs."

Hence the necessity of reviewing the plan of liturgical theology, of bringing it into a proper relationship with the object of its study and with the method of its investigation.

As we have said, the division in principle between "corporate" and "private" worship must be discarded. The purpose of worship is to constitute the Church, precisely to bring what is "private" into the new life, to transform it into what belongs to the Church, i.e., shared with all in Christ. In addition its purpose is always to express the Church as the unity of that Body whose Head is Christ. And, finally, its purpose is that we should always "with one mouth and one heart" serve God, since it was only such worship which God commanded the Church to offer. In the same way it is impossible to justify the division of the sacraments into separate liturgical departments, with the Eucharist regarded as "one among several." The Eucharist is *the* Sacrament of the Church, i.e., her eternal actualization as the Body of Christ, united in Christ by the Holy Spirit. Therefore the Eucharist is not only the "most important" of all the offices, it is also the source and goal of the entire liturgical life of the Church. Any liturgical theology not having the Eucharist as the foundation of its whole structure is basically defective.[6]

[6]Cf. Archmandrite Kiprian, *Evkharistiya* [The Eucharist] (Paris: Y.M.C.A. Press, 1947) 25ff.: "If in our time eucharistic life is weakened to the point that we have almost completely lost the proper eucharistic consciousness, and regard the Divine Liturgy being celebrated in our churches as just one of the ceremonies, considering secondary devotional services as no less important in worship, then in the times of genuine ecclesiastical life it was not so. The Eucharist was the basis and culmination of all liturgical life. But gradually

The general plan of liturgical theology proposed here is, of course, not the only one possible. But it does seem to take into account those fundamental conditions related to the subject which we have attempted to identify in the preceding pages.

A study of ecclesiastical rubrics, understood not simply as the expounding of the rules governing the Church's liturgical life but as the general and basic structure of this life, must necessarily be a preliminary step in the study of worship. Before examining the separate parts of the building we must not only sense that we are dealing with a building, but also see it as a whole, having a certain overall design or architectural plan, in which all its elements are set in a mutually dependent relationship. The task . . . is to sketch in this whole, to discover this design.[7]

Furthermore, while the Eucharist must unquestionably be placed in the center of the first part of liturgical theology, the essential nature of the Church being actualized in the Eucharist as the Sacrament of the Church's life, it is also true that the sacraments of entrance into the Church (baptism and chrismation) lead us into this life and unite us with this essential nature. They lead into the Church and into the Eucharist, and it is appropriate to relate their theological and liturgical explanation to the study of the celebration of the Eucharist itself.

That form of worship which we shall henceforth call the liturgy of time, which is by its very nature connected with "hours and days" and is expressed in three cycles, daily, weekly and yearly, forms another clear pole in the liturgical life of the Church. The structure for these cycles, their significance in the Church's "rule of prayer" and their relationship to the Eucharist—these are questions which must be answered in the second part of our liturgical theology.

Finally, that worship whose object is not the whole Church but rather her individual members will be the third area of liturgical

---

everything that was concentrated around the Eucharist as the center of liturgical life—the Sacraments, prayers, orders of service . . . were turned in the consciousness of Christians into private rites, became the private business of each individual person or family, having (apparently) nothing to do with the concept of the gathered community." Concerning the relationship of the sacraments to the Church see Fr. N. Afanassiev, "Sacramenta et Sacramentalia," *Pravoslavnaya Mysl* [Orthodox Thought] 8, no. 1 (Paris, 1951).

[7]Concerning the concept of liturgical "structures" cf. A. Baumstark, *Liturgie Comparée* (Monastére d'Amy à Chevetogne, 1939) 32ff.; J. Pascher, *L'Evolution des Rites Sacramentels* (Paris: Editiones du Cerf, 1952).

theology. We say "object," since the "subject" is always the Church herself, and the fact that a given form of worship is conditioned by the needs of individual members of the Church does not turn it into a "private" liturgy. What is accomplished in them is accomplished in the Church, and has significance for the Church; it is its initial cause which lies in the need of the individual Christian. Such worship is connected especially with the Christian's life—it includes all those rites of a non-sacramental nature which are associated with birth (the prayers of the mother and child on the first, eighth, and fortieth days); the sacrament of marriage; the sacrament of penitence and healing and the whole liturgy connected with death. Up to now liturgical scholarship has scarcely touched this whole area, and yet it occupies a prominent place in the real Church and requires therefore its own theological and liturgical evaluation and explanation.

* * *

Again let us say that this is not presented as the only possible or correct scheme. It seems to us, however, that it answers the purpose of liturgical theology better than former plans. Its intent is not to break down the Church's worship into parts, but to demonstrate it in its wholeness, as an elucidation of the rule of prayer which is always and in all places the same. It can be "justified" only *post factum*. At present we propose it only as a kind of guide line in the difficult task of reading and apprehending the liturgical tradition of the Church.

John D. Laurance

Angelus A. Häussling: Liturgy as Defining Activity of the Church

Angelus Albert Häussling was born on April 19, 1932, in Lambrecht, Germany. After schooling in the Jesuit college at St. Blasien, he entered the Benedictine Abbey of Maria Laach in 1951. Ordained a priest in 1958, he studied philosophy and theology at Maria Laach, Beuron, Innsbruck, and Salzburg, where he received his doctorate in 1965. Häussling was a lecturer in the Liturgical Institute at Trier until 1975 and then became professor of liturgy and sacramental theology in the Salesians' Theological Institute at Benedictbeuern. Since 1978 he has also been editor of the *Archiv für Liturgiewissenschaft.*

Häussling's dissertation, directed by Josef A. Jungmann, studies the Western monastic liturgy of the early Middle Ages and the history of the frequency of eucharistic celebration.[1] In it he demonstrates how a connection through the altar and its enclosed relics to the prototypical church of Rome, and not a theology of priesthood, accounts for the origin of "private masses" in the medieval Church. Häussling has published more than 375 scholarly reviews and articles on liturgically related topics, the vast majority in the *Archiv für Liturgiewissenschaft,* with a scholarly breadth and depth that have had a strong influence on the field.[2]

---

[1]*Mönchskonvent und Eucharistiefeier, Eine Studie über die Messe in der abendländischen Klosterliturgie des frühen Mittelalters und zur Geschichte der Messhäufigkeit* (Münster: Aschendorff Verlag, 1973).

[2]E.g., his observations on the relationship of liturgiology to the human sciences and the rest of theology and his highlighting the continuing value of Odo Casel's *Mysteriengegenwart* helped shape Edward J. Kilmartin's *Christian Liturgy* (Kansas City: Sheed & Ward, 1988) and *The Eucharist in the West* (Collegeville, Minn.: The Liturgical Press, 1999).

The excerpt that follows is the final section of an article written in 1970.[3] In the article Häussling gives answers to the questions: What is liturgiology—the "science" of liturgy—and what is its "critical function," that is, what reflective critique does it bring to scholarship's common task of understanding the human condition? Prior to this excerpt Häussling first reaffirms Romano Guardini's 1921 thesis that liturgiology is ultimately theology and not, as previously thought, merely a study of rubrics or even a study of the historical development of the liturgy, as necessary as that is to liturgiology.[4] Given that theology has revelation as its object, and revelation is realized only where it is understood and believed, theology is the methodic, theoretical explication of faith as faith. As such it exists only in the kingdom of God arriving in faith, that is, only in the Church. For Häussling, then, the object of liturgiology as a theological "science," that is, a methodical study, is not any particular liturgy or set of liturgies or even the liturgy itself but the Church in its defining activity of answering the call of God in the actual practice of its worship and in those expressions that are connected and bound to this practice.

Häussling next points out how in this past century liturgiology had the critical function of making the Church aware through historical investigation of how, because the liturgy changed through the ages, it could and should continue to change in order for God to speak to human beings in ever-changing cultures. It has also shifted the understanding of liturgy itself from being a duty owed to God in justice to being the highest form of Christian existence as participation through mystery in Christ's saving events.

According to Häussling, liturgiology's critical function today is threefold. First, it must constantly critique its own presuppositions not to overprivilege its own professional view of the Church and its liturgy, becoming blind to life-giving liturgical developments that may be taking place in the larger Church. Second, on the basis of historical and theological reflection, it must also give counsel to the Church in regard to modified and new liturgical forms. In the follow-

---

[3]"Die kritische Funktion der Liturgiewissenschaft," *Liturgie und Gesellschaft*, Hans-Bernhard Meyer, ed. (Innsbruck, Wien, and München: Tyrolia Verlag, 1970) 103–30.

[4]"Über die systematische Methode in der Liturgiewissenschaft," *Jahrbuch für Liturgiewissenschaft* 1 (1921) 97–108. For an overview of the history of this question, see Michael B. Merz, "'Liturgiewissenschaft,'" *Archiv für Liturgiewissenschaft* 27/1 (1985) 103–8.

ing excerpt Häussling argues in a ground-breaking way that the third and most basic critical function of liturgiology in any age is to call the whole of theology to its fundamental task of bringing people to a proper worship of God.

FOR FURTHER READING

"Breviary," "Liturgy 2," and "Liturgy 3." *Sacramentum Mundi.* Ed. Karl Rahner. Vol. 1, 236–9, vol. 3, 331–7. New York: Herder & Herder, 1968; "Liturgy: Memorial of the Past and Liberation in the Present." *The Meaning of the Liturgy.* Ed. Angelus A. Häussling, 107–18. Collegeville, Minn.: The Liturgical Press, 1994; "Messe (Expositiones Missae)," *Dictionnaire de Spiritualité Ascétique et Mystique Doctrine et Histoire.* Vol. 10, col. 1083–90. Paris: Beauschesne, 1980; "Motives for Frequency of the Eucharist." *Can We Always Celebrate the Eucharist?* Ed. Mary Collins and David Power, 25–30. Concilium 152. New York: Seabury Press, 1982; "Odo Casel—Noch von Aktualität: Eine Rückschau in eigener Sache aus Anlaß der hundertsten Geburtstages des ersten Herausgebers." *Archiv für Liturgiewissenschaft* 28 (1986) 357–87; "Was heißt: Liturgiewissenschaft ist ökumensich?" *Gottesdienst—Weg zur Einheit: Impulse für Ökumene.* Ed. Karl Schlemmer, 62–88. Freiburg-Basel-Wien: Herder, 1989.

Angelus A. Häussling

The Critical Function of Liturgiology
within Theology and in Ecclesial Life[1]

What has so far been named "the critical function" of our field of studies seems to me secondary in comparison to that critical function which urgently confronts us today, and toward which the discussion should now be directed.

Only recently did a council of the Church praise the liturgy for the first time as the "highpoint to which the action of the Church tends, and likewise the source from which all its power flows."[2] However, it appears that an unheard-of crisis in the understanding of God has also befallen us. Along with it, prayer, worship, liturgy have all been called into question. The God question has become the primary topic of theology: "Who is God, really?"[3] We live in the midst of atheists, not anti-theists, and we ourselves are also concerned that God remain a reality for us. One can read theological works today where there is no mention throughout either of God or of Christ. Where these words still do appear they seem often to be understood only as ciphers—the very words people of antiquity, in theistic ages, used for articulating the experience of change in self-understandings called "beliefs."

Where "God" becomes problematic in that way, worship, liturgy and prayer in general necessarily become meaningless. Social in-

---

[1]Excerpted from Angelus A. Häussling, "Die kritische Funktion der Liturgiewissenschaft," *Liturgie und Gesellschaft*, ed. Hans-Bernhard Meyer, translated for this volume by John D. Laurence (Innsbruck, Wien, and München: Tyrolia Verlag, 1970) 117–30.

[2]Vatican II, *Sacrosanctum concilium*, par. 10.

[3]"Wer is das eigentlich—Gott?": the title of a book by Hans Jürgen Schultz (Munich, 1969).

volvement becomes the more appropriate response, as being more in accord with the gospel. What then should be done with established symbols of salvation? What about sacrament? It no longer has any significance at all. . . . It seems to me that the crisis in the understanding of the Church expressed there lies essentially in an inability to accept the Church as a mystery, as a work of salvation of an indomitable, totally new quality. I cannot imagine how out of such a theology there could emerge a liturgy that is anything more or other than a call to action to change society. Yet our situation reflects just such a theology: God as God is no longer the obvious and uncontested source of being. He is no longer the summit of the pyramid of all beings. He is simply no longer evident. And this is the case not only for a few philosophers, poets and apostles of sociology, but for the majority of those who determine the world.

How does liturgiology fare in such an environment? Well, we might say. We could assert that God, Christ, Church, Sacrament, and faith can exist, indeed, do exist, and that we can therefore promote liturgiology unhindered. But this would be an absurd stance. It would reduce our specialty to a frivolous hobby. We would then no longer be theologians, even if we still wanted to be. The object of our discipline, the great sacrament of Jesus Christ known as the Church—insofar as it manifests itself by presenting itself in faith, expressly in word and response and in the experience of salvation and praise, before the Origin of being and of salvation—forbids us simply to abandon to others the question about what God really is (as if we ourselves were not already forced to face this question).

Once again I have to deal with the proper object of liturgiology as theology. This object is not, or is no longer, simply one liturgy or *the* liturgy. Rather, it is the work of salvation to the degree that it exists as worship. The work of salvation, which is the faith-object of Christianity, can be characterized thus: The human being is encountered in such a way that the One encountering, traditionally called "God," while remaining a Mystery, involves himself as a summoning counterpart to humankind calling for a response. This event is traditionally called Revelation and faith. Both are history-creating realities. They have one locale: the covenant of God with Israel, realized in Jesus of Nazareth, the Christ, who in turn dwells in the community of his believers, the Church, until the lordship of God, the Father of Jesus Christ, is fully realized. Revelation engages humankind now as a whole, just as the Revealer bestows himself wholly in that conversation. The goal of the economy of salvation is community in the Mystery revealing itself and the believers accepting that revelation—a *sacrum commercium* (a holy exchange). This community exists only when the other is grasped in his essential reality. He, however, who traditionally has been called "God," has shown himself essentially as One calling for a response, as a personal partner, as someone always greater but yet listening to us. Therefore prayer, that is, speech in response to God, belongs to the very nature of faith. The life of Jesus, then, would not be adequately accounted for if his prayer were not mentioned. In the same way, the believing Church, seriously accepting God as the God he is, can exist only if she prays. Or, put another way: When the Church no longer prays, perhaps she believes in the importance of changing societal structures or in an eschatological, universal evolution, but no longer in him who called her as Church. When the Church no longer prays, the work of salvation no longer takes place, because that God is no longer present whose nearness in *sacrum commercium* is salvation.

Naturally this train of reasoning has to be modified in practice. Perhaps in the temporal existence of a human being there are phases of differing ability for the word of prayer and for worship. Above all, it should be made clear that a false otherworldliness or ultra-worldliness of God ought to be foreign to Christian consciousness. Since the Word has become flesh, since a real meal has been constituted as the sign of the last offer of the nearness of God, faith in "the God and Father of Jesus Christ" exists only where the realities of our world are not avoided, but accepted. They are accepted, not because the Christian can be satisfied with them as they are—as if he could not "differentiate,"[4]— but because the God of Revelation has begun to make a new world from them, a world after his own heart. This therefore must remain true: However one wishes to demythologize and name what earlier was called God, "the God and Father of Jesus Christ" is believed in only where He is prayed to and thereby honored.

The object of liturgiology is the Church, the Church as she exists in prayer, in worship. Liturgiology is, as the Lutheran pastor Erhard

---

[4]Cf. 1 Cor 11:29: μὴ διακρίνων το σῶμα, "because he did not distinguish the body of the Lord (he did not differentiate it from common food)," F. Büchsel: *ThWB* 3 (1938) 948. On this question see the excellent observations by Heinz Schürmann, "Neutestamentliche Marginalien zur Frage der 'Entsakralisierung': Der Haftpunkt des Sakralen im Raum der neutestamentlichen Offenbarung," *Der Seelsorger* 38 (1968) 38–48, 89–104, esp. 89ff., 98.

Griese puts it, "doxological theology."[5] Here is where, it seems to me, our most important, and yet our most ticklish and difficult critical function lies: It is our task to test theology on whether, in general, it so speaks about God that in this theology God is given the honor of worship. Our critical function consists in questioning contemporary theology to see whether it is, as it were, "capable of liturgy" (liturgiefähig). To the degree that theology does not exist, it would exist were it to serve those who believe and are called to believe. It is also true that, insofar as theology does not exist, it would exist were it to lead explicitly to our responding to God as God–something that in the past happened in the liturgy as a matter of course, still happens and must always happen, if the Church is to remain the place of salvation.

In the time of a crisis about "God," our critical function also lies in being sure as well that theology today not forget this truth. It is not something we are grateful for. It is an inconvenient and thankless task and we are not eager to do it. It is such an impossible assignment because it demands that we be able to say what nobody is able to say today, that is, who God is today and how one today can speak about him and to him. But neither do *we* know how to do that. Our critical function is ticklish because, by absurd talk we can make ourselves ridiculous, harming the enterprise. Cliches are no help. Indeed, one has to wonder whether individuals engaged in our craft are not simply overwhelmed by this task. We have to be competent in so many areas and then unite them in a single overarching personal vision. We have to use the concordance tables of the Old Gelasian as well as know how to evaluate the historical significance of Karl Marx. That is asking a lot–from individuals, too much. Nevertheless, such is the task. If we do not assume the critical function of scrutinizing the doxological power of contemporary theology and Church life influenced by it, then in good time only a conventicle kind of liturgy will survive, if at all: liturgies celebrated by Johnny-come-latelies, with no symbolic power. How are we to exercise this function now in a concrete way? It seems possible to do so on two levels.

First of all, we have to be more precise about what has already been noted above as our task, that we have the right and duty to offer criticism regarding the new liturgy developed by post-conciliar

---

[5]"Perspektiven einer liturgischen Theologie," *Una Sancta* 24 (1969) 102–13, esp. 104f.

commissions. This critique is a scrutinizing whether the form of this liturgy, because it is all too naive, bespeaks a disdain for the experience of God of our time and, therefore, does more harm to worship than helps it. This critical stance does not lessen our respect for the leadership of the members of the post-conciliar commissions. In the history of the liturgy their activity is without precedent and they doubtlessly set down rules to follow. Often enough they were only able to fulfill half of their work thanks to the usual compromises. . . . [We must ask whether] those who want to create uniformity in everything, suspect how deep the crisis regarding the experience of God really is. If they do not, then we are the ones who have to inform them.

The second and truly decisive step is more urgent. It seems to me essential that we also share in attempts to solve the problem of atheism, or stated more positively, that we also make an effort to recognize who and where he or it is who is so typically named "God," and how people today can speak to and about him. It seems to me that we have to redirect our discipline in a new way. There is need from now on to look upon the liturgy of the Church as the place of the event of salvation for humankind. Liturgiology is carried on today, for the most part, in an ecclesiological way, generally, too, if those involved are modern, with an irritating tendency to critique the liturgy as a "cult" and as the place of a mindless sacralizing (meaning whatever they want by that). We see quite clearly that people around us have difficulty in performing the liturgical act. We are familiar with the question put by the eminent Romano Guardini, the question whether perhaps people of our age "might simply not be capable of the liturgical act."[6] But it seems to me that this question is stated too provisionally. It is no longer a question simply about people and their abilities or disabilities. It is obviously about the Holy One, about God. I would prefer to reforge Guardini's question into a dogmatic one: How is God, the Mystery—or whatever way one wants to express it—there, so that something like worship, like liturgy, is possible? A theological liturgiology cannot remain only ecclesiological, so as to speak now only about "community," as if community were self-sufficient and God were already included in it. Liturgiology must take the stand much more of being a true theo-logy. This of course is

---

[6]"Der Kultakt und die gegenwärtige Aufgabe der liturgischen Bildung. Ein Brief," *Liturgisches Jahrbuch* 14 (1964) 101–106. On this question see Th. Bogler, ed., *Ist der Mensch von heute noch liturgiefähig? Ergebnisse einer Umfrage.* Liturgie und Mönchtum, Laacher Hefte 38 (Maria Laach, 1966).

an unheard-of widening of our craft, one bound to cause anxiety. But it is a necessary one, because the question concerning meaning and liturgy's right to exist have been broadened in an anxiety-causing and unheard-of way. No longer are we concerned only with the forms of the liturgy. No longer is it a question whether or how far liturgy's shape fits or is able to correspond to the modern person.[7] Rather, concern is now focused simply on the event of the liturgy: that God might become real for people. Liturgy seems to have devolved definitively into "material liturgics."[8]

If we do not broaden our discipline to include the question of God, we will not only be unable to carry on our most important critical function—to recall theology to its doxological character, but we will also not be able to avoid a deadly loss of bearings. Although we can argue convincingly that there must always be liturgy in the Church, there is strong evidence in the Catholic-Christian world of a growing inability (not simply an unwillingness) to celebrate the liturgy together, at least in its customary forms. What about this loss of bearings? I dare say, and with every possibility of being wrong, that it is precisely where liturgiology does not shrink from important questions that it fulfills its critical constructive function. From theology we must first of all take seriously that God remains Mystery in his Revelation. That is, the mystery-character of his being can sometimes be bestowed on us in such a way that the salvific experience of his nearness is clouded over and can no longer be clearly grasped in his

[7]Karl Rahner finds that "modern liturgiology has taken as its object the scientifico-theological reflection on a liturgy yet to be created" and thereby "has come into the immediate neighbourhood of practical theology," but he seems to constrict the object of liturgiology to the discussion of how the liturgy can meet the conditions and needs of people today ("Practical Theology within the Totality of Theological Disciplines," *Theological Investigations,* vol. 9, tr. Graham Harrison (New York: Seabury Press, [no date]) 113. Precisely this task, it seems to us, can adequately be fulfilled only by means of a proper theological expansion. Rahner's reference to liturgiology appears insufficient even within the project of his own thesis. Nevertheless, he also states that liturgiology has become more than a subordinate discipline to Church history or, indeed, more than a glorified study of rubrics.

[8]Here Häussling refers to his observation made earlier in the article (p. 112) that theological understanding has evolved from seeing the liturgy as an exercise of the virtue of religion, the obligation to return worship to God because of his greatness and gifts, to the recognition—rediscovered by Dom Odo Casel—that participants are actually made present in the liturgy to God's saving work in Jesus Christ. Hence, "material liturgics."—Tr.

Word. If that is the case—I cannot say whether it is—it could be that there are actually times where prayer, worship, liturgy understood theologically, all recede, indeed become impossible. And not because people are diminished people, but because God as pure and simple Mystery is not nameable in an a priori way at all times. I say that more as a question, less as an assertion. If the question is correctly stated, then what happens to the liturgy of the Church? As long as the Spirit of Christ awakens people to faith in the trinitarian Source of all being, there has to be direct response of person to person—thus prayer, doxology, celebration of salvation, feasts. What then does liturgy in an atheistic age look like? Silence alone is not liturgy, even though it belongs to liturgy. I believe that we can look for answers to this question through research into two areas of concern.

We can ask who the human being is that must be formed for a Church that celebrates the liturgy, and what are the conditions that foster his existence. We know that there is no worship, no liturgy without a stirring of joy. Joy occurs when a person experiences something freshly bestowed that is decisive to human existence. The task, then, would be to explicate how a human being can newly experience his existence in such a way that what was recently called "God," the Holy One, the Source, becomes known and responded to. . . .

Given this situation, it seems to me that phenomenology can supply us with . . . telling information. Phenomenology describes a human being's existential situation as a whole in regard to its meaning, its modes of acting and its prerequisites. It can point to the fact that the experience of the Holy belongs to human existence, something that becomes apparent where the ultimate depth of meaning shines forth. The difference between sacred and profane—obviously a frequently encountered problem today—does not mean associating individual things and connections already at hand, but suggests rather different levels of understanding. Every profane reality is potentially sacred if its deepest significance is revealed. I believe that here especially, if we probe further into the general study of religion,[9] we can obtain insights that supply useful knowledge for our demanding critical function. I suggest three subject areas as examples: (a) Local community (local church)—the human connectedness to a place (the experience of home); (b) Feast, Sunday, Church Year—and

[9]In this connection, see Hansjörg Auf der Maur, "Das Verhältnis einer zukünftigen Liturgiewissenschaft zur Religionswissenschaft," *Archiv für Liturgiewissenschaft* 10, no. 2 (1968) 317–43.

the temporal nature of human existence;[10] (c) The Word- and formula-bound character of the liturgy, and language as "the house of being" (Heidegger).

As far as I know, the most useful and most important attempt to formulate phenomenologically the experience of the Holy One was undertaken by Bernhard Welte and his students.[11] The study of literature, by explaining the insights of poets, also supplies meaning. This area of studies, it seems to me, can give us a sharper vision into where people today still have experiences, or have new kinds of experiences, which both allow them to express new names for the Holy One and enable us to practice our critical function within theology. We can then point out inauthentic retrenchments if the rest of theology is not doxologically fruitful.

A possible study's first direction, to which I have already referred, is to ask how and where the Holy One can proclaim his presence in human experience. The other direction asks whether there do not now also exist quasi-"objective" possibilities of being able to know in a new way that living Reality which for generations before us was known by the name of "God." It does not take a lot of effort to become aware that the Church deals not simply with "God," but with a very specific reality, the Author of Revelation. How can he be known anew? I return to the previously cited statements about knowing and being able.[12] A human being knows something only when he knows what it has done, when he is aware of its history. Today, therefore, we are directed to history. What happened when human beings had the beginning, normative encounters with the Author of Revelation? What was revealed there, and in which media—that is, names, words, forms of speech—did it take place? I believe that liturgiology has to dedicate itself intensively to the theology of the Old Testament. For

[10]We have tried to pursue this initiative in our studies, "Breviary" and "Liturgy III: Liturgical Year," *Sacramentum Mundi*, ed. Karl Rahner (New York: Herder & Herder, 1968) vol. 1, 236–39; vol. 3, 333–37.

[11]E.g., Bernhard Welte, *Dialektik der Liebe: Gedanken zur Phänomenoligie der Liebe und zur christlichen Nächstenliebe im technologischen Zeitalter* (Frankfurt am Main: Josef Knecht, 1973).—*Tr.*

[12]"To know yourself means to know what you can do; and since no one knows what he can do before he has tried it, the only key to what the human being can do is what he has already done. Thus the value of history consists of the fact that it teaches us what the human being has done and with that what the human being is" (R. C. Collingwood, cited in Kurt H. Wolff, *Versuch einer Wissenssoziologie*, Soziologische Texte 53 [Berlin-Neuwied, 1968] 176).—*Tr.*

what is said in the Old Testament about the encounter of the LORD with his people has value beyond its own confines. Indeed, we can come to know more about God factually in the Old Testament—his name, his activity, his speaking, even the experience people have of his being and of being recalled to him, including the conditions that make it possible to answer him—than in the New Testament. Consequently, in an age where the received names of God have disappeared, this beginning history of salvation possesses a new importance and an urgent timeliness.

We of course would have to look at the Old Testament from other than what has been our accustomed perspectives. We must first of all recognize what is truly over with and past, to which doubtlessly belongs the whole Old Testament cult, even though it had been an area of great interest to our medieval colleagues. Indeed, although in principle correct, neither do I have in mind the schema of type-fulfillment which discovers the glory of the Old Testament through Christ and sees it as valuable through him. I have something else in mind. It would be to identify patterns that are constant throughout the history of God which the Old Testament portrays—laws, as it were, without which there is clearly no nearness of the revealing God in the past or present. As examples I would name: (1) The form-patterns by which God addresses the prophets (the schema of prophetic speech): possible form-patterns for a correspondingly appropriate (i.e., one that fits the address) word of prayer "in the name of Jesus" and, connected to it, "in the name of the Church;" (2) An experience of God which names God as distant and absent and still prays (especially in the Psalms): the corresponding right and duty of the Church to proclaim our situation an "absence of God" as well, doing so possibly even in the liturgy; (3) The turning of the LORD to his people in the covenant, the establishment of the People of God through the covenant, the actualizing of the covenant in continual communication— the LORD through the prophets, the people through prayers (no covenant, no People of God without prayer): correspondingly, no new People of God without communication, without liturgy; (4) And originating out of this, the communal nature of worship, of liturgy, so emphasized in recent times.

Such a theographic, as it were, valuation of the Old Testament is, if I see it rightly, new to our discipline. But it could certainly give us material and norms for our most critical function within theology, that of evaluating theology as a whole in regard to its doxological quality: does it truly deal with a God about whom and to whom we must address ourselves explicitly, that is, pray? Only that sort of liturgically-capable theology *is* theology.

How can an individual now become master of the postulates of such expanded subject matter? No one of us can, in addition to his own specialty within liturgiology, work in the area of phenomenology and simultaneously be distinguished as a specialist in Old Testament theology. But we can be aware of the questions, which in turn makes us alert to where possible answers can be found. Normally the liturgist will not be able to work in these areas nor will he need to. In the conversations among theological disciplines it is the critical function of the neighboring discipline to scrutinize our work and to give us the material which we ourselves are not able to process. Our task is now no longer as hopelessly large as it may have seemed at first glance.

If we engage at all in the critical function of liturgiology as I have just outlined it, as is our role because of the object of our craft, we will not have to complain either about lack of importance or lack of work. In regard to the relative value of its yield, liturgiology would then occupy a place next to the basic theological subjects of dogmatics, exegesis and moral theology. I do not see this as an arrogant claim of experts who have appeared only too recently on the scene, but the assertion that we see our assignment for what it is. If the liturgy is "the highpoint to which all the action of the Church tends and likewise the source from which all her power flows," then the study of theology must deal with nothing less than faith in God as God, which the Church as a whole must witness to. And that discipline is correspondingly important which deals explicitly with this aspect of God.

J. Frank Henderson

Lawrence A. Hoffman: Liturgy as Real Prayer for Real People

Lawrence A. Hoffman (1942–) was ordained as a rabbi in 1969, received his Ph.D. in 1973, and has served since then as professor of liturgy at the Hebrew Union College—Jewish Institute of Religion in New York City. From 1984 to 1987 he directed its School of Sacred Music as well. He has often been a visiting professor at the University of Notre Dame. He is past president of the North American Academy of Liturgy and serves as consultant on liturgical matters to many local congregations and organizations, including the United States Navy.

Hoffman combines research on Jewish ritual, worship, and spirituality with a deep concern for the spiritual renewal of American Judaism. He is a student of the history and development of Jewish liturgy, for example, circumcision, ordination, the Passover Seder, blessings. He is especially concerned that the meaning and spirituality of the Jewish liturgy be appreciated more deeply; he has helped to prepare renewed liturgical books for the Jewish community. He also works with Christian liturgists on matters of common concern and helps them become better informed regarding Jewish liturgy. He is able to communicate the insights and values of Jewish liturgy to Christian students especially well.

In his concern that liturgy—whether Jewish or Christian—be real prayer for real people, Hoffman considers liturgy from many points of view. Liturgy is not just texts but what individuals and communities actually do. Liturgy therefore needs to be viewed in terms of history, texts, forms, and structures; from the perspective of the human sciences—psychology, sociology, anthropology; and in terms of social environment and architectural environment, among other factors. He names and tries to understand the many contemporary challenges of liturgical worship and seeks to respond to these challenges in ways that are both creative and faithful to tradition. He seeks, in other words, a holistic approach to liturgy.

FOR FURTHER READING

The Canonization of the Synagogue Service. Notre Dame and London: Univ. of Notre Dame Press, 1979; *Beyond the Text: A Holistic Approach to Liturgy.* Bloomington: Indiana Univ. Press, 1987; *The Art of Public Prayer: Not for Clergy Only.* Washington: Pastoral Press, 1988; *Covenant of Blood: Circumcision and Gender in Rabbinic Judaism.* Chicago: Univ. of Chicago Press, 1995; *Two Liturgical Traditions* (co-editor). 6 vols. to date. Notre Dame and London: Univ. of Notre Dame Press, 1991–99; *Minhag Ami: My People's Prayer Book* (editor-in-chief and contributor). 6 vols. projected. Woodstock, Vt.: Jewish Lights Publishing, 1988–.

Lawrence A. Hoffman

A Holistic View of Liturgy[1]

Clifford Geertz [comments] regarding the incredible wealth of alternative perspectives with which contemporary theorists describe society: "The woods are full of eager interpreters," . . . each with a divining rod for uncovering the goings-on of human affairs. [My] attempt . . . to take the liturgical text as a necessary starting point, but then to go beyond it, using a holistic view of the process by which that text is actually prayed to reconstruct the identity of the people who pray it, is but one of them. . . . At issue is not any particular claim, so much as the entire enterprise, a commitment to discover the identity of a praying community—its world view (the way things are), its ethos ("the tone, character and quality of its life, its moral and aesthetic style and mood"),[2] and the place it occupies in both—and to do so through an analysis of its praying, rather than going the other way around, that is, assuming that we know enough (relatively speaking) about the community's self-perception and need most now, on the basis of that knowledge, to reproduce the recension history of its prayers.

If our goal is the ultimate unveiling of communal identity, that is, knowledge of the community as the community knew itself, and as it played out its role in the world based on that knowledge, two independent starting points are required, and both of them come to-

[1]Excerpted from Lawrence A. Hoffman, "A Holistic View of Liturgy," ch. 8, "Conclusion," *Beyond the Text: A Holistic Approach to Liturgy* (Bloomington and Indianapolis: Indiana Univ. Press, 1987) 172–82. Reprinted by permission of the author.
[2]Following the dichotomy of Geertz; see his *Interpretation of Cultures* (New York, 1970) 216–27.

gether, in a sort of pincers movement, in the liturgical study advocated here. First we have the purely textual disciplines—philology and form-criticism—by which reliable sets of prayers are attained; my indebtedness to the array of scholars, past and present, engaged in textual reconstruction should be patently evident at every turn of every argument here. We need also what has generally been the province of independent pursuits like history, which begin also with accurate facsimiles of texts, but which start from texts other than liturgical ones, and thus provide their own independent witness for a people's identity through time. Where these two directions converge is the act of prayer, in which the people, as living reality, act out the world as it sees it, and from which its members return to their several homes to shape their lives about the contours of the world as presented in prayer. It is as if we had a liturgical Heisenberg principle, in which a particle's position and momentum are replaced by a people's history and its prayers. The liturgical principle of uncertainty would state that historical evidence of a people's identity and the prayer texts by which it ritualizes its role are two interdependent entities, both of which cannot be known fully, since each step in isolating a new truth about one brings about an improvement in our understanding of the other, which in turn reflects a novel recognition of the first, and so on, *ad infinitum*. Nevertheless, physicists study particles with some success, and we can do the same for a people's identity, as long as we remember—and this is my point—that discoveries in one direction, regardless of their scope and importance, cannot obviate the need to ask questions in the other direction too. We must simply go beyond an eternal recreation of scientifically accurate texts; we need desperately to see how those texts, played out as lived liturgical practice, had consequences for the people who used them.

The focus of study should then not be the text at all, but what I have called the liturgical field, the holistic network of interrelationships that binds together discrete things, acts, people, and events into the activity we call worship—or better still, ritual. Within that field, one may single out any given relationship between or among any number of data for attention. I have here tried to isolate several such questions that seem to me crucial in the process by which ritualizing one's identity within religious communities fixes the sense of who one is.

Beginning with a look at *havdalah*, we saw the function ritual plays in establishing the categories with which we order experience. From the time of our birth, we human beings develop our capacity to encode events in meaningful patterns built on the simple recognition that to be one thing is not to be another. Whether it be the psychological development of the ego, as opposed to others; our group in contrast to theirs; the territorial imperative for our (but not their) space; or our equally serious claim that time is ours alone to name, to qualify, and even to quantify according to our own numbering system—things exist for us only if we master their patterns, and ritual seems to be above all the way we take possession of the patterns that others before us have handed down, a means of reminding ourselves that those patterns really count, and a ready-made theater for rehearsing them for our own benefit as well as for the next generation whom we socialize into them. Thus, Saturday night may be just the middle of a weekend for others, but for Jews enwrapt in (and enraptured by) *havdalah*, it is the guarantee that the very world is passing from a state of holy to one of profane.

* * *

So the study of liturgy ought first to ask how liturgical rituals encode the world for those who ritualize. Like anthropologists at work among strangers, we ask for the "why" behind the phenomena, eliciting explanations beyond what the "text" of their testimony seemed immediately able to offer; but the strangers cease being strange only when we penetrate the surface of their language, only when the underlying categories with which they order things in the first place come to light.

But if, through their ritual and its implicit categories of meaning, Jews demarcate themselves from non-Jews, choosing, as it were, an alternative social universe to inhabit, so too do different groups of Jews develop in alternative ways from one another. . . . How do simple human beings find their way through the maze of things they might be, if not, primarily, through ritual? . . .

What we have is the process of censoring in and censoring out, another conceptual model we used here, an attempt to include oneself and one's group within the dominant definition of licit religiosity, yet to define oneself as holding a special place (in contrast to the "others") inside that generally recognized framework. If the focus of study is Roman religion in general, then it is late antiquity's dominant definition of religion that everyone emulates—Jews too sacrificed animals in their Temple, with all the drama and flourish that all cosmopolitans expected of religion then.[3] But they did so in their own way. And when the Temple ceased, they patterned their prayer after the cultic model, just as Christians too, without a Temple in which to sacrifice, emphasized the sacrificial aspect of their ritual observance.

Contrary to normal expectations, our rituals rarely censor out the obvious culprits in the vicinity—they are too evidently "not us" to warrant being singled out for negative mention. They exclude, instead, the close cousins, whose very similarity to us makes it imperative that we hedge our group's ego boundaries securely against their conceivable encroachment on our ideological turf. Thus, we looked at the growth of American Judaism and saw little ritualistic demarcation between Jews and non-Jews, but a great deal of censoring out of other Jewish possibilities: Reform (German immigrants) vs. "traditionalist" (eastern European immigrants); and Conservative movement vs. Reconstructionists. To the extent that a Reform ritual polemicizes against Christian influence, it is not, strictly speaking, Christians who are being censored out, but other Jews, who are charged—at least potentially—with borrowing too freely from Christians, crossing the divide between licit self-inclusion in society's norm and illicit living in someone else's camp. Similarly, in the past: the "so-called Gnostics," against whom Irenaeus railed, were not a foreign sect of some sort, but Christians who surely had an equally opprobrious epithet for Irenaeus in return; and the *minim* cursed in early Jewish liturgy were not Christians but other Jews, accused of going too far in the direction of Christianity. The point is that group boundaries are fluid, always shifting, and observable only after the fact, where definers of group identity have successfully decided to erect them. Arbitrarily, people on the other side of the fence discover themselves marked off as strangers, even though they do not necessarily elect to be so. And after a period of years, subdivisions of people develop subdivisions of ritual, that is to say, rites.

So our study of rites documented no accident of geography, but a more basic underlying matter: the identity formation of subgroups within the larger social fabric. A second step in the holistic study of liturgy, then, is to identify changes in worship not for their own sake but so as to recognize socially significant divisions in the religious identity of the worshipers; to trace prayer book revisions

[3]Compare, for example, Ramsay McMullen's survey, *Paganism in the Roman Empire* (New Haven, 1981), with descriptions of the cult in Jewish tradition.

precisely because they entail human revisions of the worshipers' self-perception.

But identity in space through the knowledge that we keep the Sabbath precisely as it is kept by our cousins in Poland or in Jerusalem, say, is accompanied by identity through time, the myth of common origins that explains why we all do so in the first place. Hence, our next investigation dealt with what I called sacred myth, the history we tell one another in the course of our ritualizing together. Ritual is nothing if not time-bound, and specific occasions in the annual cycle take on their specificity because (among other things) they are anniversaries—either real or imagined—of occurrences in the past, occurrences that would have gone unnoticed but for the fact that the people celebrating their recurrence have chosen to remember them as their own particular way of categorizing human history. Entire mythical tales are rarely included in these annual celebrations, but references to them are, and the religious community elsewhere socializes its members to recognize these allusions.

* * *

We thus see ritual serving as the locus for what we can call *normal exegetical mythologizing.* Each ritual action is pregnant with meaning and accompanied by exegetical interpretation, either in the form of obvious historical narrative, selectively perceived and honed in size to fit the ritual moment, or just in tacit acknowledgment of these larger truths, which are merely hinted at as the ritual proceeds. . . .

Surely the liturgist's task is to unearth the system of significant history that religions present to their members at the moments most charged with religious import, the holy days and times that evoke the past.

Finally, I have made use of the common notion that religions postulate a certain "rightness" about who they are. In the course of human history, religious identity has sometimes been ascribed, sometimes chosen, but even when the latter, religious believers do more than join a group like all groups. To switch the college one attends, or to take up golf but drop racquetball, is in the realm of taste; but to assume a new religious identity is, as we say, to convert, to be born again, to be made over. By definition, conversion—like naming ceremonies for all new things—is performative in nature, in that from the perspective of the person converting, it succeeds felicitously only if he or she professes commitment to the newfound faith. In the eyes of the convert, the medieval notion of "forced conversion" is an oxy-moron, no less than forced free will or necessary choice. Religion is an identity, after all, not a pastime. It must, therefore, possess the means to impress its inherent "rightness" on those born to it, and on those who choose it, both. In part, the sacred myth accomplishes this, but inevitably, recourse is had to ultimates, that is, at least in Western religions, to God. Hence [finally one must deal] with the apprehension of the divine in worship—an appropriate ending, since it is the divine-human encounter that makes worship what it is.

Here, my commitment to conceptualizing an underlying structure that unifies diverse cases of the same phenomenon should be evident, since the analysis revealed a threefold "generic" grid composed of *Cultural Backdrop, Master Image,* and *Synecdochal Vocabulary,* which should be applicable to all liturgical instances, independent of their specific cultural content . . . .The study of prayer books was defined as a combined message of *manifest content, design or layout,* and *choreography,* for example.

What unifies this . . . is the common theme of religious community in search of self-definition through its life of prayer. At issue is an artistic impulse, however, so that if we are to ask the question, What is liturgy? without limiting our response in advance to the identification of some series of texts, we must eventually evoke the artistic potential in human behavior. There are, I think, at least three options open to us in this regard, and I should be explicit with regard to the one represented here.

* * *

In sum, the first structural model that we might employ is illustrated by Freud, whose explanatory hermeneutic takes for granted four characteristics: (1) surface phenomena from which theories are extrapolated are objectively existent, and thus observable to an impartial outsider; (2) the theory explaining phenomena, however, must penetrate beneath observations to postulate a structural connective tissue that unifies discrete and variable data; (3) truth or falsity of theories is tested by their ability to predict other surface phenomena, that is, they are of a cause-and-effect nature; (4) interpretations are thus diachronic, often mythic, in terms of extending their causal chain back through time beyond the specific phenomena in question.

A second model is given to us by Lévi-Strauss, in many ways the paragon of structuralism. He was highly influenced by Freud, he says, since the Freudian system appealed to his preference for a geological model, whereby diachronic development is nevertheless present synchronically.[4] Nevertheless, Lévi-Strauss's criteria for acceptable hypotheses differ significantly from Freud's. Of the four assumptions that Freud held, Lévi Strauss agrees with the first two, in that (1) phenomena are objectively present and empirically evident, and (2) explanations of them require the unearthing of structural grids supportive of the "seemingly incoherent mass" of "impenetrable" data.[5] Moreover, the underlying structures are mental constructs, for Lévi-Strauss, just as they are psychological ones for Freud.

But here, the similarity ceases. Lévi-Strauss's structures are not cause-and-effect relationships, but inbuilt constructs in the mind. Two events A and B are said to be explained not because A is the cause of B, but because A occurs with B as a related logical type, and so can be projected through cultural patterning upon the world we inhabit. With regard to totemism, then, Lévi-Strauss abandons cause-and-effect explanations and erects an internal logic of the system, what he calls the aesthetic component. It is "the arousal of aesthetic curiosity [that] leads directly to an acquisition of knowledge," a lesson he learned from Freud (!) he says. Thus, "ideas and beliefs of the totemic type . . . constitute codes, making it possible to ensure, in the form of conceptual systems, the convertibility of messages"; or, more specifically, in direct denial of the cause/effect hermeneutic, "How hopeless it is to attempt to establish a relation of priority between nutritional prohibitions and rules of exogamy. The relationship between them is not causal, but metaphorical."[6] Phenomena are explicable by the synchronic logical structure of the human mind itself, and we know an explanation to be true not because it predicts anything, but because it coheres aesthetically, providing "the important and valid category of the meaningful which is the highest mode of being of the rational."[7]

It is of the greatest importance to see that Lévi-Strauss has consciously crossed the boundary into the realm of art here, postulating an underlying mental structure according to which all phenomena are related not by cause and effect, nor in diachronic linear fashion,

[4]Claude Lévi-Strauss, *Tristes Tropiques* (1955; New York: Washington Square Press, 1977) 47, 49.

[5]Ibid., 49.

[6]Ibid., 49; Claude Lévi-Strauss, *The Savage Mind* (Chicago, 1963) 31, 105.

[7]*Tristes Tropiques*, 47.

but with the same logic by which a painting or a symphony is "true," that is, by its presentation synchronically, all at one time, of internal harmony. Typically, Freud took a synchronic system, totemism, and reduced it to a diachronic myth of explanation; Lévi-Strauss takes a diachronic account, myth, and reduces it to a synchronic structure, mental logic.

It may be that Lévi-Strauss's postulate of the mind's internal structure that dominates cultural categorization is correct. But at the very least, it seems premature to make that judgment.[8] So we are left with a third possibility for our analysis here, one that retains Lévi-Strauss's emphasis on meaning, eschews the need for cause-and-effect demonstrations, and is content with seeing the presentations of ritual action as a structure enforced on phenomena, without that structure existing inherently in the human mind itself. For whether, in fact, it turns out that human beings are or are not genetically constructed to think in binary opposites (or any other logical paradigm) is, in a sense, a moot point, beyond what we need to make sense of culture. As long as the ritual patterning of the universe can be seen as a projection of the human need to order phenomena artistically, it matters little whether that need is biologically given via a particular type of necessary mental operation or not.

The third mode, and the one at use in these pages, then, is . . . a combination of the perspectives in the human sciences illustrated by Peter Berger, Mary Douglas, and Clifford Geertz. As in Freud and Lévi-Strauss, (1) phenomena are assumed to be real, though not necessarily completely objective, in that it is hard to see how we can penetrate the web of culturally enforced structure in order to see nature raw. (2) Interpretations of phenomena are structural too, though these structures are not necessarily given to reality by the workings of the psyche or the logic of the mind, as Freud or Lévi-Strauss would have it. Sometimes they can be traced in a functionalist sort of way to the social structure itself (as in the case of Ottonian transcendence), and they must be studied as synchronic presentations of meaning behind disparate data, apparent to human understanding because they are forced upon the data by cultural patterns that are rehearsed in the ritual field. Therein lies the significance of ritual. And therein lies the extended study of liturgy for which I argue.

[8]See, however, essays in *Zygon* 18 (1983) 221–326, which investigate the possibility that cultural patterning is rooted in the brain's structure.

Liturgy should concern itself with the liturgical field as a whole because only there is the meaning behind the text made evident to worshipers. What we have here is no linear presentation of verbal signs, but a symbol system that Susanne Langer has characterized as nondiscursive and presentational. Ritual, like art, is "judged on our experience of its revelations." Its assertions are neither true nor false but adequate or inadequate, expressive or not.[9] They are primarily solutions to "the problem of integration," whereby meaning, pattern, composition, and rhythm are bestowed on human existence in the world.[10] Or, to revert to Geertz's analogy . . . "Analysis [I should say, *liturgical* analysis] is [or should be] the sorting out of the structures of signification . . . our constructions of other people's constructions of what they and their compatriots are up to."[11] Toward that end, the holistic study of liturgy may begin with the text but must eventually go beyond it—to the people, to their meanings, to their assumed constructs, and to their ritualized patterns that make their world uniquely their own.

[9]Susanne K. Langer, *Philosophy in a New Key* (New York: Mentor, 1941) 222–23.

[10]See Gregory Bateson on art, *Steps to an Ecology of Mind* (New York, 1971) 128–52.

[11]Geertz, *Interpretation of Cultures*, 9.

4

How Are Theology and Liturgy Related?

Sometimes the question is center stage; sometimes it lurks just around the corner. But whether conscious and explicit or not, the nature of the relationship between theology and liturgy is a concern deeply embedded in liturgical theology. No self-respecting scholar of liturgical theology ignores the issues surrounding *lex orandi, lex credendi*—although that concept itself is invoked in a bewildering number of alternative wordings, each reflecting a different nuance of meaning. If you want to be considered at all knowledgeable in the field, you will have to learn how to distinguish between them, and let the Latin terminology become embedded in your consciousness (and—among your colleagues in the field—in your speech as well!).

I have already reviewed the options for the relation between *orandi* and *credendi* in the introductory chapter under "Theology in Liturgy"; it may be helpful to review those alternatives again (see p. 11). In the readings that follow you will discover that the interrelationships are even more intricate and complex than it first appears. None of the easy alternatives will do, but get out your intellectual hip boots and wade in! If you love doing liturgical theology, you'll discover the water's fine!

That's the water of baptism, for one thing, where *orandi* and *credendi* are so interwoven in our baptismal experience as to be distinguishable but inseparable. Which brings us to Kavanagh's insistence that the liturgy is *theologia prima*—primary theology, in its own rite (*sic*). Kilmartin and Wainwright provide additional perspectives, and no treatment of this question would be complete without reference to all three.

While you're working through the conceptual relations, take time to observe how each author's presentational style embodies their perspective. Do they practice what they teach?

Gordon W. Lathrop

Aidan Kavanagh: Liturgy as *Theologia Prima*

Aidan Kavanagh is the scholar who has most persuasively articulated the influential idea that the liturgy is the primary theology of the Church, the primary enactment of the Church's faith. He has done so with a unique and memorable voice. It is a voice at once urbane yet alive to common speech, erudite yet deeply respectful of "Mrs. Murphy," elegant yet clear, Roman Catholic yet ecumenically engaged, faithful yet richly academic, humble—dutiful, even—yet imperious and epigrammatic. You will recognize that voice in the passage below.

Kavanagh is a native of Texas, with both Baptist and Episcopal background, who became a Roman Catholic and a Benedictine monk of St. Meinrad's Archabbey in Indiana. He was educated at St. Meinrad's and at the University of Ottawa, and he received his doctorate from the University of Trier in 1963, with a dissertation reflective of his past and future ecumenical engagements: "The Concept of Eucharistic Memorial in the Canon Revisions of Thomas Cranmer, Archbishop of Canterbury." He became the first professor in the graduate program in liturgical studies at Notre Dame University in 1966, and he left a profound imprint upon that program, shaping its enduring interest in both ritual studies and liturgical theology as well as liturgical history. In 1974 he became professor in the Yale Divinity School, where he exercised a similar influence in the ongoing development of the Institute of Sacred Music and where he entered into the rich dialogue of Yale University. In 1976 the first Berakah Award of the North American Academy of Liturgy was presented to him. At the occasion of that presentation he responded with an exquisitely crafted confession of the failings and unbegun work of liturgists, himself preeminently included. After all of this extensive work, it was only in 1978 that he began to publish his primary, book-length contributions to liturgical theology. He continues his contributions to this day, now as a respected professor emeritus at Yale University.

Kavanagh's major contributions to liturgical theology include his accent on *theologia prima,* his lifelong interest in conversion, initiation, and the *change* effected in liturgy, and his critical interactions with ritual *anthropology.* The discussion of all three of these crucial themes in liturgical scholarship will, at some point, always need to be traced to Aidan Kavanagh. While all three themes are pungently expressed in the excerpt included here, they may also be explored in greater detail in *The Shape of Baptism* (1978), *Elements of Rite* (1982), and *On Liturgical Theology* (1984). The same themes also animate his important 1983 response to a report on the work-in-progress of Geoffrey Wainwright.

Readers should be urged not to be so enchanted by the elegance of Kavanagh's voice nor so offended by his apodictic style as to fail to grasp the content. All of the churches are rightly called to canonical and eschatological responsibility in the Presence of the One who is saving the world. If, in Kavanagh's work, the readers do not find the secondary role of the liturgical theologian—the one who "reports the liturgy"—clearly enough distinguished from the awesome importance of liturgy itself or do not find enough realism about the actual changes that liturgy effects, then they should recall the critical humility of the 1976 Berakah laureate. This is a man at work on questions that matter. The style is only a slightly veiled self-protection before the vertiginous Presence. And the principal convert is the author himself.

FOR FURTHER READING

The Shape of Baptism. New York: Pueblo, 1978; *Elements of Rite.* New York: Pueblo, 1982; *On Liturgical Theology.* New York: Pueblo, 1984; "Liturgical Business Unfinished and Unbegun," *Worship* 50 (1976) 354–64 (Berakah response); "Response: Primary Theology and Liturgical Act," *Worship* 57 (1983) 321–24 (Response to Wainwright); VanderWilt, Jeffrey, "Aidan Kavanagh, O.S.B.: An Annotated Bibliography." *Rule of Prayer, Rule of Faith: Essays in Honor of Aidan Kavanagh,* Ed. N. Mitchell and J. Baldovin. Collegeville: The Liturgical Press, 1996, 343–51.

Aidan Kavanagh

On Liturgical Theology[1]

LITURGY, CANONICITY, AND ESCHATOLOGY

No liturgical theology can afford to ignore the basic facts that the "social occasion" which is a liturgical act is occasional, formal, unifying, and about survival. These basic facts help to throw some light not only on the liturgy's deep structures, but on the underlying congruity between the several disciplines embraced by the study of liturgy, including the discipline of liturgical theology.

That a "social occasion" is occasional, for example, suggests that liturgy is festive. It is a very special event no matter how often or how seldom it happens. Liturgy's festivity involves it necessarily in the details of time and season, details which require calculations and calendars. These are what the discipline of heortology, the study of feasts and seasons, deals with.[2]

That a "social occasion" is formal means that liturgy has a certain order of procedure about it. It is this specific order which distinguishes Christian baptism from all other forms of human bathing, which marks off Christian Eucharist from all other forms of human dining. Its order gives specific form to liturgical structure and differentiates Christian liturgical behavior from all other similar forms of human ritual behavior, while the same order relates liturgical behavior to all

---

[1] Excerpted from Aidan Kavanagh, ch. 7, "Liturgy, Canonicity, and Eschatology," and ch. 8, "Liturgy and Normality," *On Liturgical Theology* (Collegeville, Minn.: The Liturgical Press, A Pueblo Book, 1984). Reprinted by permission.

[2] See Thomas J. Talley, "A Christian Heortology," *The Times of Celebration*, Concilium Series 142 (New York, 1981) 14–21.

those other forms as well.[3] Studying the origins, growth, and comparison of liturgical orders, and analyzing their individual structures, is the main burden of *historical studies* of the liturgy.[4] These are concerned primarily with *what* will be the subject of subsequent investigations into the *why* of liturgical growth and the *how* of liturgical modulation in a given era, including one's own.

That a "social occasion" is repetitious and rhythmic suggests that liturgy is necessarily enmeshed in space and time. Worship in Spirit and in truth is never abstract, nor does it happen on some noetic level which is undifferentiated like a Cartesian grid.[5] Liturgy happens only in the rough-and-tumble landscape of spaces and times which people discover and quarry for meaning in their lives. This is an *artistic* enterprise. Liturgical repetition is thus a knowledgeable accomplishment, and its organization into definite rhythms of sounds, sights, gestures, and even smells is an act of human artistry—no more nor less so than building a house, composing a concerto, laying out a town, or playing cello. Therefore the student of liturgy must know not only heortology and history but the spatial, sonic, visual, and kinetic arts of ceremonial choreography as well. A liturgical scholar who is illiterate in the several human arts can never know his or her subject adequately. To this extent, such a one will inevitably report the liturgy to secondary theologians in a manner more or less warped.

That a "social occasion" is repetitious and rhythmic means also that liturgy is *unifying*, for repetition and rhythm have this effect upon human assemblies for worse or better. The unity which repetition and rhythm produce in social gatherings is so power-laden as to be a matter of concern. It can be so powerful as to drive a mob to violence under the orchestration of a demagogue. It may attain monstrous proportions, as at a Nazi *Parteitag* in Nuremberg. But *koinonia*, the unity of the churches of God, may be its result as well. To assure the latter and rule out the former is the main reason why Christian

[3]See Alexander Schmemann, *Introduction to Liturgical Theology* (Portland, Me., 1966), for doctrinal reflections on liturgical order.
[4]For example, Josef A. Jungmann, *The Mass of the Roman Rite* (New York, 1950) 2 vols.; A. Stenzel, *Die Taufe: eine genetische Erklärung der Taufliturgie* (Innsbruck, 1958); Paul F. Bradshaw, *Daily Prayer in the Early Church* (London, 1981); Kenneth Stevenson, *Nuptial Blessing: A Study of Christian Marriage Rites* (London, 1982).
[5]See Kent Bloomer and Charles Moore, *Body, Memory, Architecture* (New Haven, 1977) 23–24, 73–74.

orthodoxia has always been canonical, which means that it is governed by rule or *kanon*. The liturgy's canonicity goes beyond the rules of formality and aesthetics. Nor is there only a single rule or canon governing liturgy. There are several canons, all of which compenetrate and interact to assure, insofar as canons may, that the liturgy of Christians does not drift into delusion and fantasy but remains worship in Spirit and in truth. Each of the several canons is the result of innumerable complex transactions carried on within the worshiping assembly itself over considerable periods of time.

First, there is the *canon of holy Scripture.* This canon governs what the assembly deems appropriate that it should read and hear as it stands before God in worship. It is this special existential stance with respect to the divine Presence which constrains the assembly's choice to those written works which bespeak authentically that Presence to save in the world. For this reason, the canon of holy Scripture embraces written works not for their literary merit nor on the basis of the piety of their authors, but on the grounds of their being "of God" rather than just "about God." It is only with great caution that the liturgy makes use of any other written compositions in its order of service, and even then it is the close proximity of these written works to the canonical Scriptures which recommends them far more than their stylistic quality or the interest of their contents. Of all the canons which affect liturgical worship, it is the canon of holy Scripture which keeps the assembly locked into the fundamental relationship that gives it its unique character among all other human gatherings, namely its relationship to the presence in its midst of the living God.

Second, there is the *canon of baptismal faith* summed up in the several trinitarian creeds.[6] The earliest of these grew out of the three questions put to candidates for baptism as they stood naked in the font concerning their faith in Father, Son, and Holy Spirit. The creeds thus distill the substance of revealed gospel into baptismal form precisely at the instant when membership is consummated in the corporate person of him whose gospel it is. Next to the canon of holy Scripture, the credal canon of baptismal faith keeps the assembly's worship firmly rooted in relationship to a divine Presence which is not only vertiginous but communitarian and personal. The creed affirms the assembly's awareness that the living God before whom it

[6]See J. N. D. Kelly, *Early Christian Creeds* (London, 1950).

stands in worship is a community of Persons which wills to manifest itself in the world through a community of human persons wholly devoted to the world's restoration in its trinitarian Source. The canon of baptismal faith thus constrains the assembly to worship in such a way that its apostolate in the world as icon of the Holy Trinity and agent under God of the world's communion with its Source is rendered accessible to those of good will. The canon checks any temptation the assembly may be under to withdraw into itself and to worship with self-complacency. The canon of baptismal faith cautions ministers not to regard the assembly of the baptized as a clergy support group. It cautions the assembly never to forget that it is nothing less than a chosen race, a royal priesthood, a holy nation, God's own people who exist to declare the wonderful deeds of him who has called it out of darkness into his marvelous light (1 Pet 2:9).

Third, there is the *canon of eucharistic faith* which is carried in the assembly's repertoire of eucharistic prayers or "canons of the Mass." These prayers distill the substance of revealed Gospel and its baptismal creeds into strictly euchological forms of thanksgiving and petition within the corporate person of him whose Gospel is in motion for the life of the world. As the trinitarian questions generate the creed in baptism, so eucharistic prayers generate a euchological "creed" appropriate to the Banquet of the Lamb. For this reason, the eucharistic prayer must be taken as seriously in its own context as the creed must be taken in baptism, and as holy Scripture must be taken in the general life of the Church.

Fourth, there is that body of *canonical laws* which regulate the daily living and the due processes of assemblies of Christians in conformity with the foregoing canons of Scripture, creed, and prayer. Canonical laws, which are often denigrated as being unimportant, attempt to render the other three canons specific in the small details of faithful daily life. When canonical laws are overlooked too long, the other three canons are likely to drift away from a church's consciousness and to be honored only in the breach. When this happens, such a church will invariably discover its apostolate to be compromised, its faith dubious, its worship more concerned with current events than with the presence of the living God, and its efforts bent more to maintaining its own coherence than to restoring the unity of the world to God in Christ.

Finally, that a "social occasion" is about survival suggests that liturgy has an *eschatological dimension* throughout, even when its surface structures may seem to be concerned overtly with a historical commemoration (such as the day of Jesus' death) or a current event. But liturgy's deep structures always betray the continuing awareness of the faithful that the One in whose presence they stand is beyond time and time's end no less than time's beginning, Alpha and Omega. Thus even when the liturgy of Christians deals with time, as it inevitably must, it does so not in the short term but *sub specie aeternitatis*, that is, eschatologically.[7]

The liturgy is thus festive, ordered, and accomplished through a variety of artistic media. It is possible, even appropriate, that the disciplines of heortology, ritual history, and the study of the several liturgical arts be carried on according to methodologies which are not themselves theological. It does not seem possible, however, to deal with liturgy's canonical aspect, or with the eschatological dimension one meets within its deep structures, without entering into strictly theological discourse. For liturgical canonicity and eschatology are functions of that theological awareness which is native to the liturgical assembly itself. Liturgical canonicity and eschatology are, moreover, primary symptoms of that change, already mentioned, which occurs in the assembly of faithful people as they encounter the divine Presence in their act of liturgical worship. When Christians adjust to the change in them which God causes regularly in their liturgical worship, the adjustment is normally reflective and critical in terms of the four canons governing their corporate life *in the present*, and also in terms of their ultimate survival *in an eschatological future* which is already being worked out in them by God's grace and their own cooperation with that grace by faith and works. This is what it means to say that the liturgical act of Christians is not merely a mine from which scholars may dig material for second-order theological constructions. Nor is the liturgy just a dictionary from which the learned derive terms with which to write second-order theological treatises. Rather, the liturgy of faithful Christians is the primary theological act of the Church itself, and the ways in which this primary theological act carries on its own proper discourse are couched in terms of canonicity of content and structure, and in terms of eschatological survival.

When one comes to describe a liturgical theology, as distinct from a systematic theology of the liturgy, the description might be

[7]See Gregory Dix, *The Shape of the Liturgy* (London, 1945).

something like this. A liturgical theology is doxological due to the liturgy's festal quality. It is historical due to the liturgy's formal and ordered qualities. It requires critique of the sonic, visual, spatial, and kinetic arts due to the liturgy's immersion in space and time. It involves disciplined reflection on the present and actual state of life in the faithful assembly due to the liturgy's quality of canonicity— which means that a liturgical theology is inherently pastoral. And it involves no less disciplined reflection on the assembly's future discharge of its obligations in service as a corporate ministry of reconciliation according to grace and promise due to the liturgy's eschatological quality—which implies an ecclesiology no less ministerial than it is eschatological and pneumatic. The canonical "now" and the eschatological "future" frame *orthodoxia* as a life of sustained "right worship" in truth and in a Spirit who is not only consolation but promise as well.

* * *

This chapter has attempted to specify further the taxonomy of liturgy itself by calling attention to those qualities it seems to possess in common with any social occasion in which a mutuality of presences is involved. Because every social occasion is unifying and about survival, the social occasion called liturgy appears on its own evidence to be *canonical* and *eschatological*. These two qualities, which root liturgy in the present no less than in the long-term future, are those which particularly affect how primary theology is carried on by those who, beyond ordinary human efforts, live a life of one, holy, catholic, and apostolic "right worship" both inside and outside assemblies of faith. The canonical and eschatological qualities of Christian liturgy are, moreover, the ones which give specifically Christian stamp to the liturgy's being also *festive, ordered,* and *critical* as regards the various arts it uses.

On this basis, the chapter claimed that the true primary theologian in the Church is the liturgical assembly in each and every one of its members; that this primary theology is festive, ordered, steeped in the arts, canonical, and eschatological; that this primary theology discourse is what produces the body of basic faith perceptions upon which secondary theology is nurtured in its normal and healthy state. In this view, *lex supplicandi* and *lex credendi* are not detachable or opposable laws but subtly correlative, the first founding the second, the second affecting (although not founding) the first. Each law functions in concert with the other within the discourse of primary theology. This means that *lex credendi* is at root not merely something which is done exclusively by secondary theologians in their studies, as opposed to *lex supplicandi* done by nontheologians indulging in religious worship elsewhere. On the contrary, *lex credendi* is constantly being worked out, sustained, and established as the faithful in assembly are constantly working out, sustaining, and establishing their *lex supplicandi* from one festive, ordered, aesthetic, canonical, and eschatological liturgical act to the next under grace. *Lex credendi* is always in reality joined to *lex supplicandi* by an active verb as object is joined to subject, and the resulting affirmation says something central about primary theology and the relation of secondary theology to it. *Lex supplicandi legem statuat credendi* thus says something about the deepest structure and purpose of Christian worship. It also suggests a method of analytical procedure which the secondary theologian ignores to the Church's peril. For the liturgy of the faithful Christians is the primary theological act of the Church itself, and the ways in which this act carries on its proper discourse are above all canonical in structure and content, and eschatological in intent.

LITURGY AND NORMALITY

* * *

[P]art of our difficulty in grasping liturgy as a constitutive and foundational enterprise as distinct from its being little more than ceremonied adiaphora, may lie in our tendency to make secondary theology primary and primary theology secondary.

It now seems appropriate to close off this taxonomy of liturgy by pointing out in specific what liturgy and, by implication, liturgical theology are not. Such a series of negations may bring us close to what is positively normal in each.

Due to its festive nature, for example, liturgy is not ordinary, utilitarian, or for something.[8] Christians do not engage in liturgical worship to get grace or inspiration, to indulge in creativity, to become educated in matters ecclesiastical. Nor do they elaborate rite as a style of life to house nostalgia, to provide rest, to proffer moral uplift, or to supply aesthetic experience. While any or all of these results may accrue to an individual or an assembly as by-products of the

---

[8]See Josef Pieper, *In Tune with the World: A Theory of Festivity* (New York, 1965).

liturgical engagement, they constitute neither in whole nor in part the engagement's motive. The feast remains its own end. The business Christians transact in liturgy is festal business because, simply, Christ has conquered death by his death. Liturgical theology is therefore a festal endeavor, a doxological rather than any other sort of enterprise. And it is this in a way and to a degree that systematic theology, for all its other virtues, is not.

Due to its ordered character, liturgy is no more informal than any other human "social occasion" is without form. The history of Christian worship reveals an evolution of forms and formality to the detriment of makeshift, the idiosyncratic, and the aggressively enthusiastic. As the latter three characteristics turn up, they tend to be resisted by the assembly as a whole and then to be suppressed in one way or another by the assembly's ministers. A case in point may be seen in 1 Corinthians 11–14, where St. Paul cautions a particular church concerning eucharistic disorder which rends the assembly, charismatic enthusiasms which polarize the assembly, and the public behavior of certain women which causes uneasiness in Paul both as a traditional Jew and as an apostle sent to preach the gospel in as high a degree of its integrity as God's grace and his own weakness would allow. But his chastisement of the church in Corinth for liturgical disorder is for all, male and female alike. These four chapters are the first lecture in Christian history on the abuse of liturgical order. Liturgical theology is always in search of form and evangelical order.

Due to its incarnation, so to speak, in space and time, something which requires an artistic coping with creation in all its aspects, liturgy is not unworldly in that it cares nothing for the demands of matter, space, sound, and movement. Carelessness concerning these things does not produce spontaneity but confusion and anomie, an assembly intolerant of repetition, arhythmic, incoherent, bereft of form, and dissolute. Liturgical theology thus takes the arts very seriously indeed, being not merely appreciative of them, but critical of them all as they are pressed into the service of assemblies of faith.

Due to its canonical form and content, liturgy is not a battlefield of confrontation and divisiveness. The faithful do not assemble to engage in ideological combat with each other or to be rent asunder by competing special interest groups. Rather, they assemble under grace and according to the canons of Scripture and creed, prayer and common laws, in order to secure their unity in lived faith transmitted

98

from generation to generation for the life of the world. Liturgical theology's main tools in trade are therefore the canon of Scripture, the canon of the baptismal creeds, the canon of eucharistic prayers, and the canonical laws of community life. The liturgical theologian sees the liturgy as the ritual of a Word made flesh for the life of the world, as a ministry of reconciliation between God and all persons and things in Christ. This is worship in Spirit and in truth.

Finally, due to its eschatological intent, liturgy is about nothing less than ultimate, rather than immediate, survival. It is about life forever by grace and promise. Liturgy regards anything less as a trap and a delusion hostile to the gospel of Jesus Christ. Like the Sabbath, liturgy is for us rather than we for it. But also like the Sabbath, liturgy is for us in that it summons us by revealed Good News home to a Presence, to a life even now of communion in that Presence. To commune with that Presence is to be in at the end and at the center where the world is whole, fresh and always issuing new from the Father's hand through Christ in the Spirit. Unlike those who believe that Jesus came once long ago and will come again is a future more or less remote, liturgy moves within the abiding Presence of God in Christ, the uncreated creating Word, who fills the whole of time past, present and to come. Liturgical theology leans far into this eschatological wind, finding there as nowhere else not only grace's motive but its promise of judgment as well. This stance makes the liturgical theologian, like any other orthodox Christian, an unusually wary person who carries on his or her craft with great circumspection in a workshop through which cosmic storms thunder but the candle flame burns without a flicker. Like standing at a pole where everything one can see on all sides lies in only one direction, when standing here everything one can see comes already magnetized with infinity and there are no horizons beyond which one cannot see. It is an odd place filled with clouds of witnesses past, present, and to come who are very odd indeed. The liturgy happens in this odd place, and it is where the liturgical theologian works.

This is so because this is where Christian *orthodoxia* takes its normal stance and elaborates the normal way in which it looks upon all that swirls around it. Its stance and regard are highly judgmental because of its awareness of the proximity of the Presence in which it stands. The Presence is no less transcendental for its immanence in the faithful community and in all other things under heaven. The Presence is source of all that is, the first principle of the community and of all else. Because first principles can be known but not demonstrated according to the rules of human logic,[9] Christian *orthodoxia* knows its first principle only by faith, and the divine Presence thus known is radical in the extreme in what it requires of those who gather in such faith.

[9]Pace Arvind Sharma, "Playing Hardball in Religious Studies," *The Council on the Study of Religion Bulletin* 15 (February, 1984) 1, 3–4, who seems to confuse first principles such as the existence of Tao or God with matters of a different order, such as the sufficiency of ethics and the fact of whether God actually spoke to Mohammed. While one can never demonstrate a first principle, not everything which cannot be demonstrated is a first principle.

Thomas Scirghi

Edward J. Kilmartin: Reuniting *Lex Orandi* with *Lex Credendi*

Edward John Kilmartin, S.J. (1923–94) approaches the study of liturgy with the discipline of a systematic theologian. He began his career shortly before Pope John XXIII convened the Second Vatican Council. After finishing high school in 1941, he entered the Society of Jesus. He was ordained to the priesthood in 1954 and completed his doctoral studies in 1958 at the Jesuit Gregorian University in Rome, where he earned an S.T.D. His teaching career began at the Weston Jesuit School in Massachusetts. From there he went to the University of Notre Dame, and finally to the Pontifical Oriental Institute in Rome. He died in June of 1994, having suffered from bone cancer.

The council's cry for *aggiornamento* helped him realize what was lacking in his own post-Tridentine theological training. In order for the Church to speak to the society of the twentieth century it would have to include the disciplines of biblical scholarship, historical criticism, and the human sciences.

Kilmartin joins his contemporaries, Edward Schillebeeckx and Karl Rahner, in their *ressourcement,* that is, the return to the sources of the practice and doctrine of the primitive church. From his study of the primitive church he came to appreciate ritual and prayer as an important source for practicing theology. He then argues for reuniting the *lex orandi* with the *lex credendi* and that precedence must be given to the former. Consequently much of his study focuses on the liturgical rites.

The liturgy needs to be experienced and understood as an integral act of worship. Kilmartin is critical of the exaggerated focus upon the moment of consecration, which diminishes the rest of the liturgy. Such focus fails to recognize the integrity of the liturgy, that is, the orchestration of Scripture, elements, prayer, song, and gesture into a unity of worship. It also obscures the presence of Christ, who is manifest in the assembly as well as in the elements and with the priest. His emphasis on the active participation of the assembly in the Eucharist offers a renewed appreciation of the roles of the baptized and ordained in the mission of the Church. He argues that the priest functions *in persona ecclesiae* rather than *in persona Christi*. The role of the priest, then, is not limited to the moment of consecration but includes all the activity of the priest, who acts *in persona ecclesiae.*

In studying liturgical theology one finds little change of thought between the Middle Ages and the twentieth century. Kilmartin strives to advance theology by entering into dialogue with the human sciences. He is aware that if the Roman Catholic Church is to adequately express the faith of its members, then its theology of worship will have to build a bridge between theology and anthropology and to link the sacraments with human experience. The connection of theology and anthropology is significant to him because human beings experience the holy in those human situations in which the question of ultimate meaning is raised. Through the connection of these two disciplines we will deepen our understanding of the human condition and find the appropriate means to express this meaning in worship.

FOR FURTHER READING

Christian Liturgy: Theology and Practice. Kansas City: Sheed & Ward, 1988; *Toward Reunion: The Roman Catholic and the Orthodox Churches.* New York: Paulist Press, 1979; *The Eucharist in the Primitive Church.* Englewood Cliffs, N.J.: Prentice Hall, 1965; *The Eucharist in the West: History and Theology.* Ed. Robert J. Daly. Collegeville, Minn.: The Liturgical Press, 1998; "Apostolic Office: Sacrament of Christ." *Theological Studies* 36 (1975); "The Catholic Tradition of Eucharistic Theology: Towards the Third Millennium." *Theological Studies* 55 (1994).

Edward J. Kilmartin

Theology as Theology of the Liturgy[1]

The phrase "theology as theology of the liturgy" is open to more than one meaning. For example, one speaks of liturgy's theology, employing the subjective genitive. The witness of faith, in the form of the Church's liturgical prayer, is a speaking *(logos)* about God *(Theou)* in the form of a speaking to God. As such, liturgy is a source of theological knowledge. On the other hand, theological reflection on the content and meaning of liturgical practice can also be called "theology of liturgy," employing the objective genitive. Here it is a matter of theological understanding of liturgy, formulated by reflection on the liturgy as object of study.

Understood in the latter sense, two questions can be asked. Is there a sense in which all systematic theological reflection on various aspects of the economy of salvation should qualify as theology of the liturgy? The principle of intelligibility in systematic theology is the relation of one aspect of the revealed mystery of salvation to *all the others*. For example, a theology of grace would be deficient if it did not include the considerations drawn from christology, pneumatology, etc. Correspondingly, a theological exposition of christology would not be complete without reflection on the relationship of Christ to the liturgical activity of the Church. But to what extent

[1]Excerpted from Edward J. Kilmartin, "Theology as Theology of the Liturgy," ch. 6, *Christian Liturgy: Theology and Practice*, vol. 1, "Systematic Theology of Liturgy" (Kansas City: Sheed & Ward, 1988) 93–99. Reprinted by permission of Sheed & Ward, an apostolate of the Priests of the Sacred Heart, 73737 South Lovers Lane Road, Franklin, WI 53132 (1-800-558-0580). The editor wishes to express his appreciation to Mary M. Schaefer, Atlantic School of Theology, Halifax, Canada, for providing corrections to the printed text.

should all systematic reflection of the various branches of theology be a theology of liturgy, that is, explicitly draw out the implications of their subject for a theology of liturgy?

The second question concerns the value to be awarded to liturgy as a source of theological knowledge. One might presume that liturgy is *the* unique source of knowledge, under which other traditional sources should be subsumed. Or, liturgy might be considered among several sources, each of which has its particular and indispensable contribution to make to the understanding of the life of faith. How should the role of liturgy, as source of theology, be understood in the task of working out a systematic theology of any aspect of the economy of salvation and, in particular, a systematic theology of the liturgy?

A response to these two questions is given in this chapter. First, it is explained why all so-called branches of theology should endeavor to demonstrate the relevance of their particular subjects for the understanding and practice of the liturgy. Second, the relative value of the liturgy for the formulation of a systematic theology of the liturgy is discussed.

SYSTEMATIC THEOLOGY AS THEOLOGY OF LITURGY

An answer to the first question, posed above, follows as a corollary to certain anthropological observations. . . . The subject of the relationship between culture, cult, and religious worship, and the application of this data to Christian worship, need not be repeated here. It may only be noted that liturgy is the most important place in which the Christian community expresses its nature. Liturgy serves the indispensable function of establishing and maintaining Christian identity, mediating the meaning whereby the community is held together and grows.

It is a matter of the highest importance that the connection be recognized *by all*, between the world of meaning, constitutive of the community, and its crystallization in the basic symbolic language, verbal and gestural, of the liturgy. If the correspondence is gradually obscured, if the shape of meaning of the life of faith, expressed in the liturgy, no longer serves as the symbolic expression of the community's self-understanding, then the free acceptance of, and commitment to, the complex world of meaning of the Christian faith will be seriously affected.

From the consideration of the role of liturgy in the life of faith, this conclusion follows: Systematic theologians, working in all branches of theology should consider it a matter of the highest priority to show how their subjects can contribute to a better understanding and practice of communal worship.

SYSTEMATIC THEOLOGY OF LITURGY AND ITS SOURCES

A systematic theology of the liturgy differs from the various specialized fields of theology which focus on specific themes. Its object is the liturgical symbolic activity, which expresses in a synthetic way all that goes to make up the life of the faith. In the liturgical symbolism all the themes of theology are brought together. The liturgical-sacramental practice implies a comprehensive interpretation of reality, which can be unfolded with constant reference to the practice itself. Hence it may be said that the liturgical symbolism *per se* mediates the Christian global perception of the world of faith, and so the Christian identity. But *per accidens* the practical connection may not be grasped.

The formulation of the relationship between the Christian perception of the life of faith and the practice of faith has been the subject of discussion in recent years.[2] The linguistic hybrid "orthodoxy-orthopraxies" was first formulated in recent years by Johannes B. Metz, a German Catholic professor of theology, to express this relationship. However, the concept goes back to the patristic period and is perhaps best expressed by Maximus the Confessor: "Practice is the reality of the theory; the theory is the intimate and mysterious nature of the practice."[3] Here ortho represents a quality proper to a theory which intrinsically affects practice, and is not the quality of a theory, previously established, of which practice is a casuistic adaptation. Maximus applies this principle to the spiritual life.[4] But it has important applications in the whole range of the practice of the faith, including liturgy.

[2]P. Schoonenberg, "Orthodoxie und Orthopraxie," *Der Antwort der Theologen* (Düsseldorf: Patmos, 1968) 29–34; O. Semmelroth, "Orthodoxie und Orthopraxie: Zur wechselseitigen Begrünsung von Glaubenserkennen und Glaubenstun," *Geist und Leben* 49 (1969) 359–73; C. Dumont, "Orthodoxie vor Orthopraxie?" *Theologie der Gegenwart* 13 (1970) 184–91; T. Schneider, "Orthodoxie und Orthopraxie: Überlegungen zur Struktur des christlichen Glaubens," *Trierer Theologische Zeitschrift* 81 (1972) 140–52.
[3]*Quaestiones ad Thalassium* 63 (PG 90.681).
[4]I. H. Dalmais, "La doctrine ascétique de s. Maxime le Confessor d'après le *Liber Asceticus*," *Irenikon* 17–39; L. Thudberg, *Microcosm and Mediation: The Theological Anthropology of Maximus the Confessor* (Lund: G. Leerup, 1965) 355–56; 360–63.

The practical connection between the world of meaning of Christian faith and communal worship was established with the birth of Christian liturgies. In the patristic period, a good deal of effort was exerted in working out and communicating an ever-deeper grasp of the meaning of liturgical symbolic activity. This can be verified by reading the mystagogical catecheses of Cyril of Jerusalem, John Chrysostom, Theodore of Mopsuestia, and Ambrose of Milan. It is the task of a systematic theology of liturgy to maintain or recover this coherence and do this by a consistent interpretation of the central symbolic activity of the liturgy.[5] It may be expected that a theology with this orientation will contribute to the building up of the life of faith, which is grounded on, and nourished by, the liturgy.

The study of the theology of liturgy can be undertaken in one of two directions. One may ask about the understanding of the faith reflected in a specific liturgical tradition at some stage of the past history of the Church. By analyzing the relevant data of the historical context in which the liturgy was formulated or used, the particular global theory that grounds the complete practice can be worked out. A Catholic systematic theology of liturgy is not concerned directly with this kind of historical question. Rather it asks: How is one to explain the connection between the liturgical symbolic activity and the central mystery of the life of faith within the scope of the comprehensive Catholic tradition?

A response to this question requires taking into account the *law of prayer (lex orandi),* but also the other sources of theological knowledge. The help of a variety of sources of theology is needed besides the liturgical practice. Each of these sources has a particular contribution to make to the theological enterprise. We can learn much from the liturgy itself about the profound mystery which it represents. But discursive thought is required to bring to the surface the Christian potential of meaning symbolized in liturgy. Special attention must be given to the *law of belief (lex credendi),* understood as the doctrinal formulation of aspects of Christian revelation.

Lex orandi–Lex credendi

The axiom "law of prayer–law of belief" has become representative of two points of view regarding the value of liturgy as a source of

---

[5]A. Schilson, *Theologie als Sakramententheologie: Die Mysterientheologie Odo Casels.* Tübinger Theologische Studien (Mainz: Matthias-Grünewald, 1982) 19–21.

theology. Odo Casel has to his credit the great merit of bringing to the foreground of theological thought the importance of understanding theology as theology of the liturgy. But he tended to make the law of prayer a law "unto itself." According to him, the truth of the faith is made accessible not simply in a unique way through the liturgical celebration of the faith of the Church. Rather the liturgical expression of the self-understanding of the Church, while not rendering other modes of expression of faith superfluous, is clearly superior from all points of view. The authentic liturgical traditions are not simply one among many sources of knowledge of faith, but *the source and central witness* of the life of faith and so of all theology. As a consequence of this one-sided stress on the value of liturgical-practical grounding of theological knowledge, Scripture and the other sources of theology are placed in the background of his theological reflection.[6]

While Casel tends to formulate the axiom in the direction of "the law of prayer is the law of belief," Pope Pius XII's encyclical letter *Mediator Dei* reverses the accent: "Let the law of belief determine the law of prayer."[7] There is no doubt that he had in mind the problems raised by the reduction of the sources of theology to the law of prayer. His solution is to admit that liturgy is a source of faith to the highest rank, but to accentuate, by reversing the axiom, the unique value of the law of belief, guaranteed by the teaching authority of the Church.

Both of these approaches, which tend toward an overdrawn identity between theory and practice, threaten to obscure the unique value of two different kinds of expression of faith. In order to avoid either extreme, it should be recognized that the traditional axiom itself is open to either accent in specific cases. The slogan "law of prayer–law of belief" leaves in suspense which magnitude might be the subject and which the predicate, in particular instances. Consequently, it seems legitimate to state the axiom in this way: *the law of prayer is the law of belief, and vice versa.*

This latter formulation conveys the idea that the two sources of knowledge are neither independent of one another nor serve precisely the same purpose. On the one hand, the law of prayer implies a comprehensive, and, in some measure a pre-reflective, perception

---

[6]A. Schilson, *Theologie als Sakramententheologie*, 128–31.
[7]*AAS* 39 (1947) 540: "Lex credendi legen statuit supplicandi."

of the life of faith. On the other hand, the law of belief must be introduced because the question of the value of a particular liturgical tradition requires the employment of theoretical discourse. One must reckon with the limits of the liturgy as lived practice of the faith. History has taught us that forms of liturgical prayer and ritual activity, however orthodox, often had to be dropped or changed to avoid heretical misunderstanding. Moreover, in new historical and cultural situations, the question of the correspondence between the community's understanding of Christian truth, and its expression in the liturgy and that of the authentic whole tradition must continually be placed. To respond responsibly to this problem, other sources of theology must be introduced along with the liturgical-practical grounding of the knowledge of faith.[8]

CONCLUSION

Theology, conceived as the systematic reflection on liturgical practice, can be developed in various ways. But the aim is always the same: to attain more precise knowledge of the depth dimension of all forms of Christian communal worship, as well as the peculiar significance of the various forms in which the liturgy is celebrated. Since the mystery of salvation is one, and not many, the one and the same mystery is realized in all forms of the liturgy of the Church. Because this mystery is the ground and goal of all activity of the life of faith, it determines ultimately all aspects of liturgy.

Systematic theology, as systematic theology of liturgy, completes its task only when it demonstrates how the liturgy serves in its particular way as transparency for the mystery of salvation. The reduction of the theology of liturgy to the one divine plan of God is the aim of this theology. The one mystery of Christian faith is the Triune God in his self-communication to humanity. All classical liturgies confess this Trinitarian grounding and goal of the economy of salvation. In different ways, the forms of liturgy express the conviction of faith that the Triune God, in their economic activity, is the mystery of Christian worship. Consequently, theologians are challenged to show

---

[8]On the subject of the original meaning of the axiom: *Lex orandi–Lex credendi*, cf. P. De Clerk, "'Lex orandi–Lex credendi': The Original Sense and Historical Avatars of an Equivocal Adage," *Studia Liturgica* 24 (1994) 178–200. Also, K. Lehmann offers a good analysis of the problem of the relationship between dogmas and liturgical expression of faith: "Gottesdienst als Ausdruck des Glaubens," *Liturgisches Jarbuch* 30 (1980) 197–214.

how theology of liturgy can be formulated as theology of the economic Trinity.[9]

[9]L. Lies, "Trinitätsvergessenheit Gegenwärtieger Sakramententheologie," *Zeitschrift für Katholische Theologie* 105 (1983) 290–91, notes the importance of the reduction of theology of liturgy to a theology of the Trinity in a critical review of several new contributions to the theology of sacraments.

Byron David Stuhlman

Geoffrey Wainwright: Systematic Theology from a Liturgical Perspective

Geoffrey Wainwright was born in Yorkshire, England, in 1939 and received his education at Cambridge (B.A., M.A., D.D.), the University of Geneva (Docteur en Théologie), and the Waldensian Faculty of Theology, Rome. Ordained a presbyter of the British Methodist Church, he has served as a pastor in England and the Cameroon and has held faculty appointments at the Faculté de Théologie protestante, Yaoundé, Cameroon (1967–73); Queen's College, Birmingham, England (1973–79); Union Theological Seminary, New York (1979–83), and Duke University, Durham, North Carolina (since 1983), where he is currently the Robert E. Cushman Professor of Christian Theology. His professional memberships and appointments reveal the systematic, liturgical, and ecumenical dimensions of his theology: a member of the American Theological Society, he served as president 1996–97; a member of Societas Liturgica, he served as editor of its journal, *Studia Liturgica*, 1974–87, and president 1983–85; a member of the Faith and Order Commission of the World Council of Churches 1977–91, he chaired the final redaction of the Lima document, *Baptism, Eucharist, and Ministry.*

By vocation primarily a systematic theologian, Wainwright is distinguished by his commitment to do theology from a liturgical perspective, as he reveals in the title of his major work, *Doxology: The Praise of God in Worship, Life, and Doctrine. A Systematic Theology,* and explicitly declares in the preface to that book. Most liturgical theologians focus their attention on the theology of worship. While Wainwright has published works on the theology of Christian initiation

110

and the Eucharist, he focuses primarily on systematic theology which is rooted in the Church's life of worship. For a succinct example of such work, see his entry, "Doctrine, Liturgy and," in *The New Dictionary of Sacramental Worship*.

"The Praise of God in the Theological Reflection of the Church," which is reprinted below, is an excellent introduction to Wainwright's "theology written from a liturgical perspective." The first section of the article identifies praise as the Church's joyful response in "duty and delight" to God's self-disclosure. The second section then goes on to explore the proper relations between worship and reflective theology: worship as a witness to the Church's doctrine, liturgical theology as an exposition of liturgy that allows intelligent participation in the worship of the Church, worship as an epistemological resource for reflection on other theological issues, theological reflection as a prophetic critique of worship, and the final doxological offering of theological reflection when it reaches its own boundaries in the ultimate mystery, which faith grasps but reason cannot exhaust.

FOR FURTHER READING

Eucharist and Eschatology. London: Epworth Press, 1979; New York: Oxford Univ. Press, 1981; *The Study of Liturgy*. Co-edited with Cheslyn Jones and Edward Yarnold. London: SPCK, 1978. Second edition co-edited with Cheslyn Jones, Edward Yarnold, and Paul Bradshaw. London: SPCK, 1980; *Doxology: The Praise of God in Worship, Doctrine, and Life. A Systematic Theology*. London: Epworth Press; New York: Oxford Univ. Press, 1980; *Worship with One Accord: Where Worship and Ecumenism Embrace*. New York: Oxford Univ. Press, 1987; "Doctrine, Liturgy and." *The New Dictionary of Sacramental Worship*. Ed. Peter E. Fink, 349–58. Collegeville, Minn.: The Liturgical Press, 1990; *For Our Salvation*. Grand Rapids: Eerdmans, 1997.

Geoffrey Wainwright

The Praise of God in the Theological Reflection of the Church[1]

Words and God: The language of theological reflection is less direct
than some other types of speech involving God. Christianity knows
the word *of* God addressed to human beings in revelation. There is
then the word *to* God expressing the human response. There is also
the word *about* God which bears witness to the encounter and invites
participation in it.[2] Scripture, worship, and preaching take precedence over faith seeking understanding, over teaching on prayer,
over a hermeneutic of proclamation. In the latter cases, the logos of
theology has something of a "scientific" character: it gives a rationale
for beliefs held, draws up rules for appropriate linguistic behavior
toward God, and offers a theory of communication for transmitting
the gospel. The distinction between theological reflection and the
more primary types of speech involving God, however, takes place
on a continuum; there is no sheer disjunction. Theological reflection
tries for adequacy to the primary types of speech and the reality
which they enact. It aims to clarify our knowledge of both the reality
and its linguistic expression, and they in turn should illuminate and
affect the content and character of theological reflection. Theological

[1]Geoffrey Wainwright, "The Praise of God in the Theological Reflection of
the Church," *Interpretation: A Journal of Bible and Theology* (January 1995)
34–45. Reprinted by permission of the author.
[2]For this primary pattern of words from God, to God, and about God, see
most recently Maria-Judith Krahe, "'Psalmen, Hymnen und Lieder, wie der
Geist sie eingibt': Doxologie als Urspurung und Ziel aller Theologie," *Liturgie
und Dichtung: ein interdisziplinäres Kompendium II*, ed. H. Becker and R.
Kaczynski (Sankt Ottilien: EOS-Verlag, 1983) 921–57.

reflection may be critical, provided it is loyally attempting to improve on previous formulations of the relation between God and humanity. Criticism passes beyond the church when it strikes at the heart of the faith, desires to subvert Christian identity, wishes to alter the message; it may then be the beginning of a new religion, which need not have more than one adherent.

Praise is a linguistic act with an ontological basis and consequences: "That we may be to the praise of God's glory" is how the hymn in Ephesians 1:13-14 puts it (v. 12). The present article will engage first in theological reflection on the praise of God in order to discover what the church's practice in this matter implies about God, God's nature and dealings with the world, the relation of humanity to God, and the human destiny in the purpose of God. We shall be drawing on some classical examples of the church's laudatory repertoire.[3] A second half will illustrate how doxology has in fact affected dogma and show how the praise of God ought to inform all theological reflection.

REVELATION AND RESPONSE

A magnificent hymn by the English nonconformist Isaac Watts (1674–1748) supplies a text for our reflections:

"Praise ye the Lord! 'Tis good to raise
Your hearts and voices in his praise:
His nature and his works invite
To make this duty our delight."

This single stanza (1) names the object and grounds of praise, (2) states the obligation and benefits of praise, and (3) issues a call to join in the act. Under those headings we shall examine praise as the church's response to God's self-revelation.

God's Nature and Works

The object and ground of praise are the *aretai tou Theou,* the *magnalia Dei* (1 Pet 2:9), the greatness of God in virtues and deeds. Guided by Psalm 147, Watts's hymn goes on to praise the qualities of God in his acts of creation, providence, and redemption:

---

[3]For praise as the dominant note of the liturgy, see A. Verheul, "La Liturgie comme louange à Dieu," *Questions Liturgiques* 64 (1983) 19–44.

"He formed the stars, those heavenly flames,
He counts their numbers, calls their names;
His wisdom's vast, and knows no bound,
A deep where all our thoughts are drowned.

"Sing to the Lord! Exalt him high,
Who spreads his clouds along the sky;
There he prepares the fruitful rain,
Nor let the drops descend in vain.

"He makes the grass the hills adorn,
And clothes the smiling fields with corn;
The beasts with food his hands supply,
And the young ravens when they cry. . . .

"But saints are lovely in his sight,
He views his children with delight;
He sees their hope, he knows their fear,
And looks, and loves his image there."

The trinitarian precision made possible by the history of salvation comes to expression in the *Te Deum,* a hymn used in the Western church since the fourth or fifth century:

"We praise thee, O God, we acknowledge thee to be the Lord.
All the earth doth worship thee, the Father everlasting.
To thee all angels cry aloud, the heavens, and all the powers therein.
To thee cherubim and seraphim continually do cry:
Holy, holy, holy Lord God of Sabaoth,
Heaven and earth are fully of the majesty of thy glory.
The glorious company of the apostles praise thee,
The goodly fellowship of prophets praise thee,
The noble army of martyrs praise thee,
The holy Church throughout the world doth acknowledge thee:
The Father of an infinite majesty,
Thine honorable, true and only Son,
Also the Holy Ghost the Comforter.

"Thou art the king of glory, O Christ,
Thou art the everlasting Son of the Father.
When thou tookest upon thee to deliver man,
Thou didst not abhor the Virgin's womb.

When thou hadst overcome the sharpness of death,
Thou didst open the kingdom of heaven to all believers.
Thou sittest at the right hand of God, in the glory of the Father.
We believe that thou shalt come to be our judge.
We therefore pray thee, help thy servants, whom thou hast redeemed
    with thy precious blood.
Make them to be numbered with thy saints in glory everlasting.

"O Lord, save thy people and bless thine heritage,
Govern them and lift them up for ever.
Day by day we magnify thee,
And we worship thy name ever world without end.
Vouchsafe, O Lord, to keep us this day without sin.
O Lord, have mercy upon us, have mercy upon us.
O Lord, let thy mercy lighten upon us, as our trust is in thee.
O Lord, in thee have I trusted, let me never be confounded."

It has been suggested that the *Te Deum* was originally the Preface,
Sanctus, and Post-sanctus of a Mass for the Easter Vigil.[4] Certainly
the Eucharistic preface is a high point of the church's praise.[5] Here
"preface" is related to *prae-fari*, to "speak before" God and the world.
It is that part of the Eucharistic prayer which stretches between the
introductory dialogue ("Lift up your hearts") and the Sanctus ("Holy,
holy, holy"). In Syrian anaphoras, the preface tends to be restricted
to the adoration of the Creator in his heavenly being. The seasonal

[4] E. Kähler, *Studien zum Te Deum* (Göttingen: Vandenhoeck & Ruprecht, 1958).
[5] In this systematic essay, it is not my purpose to delve into the historical
question of the relations between the Christian genre of *eucharistia* and the
Jewish forms of blessing *(barak, berakah)* and thanksgiving *(yadah, hodaah,
todah)*. Relevant studies, which would also supply much substantial material
on our theme of praise, are J. P. Audet, "Esquisse historique du genre littéraire
de la 'bénédiction' juive et de 'l'eucharistie' chrétienne," *Revue Biblique* 65
(1958) 371–99; Louis Bouyer, *Eucharistie* (Tournai: Desclée, 1966). English trans.
Eucharist (Notre Dame: Notre Dame, 1968); Robert L. Ledogar, *Acknowledgment: Praise-verbs in the Early Greek Anaphora* (Rome: Herder, 1968); L. A. Ligier,
"From the Last Supper to the Eucharist," *The New Liturgy*, ed. L. Sheppard
(London: Darton, Longmann & Todd, 1970) 113–50, and "The Origins of the
Eucharistic Prayer," *Studia Liturgica* 9 (1973) 161–85; T. J. Talley, "The Eucharistic Prayer of the Ancient Church According to Recent Research," *Studia Liturgica* 11 (1976) 138–58; Cesare Giraudo, *La struttura letteraria della preghiera
eucaristica* (Rome: Biblical Institute, 1981); José Manuel Sánchez Caro, *Eucaristía
e historia de la salvación* (Madrid: Biblioteca de Autores Cristianos, 1983).

prefaces for the West focus rather on thanksgiving for the various events of salvation history. The Byzantine anaphora of St. John Chrysostom interweaves the two approaches:

"It is fitting and right to hymn you,
to bless you, to praise you, to give you thanks,
to worship you in all places of your dominion.
For you are God, ineffable, inconceivable,
invisible, incomprehensible, for ever the same,
you and your only-begotten Son and your Holy Spirit.
You brought us out of non-being to being;
and when we had fallen, you raised us up again,
and did not cease to do everything
until you had brought us up to heaven,
and granted us the kingdom that is to come.
For all these things we give thanks to you
and to your only-begotten Son and to your Holy Spirit,
for all that we know and do not know,
your seen and unseen benefits that have come upon us.
We give thanks also for this ministry;
vouchsafe to receive it from our hands,
even though thousands of archangels and ten thousands of angels
   stand before you,
cherubim and seraphim, with six wings and many eyes,
flying on high and singing the triumphal hymn,
proclaiming, crying, and saying:
Holy, holy, holy. . . ."

It is generally held that Israel's experience of redemption influenced its understanding and celebration of creation; the New Testament hymns which ascribe a role to Christ in creation no doubt draw on speculative extrapolation from his experienced mediation in redemption. Rather similarly, the universal and transcendent epithets heaped in praise on God in this Eucharistic preface spring from reflection on the events of salvation history in which God's loving sovereignty was made manifest. They become a doxological anticipation of the day when God will *reveal* himself to be "all in all" (1 Cor 15:28).

In the course of the liturgy, the Eucharistic prayer is preceded by a doxological profession of faith. The creed was introduced into this context first in the East in the sixth century and finally at Rome in the

eleventh. From their earliest days, there existed great thematic similarity between the baptismal creed and the Eucharistic prayer.[6] In its
Byzantine position just before the Eucharistic anaphora, the recitation
of the creed reconstitutes the baptismal community as those who will
once more offer thanks. The creed's western location in the service of
the word make it a remembrance of the baptismal response to the
preaching of the gospel. The ascription of praise with which a
Chrysostom, an Augustine, or a Calvin ended their sermons was no
mere formality: It indicated the intention of the sermon itself and its
aim of bringing others also into the praise of God on account of what
had been proclaimed in Scripture and sermon.[7] For the sermon expounds the story of God's dealings with the world and invites hearers to maintain their identity among the people who enthrone God
on their praises (cf. Ps 22:3). It does so on the basis of the reading of
Scriptures which, themselves peppered with outbursts of praise, recall the nature and works of God as revealed to Israel and made
known in Jesus Christ. Thus the Eucharistic prayer constitutes for the
believing community a climax of praise, toward which the liturgical
sequence of Scripture lessons, sermon, and creed has been leading.

Our Duty and Delight

As Watts' raising of "hearts and voices" echoes the *Sursum corda,*
so his "'tis good" and the binome of "duty" and "delight" recall the
opening words of the Eucharistic preface: "It is right and just, our
benefit and salvation, to give thanks to you, Lord. . . ." *(Vere dignum
et iustum est, aequum et salutare. . . .)* The Westminster Catechism
teaches that "Man's chief end is to *glorify* God and to *enjoy* him forever." There is no contradiction, but only coincidence, between God's
will and the good of humanity, between human salvation and the divine kingdom.

The Anglican collect prays to God, "whose service is perfect freedom"; and the early Roman model is perhaps even more striking:
"God, whom to serve is to reign" *(Deus auctor pacis et amator . . . cui
servire, regnare est).* St. Irenaeus declared: "The glory of God is living
humanity" *(gloria Dei vivens homo),* that is, alive with the abundant

---

[6]Marc Lods, "Préface eucharistique et confession de foi—aperçu sur les pre-
miers textes liturgiques," *Revue d'Histoire et de Philosophie Religieuses* 59 (1979)
121–42.

[7]See G. Wainwright, "Preaching as Worship" and "The Sermon and the
Liturgy," *Greek Orthodox Theological Review* 28 (1983) 325–36, 337–49.

life Jesus came to bring (John 10:10); and "the life of man is the vision of God" *(vita autem hominis visio Dei).*[8] Augustine confesses that God made us for himself so that our hearts find their rest only in God.[9] God, then, is our "delight."

Yet Hebrews 13:15 can speak precisely of a *"sacrifice of praise"* (a traditional designation of the Eucharist is the *sacrificium laudis*). Jesus loved his own "to the end" (John 13:1). The human love that responds to the divine love is likewise to be all-consuming, a sacrificial love of the heart, soul, mind, and strength (Luke 10:27). Therefore Isaac Watts can also sing (following Ps. 146):

"I'll praise my Maker while I've breath;
And when my voice is lost in death,
Praise shall employ my nobler powers:
My days of praise shall ne'er be past,
While life, and thought, and being last,
Or immortality endures."

The communion between God and human beings is reciprocal, but not symmetrical. John Chrysostom puts it thus:

"God does not need anything of ours,
but we stand in need of all things from him.
The thanksgiving itself adds nothing to him,
but causes us to be nearer to him" (Homily 25.3 on Matthew, *PG* 57.331).

Our praise is not flattery of God but a loving self-offering of creatures to the beneficent Creator. It is indeed "to the greater glory of God" *(ad majorem Dei gloriam)*—the motto of the Jesuits—insofar as the creatures, loved by God for their own sake, are thereby fulfilling the blessed destiny of communion for which they were made. And in that sense, although God does not need us in order to be God, our praise brings the purpose of God to completion and so is our "duty."

Praise Ye the Lord!
All are invited to share in the destiny of glorifying and enjoying God. If Israel was summoned to proclaim God's name "among the nations" (1 Chr 16:8-36; Pss 57:9; 67:1ff.; 86:8-10; 108:3; 113:1ff.; 117;

[8]*Adversus Haereses* 4.20.7, *PG* 7.1037.
[9]*Confessions* 1.1

145:10-12; Isa 42:10-12; 66:18ff.), the intention was that the peoples might come to recognize Israel's God. According to the apostle Paul, the purpose of preaching the gospel is to augment the Eucharistic chorus: "Since we have the same spirit of faith as he had who wrote, 'I believed, and so I spoke,' we too believe and so we speak . . . so that as grace extends to more and more people, it may increase thanksgiving, to the glory of God" (2 Cor 4:13-15). Under the New Covenant, the universalization of praise passes through a christological mediation, as the hymn in Philippians 2:9-11 makes clear:

"Therefore God has highly exalted him
and bestowed on him the name
which is above every name,
that at the name of Jesus
every knee should bow,
in heaven and on earth and under the earth,
and every tongue confess
that Jesus Christ is Lord
to the glory of God the Father."

That praise will lead to praise is the theme of the hymn which has opened successive Methodist hymnals since the Wesleys' *Collection of Hymns for the Use of the People called Methodists* (1780):

"O for a thousand tongues to sing
My dear Redeemer's praise!
The glories of my God and king
The triumphs of his grace!

"My gracious Master, and my God,
Assist me to proclaim,
To spread through all the earth abroad
The honors of thy name.

"Jesus the name that charms our fears
that bids our sorrows cease—
'Tis music in the sinner's ears,
'Tis life, and health, and peace.

"Hear him, ye deaf; his praise, ye dumb,
Your loosened tongues employ;

Ye blind, behold your Savior come,
And leap, ye lame, for joy!

"Look unto him, ye nations; own
Your God, ye fallen race;
Look, and be saved through faith alone,
Be justified by grace!"

Some Eastern anaphoras call the praises of God not *doxologiai*, but *theologiai*.[10] We turn now to look at how these primary "theologies" have influenced the dogmatic statements of the church, and how they are related to theological reflection.

DOXOLOGY AND DOCTRINE

A highly selective historical account of the effects of liturgy on official dogma will be followed by a systematic consideration of the proper relations between worship and reflective theology. Since praise remains their dominant note, in this second half I will take the liberty of using the terms liturgy and worship in a comprehensive sense which includes also their other modes.

Liturgy and Dogma

The old tag "the law of praying [sets] the law of believing" (*lex orandi, lex credendi*) derives from a fifth-century argument that long went under the name of Pope Celestine I but was actually put forward by Prosper of Aquitaine.[11] Against semi-pelagianism he argues that the apostolic injunction to *pray* for the whole human race—which the church obeys in its intercessions—proves the obligation to *believe* that all faith, even the beginnings of goodwill as well as growth and perseverance, is from start to finish a work of grace. Doctrinal appeal to liturgical practice had already been made by Augustine, Prosper's literary mentor, when he adduced in favor of original sin the exorcisms performed on infants before their Baptism, which was itself "for the remission of sins." The principle goes back much farther: Irenaeus and Tertullian invoked the sacraments against the gnostic depreciation of matter. Already Ignatius of Antioch saw abstinence from the Eucharist as a denial of the reality of Christ's incarnation, passion, and resurrection.

[10]Thus the liturgies of St. Mark and St. Basil; see *Prex Eucharistica*, ed. A. Hänggi and I. Pahl (Fribourg: Éditions universitaires, 1968) 110, 234.
[11]See K. Federer, *Liturgie und Glaube: eine theologie-geschichtliche Untersuchung* (Fribourg: Paulus Verlag, 1950).

In the Arian controversy, Athanasius argued that the denial of the Son's divinity would, unthinkably, make Christians into idolators, creature-worshipers; and it seems unquestionable that the address of praise and prayer to Christ historically played a part in the Nicene recognition of his deity. Against the pneumatomachian tendency, Athanasius and Basil appealed to the Holy Spirit's inclusion in the baptismal name: Only God can give participation in God. The Council of Constantinople (381), in affirming the deity of the Spirit, declared that "with the Father and the Son together he is worshiped and glorified." Cyril of Alexandria's insistence on the role of Christ's humanity in his mediation of the church's worship to the Father is proof that Cyril was not "monophysite" in any but a terminological sense.[12]

In such cases, worship largely led doctrine, but worship may get out of hand. The Reformation may be read as a doctrinal revolt against a deformed liturgical practice and understanding focused on "the sacrifice of the Mass." The issues that are thereby raised will be briefly treated in the following final section, especially under (2).

Worship and Theology

Here I want to mention (1) the motivation of the theologian, (2) the relations between worship and the functions of reflective theology, and (3) the limits of theological reflection.

(1) *The motivation of the theologian.* To mention the praise of God as the theologian's motivation runs the risk of provoking dissent from colleagues anxious for academic neutrality. Yet scholars who wish simply to describe the Christian faith had better call themselves historians, although good historical description usually calls for at least a certain empathy with the subject, and very little historiography proves to be ideologically "value free." Again, those who wish to undertake an independent "search for truth" are better called philosophers, for Christian theology does not start from scratch with every thinker but takes place within a tradition and community of faith and praise. The old "faith seeking understanding" remains a good definition of reflective theology.[13] The search can carry with it

---

[12]See Thomas F. Torrance, "The Mind of Christ in Worship: The Problem of Apollinarianism in the Liturgy," *Theology in Reconciliation* (London: Chapman, 1975) 139–214.

[13]I should myself be even happier with faith seeking *greater* understanding, so as not to risk eliminating the element of understanding from the initial gift

the intellectual excitement of exploration. The context of worship, the "playfulness of liturgy" (R. Guardini), is there to set the spirit of the inquiry.

(2) *The tasks of reflective theology.* Three may be mentioned in relation to worship. First, theology has the task of reflectively expounding the worship of the church in order to facilitate an intelligent participation in it. A modest example of that function is found in the first half of this article. In *For the Life of the World*[14] and *Of Water and the Spirit*,[15] Alexander Schmemann undertook this task in a way which followed very closely the actual *déroulement* of the rites in the Orthodox Church. Such work may be called liturgical theology. It helps to keep theology as a handmaid of worship, performing a service ancillary to a primary activity of the church. When a theological interpretation has found official and widespread acceptance in the church, it may in turn influence worship: that was at stake in the Arian controversy, and the triumph of the Nicenes eventually opened the way to a more frequent liturgical address of prayer to Christ.

Second, theology, which also addresses other issues than those which come directly to expression in worship, can and should draw on the experience of the church in worship for its reflection. I attempted that in my book *Doxology*.[16] After a long period of neglect, it is interesting to note that German Protestant systematicians are now starting to recognize worship and prayer as a dimension of the Christian faith which theological reflection must take into account throughout its endeavors, rather than domesticating them as mere "topics" to be treated separately and in any case preferably left to "practical theology." After an article on "the necessity of Christian worship," Gerhard Ebeling in his *Dogmatics* made prayer the basis of his whole "relational ontology."[17] After a seminal article in which he advocated the resolution of confessional differences through bringing them back to their common basis in worship, Edmund Schlink concluded his life's work in an *Ecumenical Dogmatics* governed by doxol-

---

and act of faith itself. Thus the genitive in *intellectus fidei* ("the understanding of faith") is in the first place subjective.

[14]Crestwood, N.Y.: St. Vladimir's, 1973.

[15]Crestwood, N.Y.: St. Vladimir's, 1974.

[16]New York: Oxford Univ. Press, 1980.

[17]"Die Notwendigkeit des christlichen Gottesdienstes," *Zeitschrift für Theologie und Kirche* 67 (1970) 232–49; *Dogmatik des christlichen Glaubens*, 3 vols. (Tübingen: Mohr, 1979).

ogy.[18] Dietrich Ritschl sees the liturgically transmitted "story" as provoking theological reflection and (only then? or once more?) issuing in doxology.[19] Gerhard Sauter considers prayer as an elementary fact and experience, epistemologically productive, rather than something one might or might not come to as a result of reflection upon the self and its relation to reality.[20] This movement has gone so far that I. U. Dalferth feels he must insist that Tübingen Protestants believe theological reflection "still" to be necessary.[21] Even some philosophers of religion, admittedly Catholic, are again taking worship and prayer seriously.[22]

Again, reflection on theological problems in the light of worship may eventually have a return effect on the liturgy. For instance, worship shows Christians ascribing salvation to God's grace alone yet themselves engaged in the active dynamic of faith. Many collects in the ancient Western sacramentaries then appear to have been deliberately composed with an anti-pelagian intent and yet a due acknowledgment of the place of works in the salvation of believers.

Third, reflective theology has the responsibility, where necessary, of criticizing particular acts of worship and the formulations and practices of the liturgy.[23] It can do so, because the liturgy is not its *only* source. Theology also draws on the Scriptures which, although they are largely a liturgically composed, defined, and transmitted body of material, possess a certain independence in virtue of their recognized canonical status. Theology draws, too, on the Tradition of the Church, in which certain elements or periods impress themselves as

[18]"Die Struktur der dogmatischen Aussage als ökumenisches Problem," *Kerygma und Dogma* 3 (1957) 251–306; *Oekumenische Dogmatik* (Göttingen: Vandenhoeck & Ruprecht, 1983).

[19]*Memory and Hope* (New York: Macmillan, 1967), especially 89–101, 143–80, 202–30; "'Story' als Rohmaterial der Theologie," which is the title piece of no. 192 in the series Theologische Existenz heute (Munich: Kaiser, 1976) 7–41; *Zur Logik der Theologie* (Munich: Kaiser, 1984), especially 130–37, 329–38.

[20]"Reden von Gott im Gebet," *Gott nennen*, ed. Bernhard Casper (Munich: Alber, 1981) 219–42.

[21]*Existenz Gottes und christlicher Glaube: Skizzen zu einer eschatologischen Ontologie* (Munich: Kaiser, 1984) 25; cf. the same author's *Religiöse Rede von Gott* (Munich: Kaiser, 1981).

[22]Ferdinand Ulrich, *Gebet als geschöpflicher Grundakt* (Einsiedeln: Johannes, 1973). Richard Schaeffler, *Fähigkeit zur Erfahrung: zur transzendentalen Hermeneutik des Sprechens von Gott* (Freiburg: Herder, 1982), especially 80–110; and *Religionsphilosophie* (Munich: Alber, 1983), especially 143–96.

[23]See G. Wainwright, *Doxology*, particularly chapters 7 and 8.

more authentic and hence serve as standards. Theology, again, must test particular liturgical practices for their ethical presuppositions and consequences: Theologians must heed, and perhaps even exercise, the prophetic critique of the cult at a given time. Finally, and gingerly, theology must use reason. At this point in the history of ideas, perhaps particularly in the United States, care is necessary because the word "reason" carries a suggestion of that quasi-divine yet thoroughly secular entity which the Enlightenment wrote with a capital letter: Reason. The matter is in any case delicate and complicated, in that (theologically) reason's use may be subjected to a perverted will, and (anthropologically) thought patterns and even the "best" available human knowledge are always culturally conditioned. Nevertheless, reflective theology obviously cannot abandon what is in fact its most characteristic tool.

As already mentioned, the Reformation was a striking example of doctrinal critique upon current worship. The Reformers then put out their own orders of worship. The reform was doubtless necessary, but an unfortunate result of the doctrinal thrust has been the preponderance of the didactic over the latreutic in Protestant services.

(3) *The limits of theology.* Even, perhaps especially, the best of Christian theologians have found that reflection runs into mystery. That is not an intellectual excuse, but a religious fact. This "open-endedness" of faith and of reflection upon it leads Dietrich Ritschl to say that theology has a "doxological edge" *(einen doxologischen Rand):* Its final thoughts are simply offered to God.[24] A trinitarian hymn of Isaac Watts, "We Give Immortal Praise," which is firmly rooted in the history of salvation, ends thus:

"Almighty God, to Thee
Be endless honors done,
The undivided Three,
And the mysterious One.
Where reason fails, with all her powers,
There faith prevails, and love adores."

---

[24]*Zur Logik der Theologie,* 337; cf. W. Pannenberg, "Analogie und Doxologie," *Dogma und Denkstrukturen,* ed. W. Joest and W. Pannenberg (Göttingen: Vandenhoeck & Ruprecht, 1963) 96–115.

5

How Does Liturgy Embody
Theological Themes?

Like many of the other chapters, this one deserves a whole book—
make that a library of books—itself. We could look at the ways in
which the themes of Christology, pneumatology, ecclesiology, and eschatology are manifested in the liturgy, or analyze the ways in which
the Trinity is invoked or how justification or sanctification is treated.
For that matter, you could take any of the above themes (or any other
studied in systematic theology) and investigate what liturgical theologians themselves have to say about the way in which it is present
in the liturgy.

Given the limitations of time and space, however, I've chosen three
essays that reflect three different ways of talking about theological
themes in the liturgy. They illustrate three different perspectives—
Reformed (von Allmen), Orthodox (Taft), and Roman Catholic (Collins).

The excerpt from von Allmen deals with the broad sweep of the
liturgy, while that of Taft focuses on a series of explicit theses regarding soteriology. After providing a theoretical framework, Mary
Collins illumines the way in which changing liturgical practice reflects (and helps form) changing theological understanding. In all
three the relationship between *orandi* and *credendi* is recognized in
specific ways.

After you see how these liturgical theologians do it, take a theological theme you have studied and hold it in one hand and the
liturgy (as a total experience, not merely as a text) in the other, and
let the dynamic interaction between the two be the basis for your further reflection.

Arlo D. Duba

Jean Jacques von Allmen: Christian Worship: A Reformed Perspective

Jean Jacques von Allmen (1917–1994) was born in Lausanne, Switzerland, grew up in Basel, and received his theological education first with the theological faculty of the Free Church in Lausanne and then with the Reformed faculties of Basel and Neuchâtel. He received his degree from Neuchâtel in 1941 and shortly thereafter was ordained and married. His students report that his wife was an enthusiastic partner and supporter of his ministry, both in the parish and the academy, and that they had a particularly happy marriage. His book *Maris et femmes d'après saint Paul* appeared in English as *Pauline Teaching on Marriage* (London: Faith Press, 1963).

Von Allmen served for seventeen years as a parish pastor, many of them in the French-speaking church in Lucerne. In 1948 in Neuchâtel he received his doctorate in church history. He was a trained and disciplined historian, but his interests ranged widely. He was a biblical scholar and a theologian, but preeminently he was a liturgical theologian, focusing his broad interests in the area of worship, often quoting his friend, Karl Barth, who said, "Christian worship is the most momentous, the most urgent, the most glorious action that can take place in human life" (*Worship: Its Theology and Practice*, p. 13). His book *Vocabulaire biblique*, written while a parish pastor in 1954 (*A Companion to the Bible*, N.Y.: Oxford Univ. Press, 1958), catapulted him into prominence in the biblical field. In 1958 von Allmen was called to the Protestant Theological Faculty of the University of Neuchâtel, where he remained until the end of his ministry. He died in 1994.

126

While a student von Allmen studied briefly in England, where he was excited by the Anglican Church. As pastor and professor he became closely related to Lutherans, Eastern Orthodox, and Roman Catholics. These relationships and his writing in the early 1960s made him a significant source for conversation at Vatican II and led to an invitation to take a brief leave from Neuchâtel to be the director of the Tantur Ecumenical Biblical Institute near Jerusalem (1971–1974), established in the exhilarating days following Vatican II.

His 1962 book, *Preaching and Congregation,* has been called by Thomas Long "a high water mark in Reformed homiletics." His 1964 publication of *Prophétism sacramental,* a discussion of the prophetic sacramentalism of the Taizé Community (not available in English), expresses his commitment to ecumenism as well as his pastoral, missional thrust.

However, it was *Worship: Its Theology and Practice* that established von Allmen as a premier liturgical theologian in and for the Reformed tradition. The chapter before us sets out his views on anamnesis and epiclesis, which were at once stimulating and controversial. This theology from a Reformed point of view introduces five theological chapters. These are the basis for part 2 of the book, which then examines "problems of celebration," in which he sounds as if he were speaking to our cultural situation when he says, "the world participates in the church's praises, not vice versa."

FOR FURTHER READING
Preaching and Congregation. Ecumenical Studies in Worship. No. 10. London: Lutterworth Press, 1962; Richmond, Va.: John Knox Press, 1962; *Worship: Its Theology and Practice.* New York: Oxford Univ. Press, 1965; *Le saint ministère* (on the ministerial office). Neuchâtel: Delachaux et Niestlé, 1968; *The Lord's Supper.* Ecumenical Studies in Worship. No. 19. Richmond, Va.: John Knox Press, 1969.

Jean Jacques von Allmen

The Cult as Recapitulation of the History of Salvation[1]

We have seen that the worship of the Church is possible only because Jesus Christ in his earthly ministry lived a sufficient and perfect life of worship. We have also seen that the worship of the Church is true and real because Jesus Christ is freely present therein as Lord, abiding with those who are gathered together in his name. We must now consider what takes place in Christian worship.

Lancelot Andrewes (1555–1626), who was successively Bishop of Chichester, Ely and Winchester, put forward in a Christmas sermon the bold idea that "for as there is a recapitulation of all in heaven and earth in Christ, so there is a recapitulation of all in Christ in the holy sacrament." The worship of the Church would be thus a recapitulation of the major event in the history of salvation and so, implicitly, of the whole story of salvation.

This idea, as we shall try to demonstrate, is true. However, one might question whether the term "recapitulation" is well-chosen. Does not the word necessarily mean—like the ἀνακεφαλαιώσασθαι of Eph 1:10—"to give or to restore a head to what was without one or had the wrong one," and thus, in short, to give to what is "recapitulated" a justification, a *raison d'être*, an orientation, a fulfillment. In this meaning it is not Christian worship but Jesus Christ who recapitulates, i.e., who fulfills and justifies the process of saving history, imparting to it its true purpose. Now nothing could be worse than to

---

[1]Excerpted from Jean Jacques von Allmen, "The Cult as Recapitulation of the History of Salvation," pt. 3 of ch. 1, "Christian Worship Considered as the Recapitulation of the History of Salvation," *Worship: Its Theology and Practice* (New York: Oxford Univ. Press, 1965) 32–41.

128

reverse the order of Christ and worship, to cephalize Christ by worship, whereas in fact it is worship which is cephalized in Christ.* However, *recapitulare* normally means more simply to "sum up" or "confirm" or "repeat," and in this sense the term is perfectly appropriate: the cult sums up and confirms ever afresh the process of saving history which has reached its culminating point in the intervention of Christ in human history, and through this summing-up and ever-repeated confirmation Christ pursues his saving work by the operation of the Holy Spirit. This recapitulation concerns the history of salvation both from a chronological and theological point of view.

(a) Let us begin by speaking of the cult as a recapitulation of the history of salvation in the chronological sense. But, first of all, what is the chronological structure of this saving history? It is known that it is entirely governed by the work of the incarnate Christ, by his death and resurrection. "The center of God's economy of salvation is the incarnation of the eternal Son of God in Jesus of Nazareth, His cross and His resurrection."[2] This is its obligatory point of reference, its justification. The whole history of the world is here in principle brought to its conclusion and completed. Like a watershed it dominates on the one side the OT period, all history preceding the Nativity back to pre-history and the mystery of the creation; on the other side the NT period, all history following the Ascension, to beyond all present knowledge, even to the mystery of the end of the world. This history *post Christum natum* brings nothing new, moreover; it is simply a perpetual struggle against the Evil One, who is unwilling to surrender; it is a dramatic exploitation of Christ's victory up to the day when it will shine forth triumphantly before the whole world, on the day of the parousia of the Lord.

To say that the Christian cult recapitulates the process of salvation in a chronological sense is then to say that it sums it up and confirms it insofar as this process itself is recapitulatory; in other words, inasmuch as it is essentially a summing up of the work of Christ.

The cult is firstly an anamnesis of the past work of Christ. In instituting the Eucharist, i.e., Christian worship, Jesus said: τοῦτο ποιεῖτε εἰς τὴν ἐμὴν ἀνάμνησιν (1 Cor 11:24ff). This anamnesis or memorial

*Editor's note: "cephalize" = to make the head.
[2] P. Brunner, "Zur Lehre und sur Feier der in Namen Jesu versammelten Gemeinde," *Leiturgia vom Gottesdienst*, vol. 1 (Kassel, 1954).

(ἀνάμνησις, words belonging to the family ZKR) is something quite different from a mere exercise of memory. It is a restoration of the past so that it becomes present and a promise. In the world of biblical culture "to remember" is to make present and operative. As a result of this type of "memory," time is not unfolded along a straight line adding irrevocably to each other the successive periods which compose it. Past and present are merged. A real actualization of the past in the present becomes possible. It is on this doctrine also that is based the paschal rite, of which Exod 12:14 says that it was instituted le-Zikaron, i.e., for a memorial. This implies that every one, as he calls to mind the deliverance from Egypt, must realize that he is himself the object of the redemptive act, to whatever generation he belongs. When it is a question of the history of redemption, the past is reenacted and becomes present. Thus, similarly, at each Christian act of worship and so—within the perspective of the NT—at every Eucharist, those who participate learn that they are themselves the objects of the redemptive action of the cross.

But the cult, while being an anamnesis, is not merely "a re-enactment of the past," it is, further, an engagement in his service and a confession of faith on the part of those who thus remember the death of Christ. "To Him who is remembered, the worshiper pays homage and confesses allegiance."[3] Consequently, Christian worship, and supremely the Eucharist, is what the OT would describe as an *oth*, a sign which, by the power of God, brings to life what it represents, if it is anamnetic; or brings it to pass if it is prefigurative.

But the Christian cult does not merely recapitulate the life, death, and resurrection of Christ by making them operative in the present. The history of salvation, in fact, is not only something past: it is also what is to come. Not that the future can add to the focus of the whole process of saving history, the incarnation of the Son of God, and especially his death and resurrection. But the future will bring its confirmation, manifestation, and ultimate and eternal fruition. In summing up the process of salvation, the cult is also directed towards the future. It is not merely a representation of the death and victory of Christ, it is also an anticipation of his return and foreshadowing of the kingdom which he will then establish. It does not merely commemorate Jesus' last meal with his disciples; it also prefigures the messianic feast at which, with his disciples, Christ will

[3]Michel, art. μνημονεύω, *Theological Wordbook of the New Testament*, 4, 686.

drink the new wine of the kingdom of his Father (Matt 26:29). Thus in sharing in the Eucharist the faithful are invited to receive the sign of their belonging to the kingdom that is to come. And the prefiguration of the future is no more of an exercise of imagination than the representation of the past is an exercise of memory: in the cult—and we shall see that this is the work of the Holy Spirit—past and future, the chief event of the saving process and its glorious manifestation becomes effectually present.

In our survey of the chronological recapitulation of the saving process, effected by the Holy Spirit in the Christian cult, there remains a third dimension. It is not merely the past which becomes again present; nor is it merely the future which is already dawning. There is also the present itself which is affirmed, and the present of the history of salvation is the heavenly offering which Jesus Christ renders to his Father in the glory of the Ascension. Here, however, we leave the temporal for the spatial framework. Just as in Christian worship past and future meet in an effective present, so also heaven touches earth or earth is lifted towards heaven: "The worship of God in the Church . . . is a participation in the one world-saving and uninterrupted offering of the crucified and ascended Lord before the throne of God."[4]

Because it recapitulates the drama of salvation in the sense that it makes the past effectively present, foreshadows the future and glorifies the messianic present, the cult may be called an eschatological phenomenon. And this is why, despite the ambiguity in which it is still celebrated, it is a joyful phenomenon, for the Christ who gave himself for the world did not remain enslaved by death, and it is as the Risen Lord, as at the time of his Easter appearances, that he is present among his followers. How then can they repress the ἀγγιάσει , the exultation of worship (Acts 2:46; 16:34; 1 Pet 1:8, cf 1 Pet 4:13; Jude 24)? Here we have an absolutely basic element in Christian liturgy; the cult, because it recapitulates the process of salvation, is an act of joy. Certainly it also proclaims the death of Christ (1 Cor 11:26), but, because of the victory which crowned that death, it becomes, for those who share its benefits, less an occasion of sorrow than an inexhaustible source of joyful thanksgiving. This should have a clear impact on liturgical formulation in general, and in this respect our Protestant liturgical tradition has much to learn.

[4]P. Brunner (see n. 2, above).

One further question: We have seen that the cult makes present and operative the perfect and sufficient act of worship offered once for all by Christ on the cross, that it foreshadows the joy of the undisputed worship in eternity, and that it enables the Church to share in the heavenly offering that accompanies the drama of salvation. We might go on to ask whether the worship of the Church restores the primordial, paradisial life of worship which God had willed, not only in making man the liturgical representative of creation, with the task of leading the whole world in thanksgiving, adoration and praise, but also in fixing—in a supralapsarian manner—a day of worship, and perhaps even—if we are to follow Luther here—a place of worship (the tree which was the limit of good and evil) and a form of worship (Ps 148).

I think that we must give a positive reply to this question, since Christ, the new Adam, has, by his coming, restored and fulfilled the plan of the Creator and has rehabilitated those who find in him the true purpose of their manhood, and the basic liturgical orientation which God willed in creating man in his image. In summing up the process of salvation which culminates in the incarnate intervention of Christ, the Christian cult thus regains and restores to its place that supralapsarian cult which had no sacrifice, and it regains it not simply by way of anamnesis but also by way of prolepsis: I am thinking of what has been said earlier about the cult which is no longer expiatory but purely sanctifying, and over which Christ will preside so that God may be all in all.

But just as the worship of the Church is but a prolepsis of the messianic feast and the joys of the kingdom—so ambiguous so as to be perceptible only to faith—so also is it with regard to the anamnesis of worship before the Fall. While it is true that in the cult of the Church man rediscovers the purpose for which he was created—to be a royal priest, and his right to summon the whole creation to join with him in adoration and praise of the Lord . . . yet this rediscovery is constantly compromised by sin, so that it is not possible to say more than this: the Christian cult, because it is based on the reconciliation of all things in Christ, is the advance-guard of that cosmic quest of which St. Paul speaks, that cosmic longing for a restitution of what God, in his love, had established at the first (Rom 8:18ff.). It does not in any evident way restore paradise any more than it brings about the kingdom; it justifies the hope and furnishes the pledge of these; it offers the day and the place in which the past before the Fall, and the future after the Judgment, still survives or already breaks forth. And because of that, we may not say that this present reality is too ambiguous to be expressed. On the contrary, to refuse it the possibility of expression shows that we do not love it. If we love the kingdom which will both restore and complete the mystery of the first creation, we cannot refuse it—where its self-expression is most appropriate, i.e., in the cult of the Church—some means of expression, even if that means is ambiguous and unsatisfactory. The Church's worship—and we shall often return to this point—is the most splendid proof of love for the world. Those who do not love the cult do not know how to love the world.

(b) We have, all too briefly, reminded ourselves that the cult sums up the drama of salvation from a chronological point of view; in it the messianic past, present and future meet and are joined. But the cult also sums up this drama from a theological standpoint. What does this mean? In answer, we must remember of what elements the history of salvation is constituted. If we adopt the traditional scheme we can group these under three heads and say that the history of salvation is composed of a revelation of the divine will for salvation, a reconciliation which makes possible the fulfillment of this will, and a protection which safeguards the efficacious operation of this will. Thus it has a prophetic, a priestly and a royal aspect.

Here again, examining the drama of salvation not chronologically but theologically, we must recognize that its culmination, which wholly justifies it, explains and sums it up, is the work of Christ. Christ is the supreme prophet, because he is both the bearer and the contents of the revelation of God. He is the supreme priest, because he is both the great high priest and the Lamb that was slain. He is the supreme king, because he is both Lord and the Servant, he who commands and he who carries out the command.

Thus the cult will be a recapitulation of the history of salvation by being—in relation to Christ who is and was and is to come—at once prophetic, priestly and royal. The cult, in which the Word of God is proclaimed, sums up all that God has taught us of his will for the world. The cult in which the Eucharist is celebrated sums up all that God has done to reconcile the world to himself. The cult, where the people of God come together in freedom and joy before him whom they worship, sums up all that God has made of those who accept reconciliation with himself; men delivered from the fear of death, freed from bondage and thus capable, like Moses and Miriam at the Red Sea, of rejoicing in the defeat of the Evil One and the victory of the Lord (Exodus 15).

* * *

(c) Among all the systematic problems which should be examined, I take only one, but one which is important: that of the relation between the cult of the Church and the continuance of the history of salvation, after the latter has, in Jesus Christ, reached both its culminating point and fulfillment. There is no question of going deeply into this matter. We shall confine ourselves to suggesting the direction in which the solution appears to lie. This is of capital importance for what follows.

The history of salvation is completed in Jesus Christ. God has nothing further to say or to do than what he has already said and done in Jesus Christ. Why then does the history of salvation continue and how does it continue?

One thing strikes us constantly: it is clear that, as far as the witness of the NT is concerned, the death of Christ has accomplished all things and that his ascension has crowned forever this final fulfillment. And yet at the very moment when he ascends into heaven, angels proclaim that he will return (Acts 1:11). Thus it is implied that the history of salvation is not ended. It will continue for centuries or millennia, which will not bring it any new feature, for all is accomplished. If the history of salvation continues—as is proved both by the fact that history itself continues and above all by the fact that Jesus Christ has promised to return—it is because the central event of this saving process, the cross and the resurrection of Christ which had as it were absorbed, concentrated into itself, the whole history of salvation from the expulsion from paradise up to the morning of Good Friday, must in some way pour itself out, bringing into operation its full efficacy,[5] a process which will however be interrupted before its term by God's plan to put an end to the world. What was once concentrated in Jesus alone, in that "baptism" (Luke 12:50) by

---

[5]That which is a central event will never happen. In itself it would suffice for an unending history of this world, hence the end of this world will not come when the central event of the saving process has exhausted its efficacy—like an electric battery that is exhausted—but when God has determined "to shorten the days" (Mark 13:20).

which he substituted himself for the whole world, must now shed itself abroad, bear its fruit, be exploited. "The virtual inclusion of all
human existence in the crucified body of Jesus must be realized and
actualized in the concrete historical existence of every single man
until it becomes an ontically real and personally apprehended inclusion, until it culminates in its ultimate form."[6] In this sense, according
to the normal mode of biblical revelation, the εφάπαξ [once for all]
brings into being an οἰκονομία [literally, economy]. Christian worship preeminently forms part of this οἰκονομία. That is why the saving process continues even after finding its fulfillment in Jesus Christ.

But how does it continue? It seems to me that the correct answer is
that it continues as a result of the anamnesis which springs from it. But
in saying this we must give to the term anamnesis its fullest significance. It is not merely a question of informing men of past events but
rather of launching them on the full flood tide of salvation. If I may
dare to use such expressions, it is a question of the act by which a man
(or an event) is grafted onto the cardinal act of Good Friday and Easter
and of the act by which this cardinal event of the saving process is
grafted, in the course of the following centuries, onto such a man (or
such an event). By anamnesis the Christian is brought to share in the
benefits of that event which was remembered, and by the same action,
the recalled event is made effectively present and operative.

"What God does, He always does once only *for* all the other times
and *in view of* all the other times when his intervention will continue
to show itself in a saving way. On the level of the life of faith, nothing
is more actual and operative than what God has done once for all"
(Fr. J. Leenhardt).

What we are here describing is the work of the Holy Spirit, which,
since Easter Day, does not consist in producing a new ἐφάπαξ, or in
repeating the former one as though it were not eternally sufficient. It
consists on the one hand, in efficaciously applying what God has
done *illic et tunc* [there and then] in Jesus Christ to the *hic et nunc*
[here and now] of such and such a man or community (or event)—
the Holy Spirit thus mediates Christ to us—and, on the other hand,
in efficaciously referring the *hic et nunc* of such and such a man or
community (or event) to the *illic et [t]unc* of what God has done in

---

[6]P. Brunner (see n. 2, above).

Jesus Christ at Golgotha and in the garden of Joseph of Arimathea—the Holy Spirit brings us into communion with Christ.

We need not here enter into details of liturgical or eucharistic history. Suffice it to say that if we do not deprive the idea of anamnesis of its true nature; if we refuse to make of it a simple memorial; then there is no need, in order to emphasize the efficacious character of this anamnesis and its eschatological bearing, to have recourse to a doctrine which would threaten the oneness of the ἐφάπαξ and multiply the sacrifice of Christ by the number of its celebrations. But let us say especially that the remedy for any weakening of the character of the anamnesis lies in a reverent doctrine of the Holy Spirit. We deny the power of the Spirit if we deny the efficacious virtue and the eschatological bearing of the anamnesis. But we do so no less, if we call in question the uniqueness of the death (and the resurrection) of Christ by allowing it to be supposed that that event must be repeated to retain its efficacity, that its uniqueness is not sufficient for the salvation of the whole world. And it is perhaps because the Eastern Orthodox Church has quite another doctrine of the Spirit, far more powerful than that which characterizes the West, that it has escaped the Western dilemma with regard to the interpretation of the Eucharist.

The history of salvation thus continues, efficaciously operative, in the form of an anamnesis of its central event. What then took place in a substitutionary way on behalf of the whole world is shed abroad by the power and work of the Holy Spirit, to become the ontological reality of those who rejoice in it and live by it. And because the worship of the Church—its baptismal and eucharistic sacraments both of which are acquainted with the power of the proclaimed Word—is the privileged sphere where this application, this actualization takes place, it may be said that Christian worship is one of the most conspicuous agents in the process of saving history. Through the Christian cult—not exclusively, but as one agent and in a very special way—the history of salvation continues. That is one of the reasons for its necessity; it is an instrument which the Holy Spirit uses to carry on his work, to render efficacious today the past work of Christ, and also to bring into saving contact with this work of the past the men and the events of today that they may enter into its benefits.

David W. Fagerberg

Robert F. Taft: Breathing with the Second Lung

There is no other figure in contemporary liturgical scholarship who has been more influential in interpreting the Eastern Rite to Western Christians than Robert Taft. His work as an Orientalist has advanced the goal urged by John Paul II that the Church might learn again to "breathe with both its lungs" *(Ut unum sint)*. Born in 1932, Taft entered the Society of Jesus in 1949 and was ordained a Catholic priest in the Byzantine-Slavonic (Russian) Rite in 1963—the Rite that has been the primary focus of forty years of scholarship and over five hundred publications. In progress now is a five-volume history of the liturgy of St. John Chrysostom. Professor since 1970 and now vice-rector at the school from which he received his doctorate, the *Pontificio Istituto Orientale* in Rome, Taft has rendered service to the academy both as visiting professor in America and Europe and as editor of liturgical journals, to the Roman Catholic Church as appointed member of numerous liturgical commissions, and to Eastern Rite churches where his historical erudition and fluency in over a dozen languages has aided the revision of liturgical books.

For Taft liturgical theology is the spark that arcs between the poles of history, ritual structure, and theological mystery. One must therefore first take history seriously. It is impossible to understand liturgical meaning without understanding liturgical development. Second, liturgical symbols must be seen as they function within the whole ritual structure. No symbol can be accurately interpreted in isolation; its meaning is connected to the structure of the rite. The liturgy must be understood in motion, he wrote, just as the only way to understand a top is to spin it. This structural methodology derives from Mateos and Baumstark. Third, liturgy is the community's encounter with

God's theological mystery every eighth day. Liturgy is not only ritual act, it is soteriological act, as the following article attests.

Theologians cannot understand liturgy in the abstract, they need the historian's guidance through the maze of structural development; but historians cannot understand liturgy if they eclipse God from the subject. God is the subject of liturgy—both the acting subject and the subject matter being celebrated. Liturgy is the faith of the Church in motion; it is the vortex wherein God and humanity entangle; it bridges the gap between the life-giving gesture of God and human response. A thin definition thinks of liturgy only as embellished human piety corporately expressed. Taft's thick definition of liturgy perceives the entire *oikonomia* of God in every encounter. This iconic and epiphanic quality of the Eastern Rite informs his thinking and holds the promise of dilating ours.

FOR FURTHER READING
"The Structural Analysis of Liturgical Units: An Essay in Methodology." *Worship* 52 (1978) 314–28; "The Liturgical Year: Studies, Prospects, Reflections." *Worship* 55 (1981) 2–23; *Beyond East and West: Problems in Liturgical Understanding.* Rev. ed. Rome: Pontifical Oriental Institute, 1997; *The Liturgy of the Hours in East and West.* Collegeville, Minn.: The Liturgical Press, 1986; *The Byzantine Rite: A Short History.* Collegeville, Minn.: The Liturgical Press, 1992; *Eastern-Rite Catholicism, Its Heritage and Vocation.* Glen Rock, N.J.: Paulist Press, 1963.

Robert F. Taft

What Does Liturgy Do? Toward a Soteriology of Liturgical Celebration: Some Theses[1]

* * *

In 1513 Michelangelo Buonarroti completed the frescoes that still grace the Sistine Chapel four and three-quarter centuries later. In the magnificent creation scene, the life-giving finger of God stretches out and almost—but not quite—touches the outstretched finger of the reclining Adam. Liturgy fills the gap between those two fingers. For God in the Sistine metaphor is a creating, life-giving, saving, redeeming hand, ever reaching out toward us, and salvation history is the story of our hands raised (or refusing to be raised) in never-ending reception of, and thanksgiving for, that gift. And isn't that what liturgy is all about? Of course here I am using the term "liturgy" in the broadest, Pauline sense, to include what the Fathers of the Church called the entire *oikonomia* or *commercium*, that ongoing, saving, give-and-take between God and us, the Jacob's ladder of salvation history.

Now surely that is a bold claim, to say that liturgy is the salvific relationship between God and us, and that our liturgies, a privileged ground of this saving encounter, embody and express that relationship. . . . I shall try to justify that claim, and to reflect on its possibility and meaning, via a series of propositions or theses, an artifice I borrow from the German Franciscan theologian Bernhard Langemeyer,[2] one

[1]Excerpted from Robert Taft, "What Does Liturgy Do? Toward a Soteriology of Liturgical Celebration: Some Theses," *Worship* 66, no. 3 (May 1992) 194–211. Reprinted by permission of the author.
[2]See his study, "Die Weisen der Gegenwart Christi im liturgischen Geschehen," *Martyria, Leiturgia, Diakonia: Festschrift für Hermann Volk, Bischof*

that suited the scholastics as well as Martin Luther, and lends itself well to what I am trying to do here: summarize a Catholic vision of what liturgy is all about within the compass of one brief article. . . .

Here, then are the theses, one by one:

1. *The liturgy of the New Covenant is Jesus Christ.*

As the classic Antiochene-type eucharistic anaphoras never tire of repeating, when we were mired in sinfulness, Jesus died for our sins and rose for our salvation, bringing us into unity with God and with one another in him. According to the New Testament, it is this incarnate Lord and savior in his self-giving, reconciling obedience to the will of the Father that for the followers of Jesus is the new liturgy. It is this, and not a new ritual system, that fulfills and replaces what went before: the new temple and its priest and sacrifice and victim; the new creation and the new Adam; the new covenant and the new circumcision and the new Sabbath rest; the new Pasch and its Paschal Lamb—are all Jesus Christ in his saving life-for-others. . . .

2. *Christian liturgy in the Pauline sense is this same reality, Jesus Christ, in us.*[3]

Our liturgy, our service, is to be drawn into him, who is our incarnate salvation, and to live out his life, the same pattern he has exemplified for us, dying to sin to rise to new life in him. In short, our salvation is God's glorification, and he gives it to us, not we to him. He does this through his Spirit dwelling and moving in his Church.

3. *This reality is a personal experience operative only through faith.*

Given by God and received by us, this experience of salvation through faith is an encounter with God, by means of God's epiphany who is Jesus Christ, continued among us today through the indwelling of Christ's Spirit in the community he calls his own. His action is prior: he must call. That is why the Church is a *"calling together"*—*ekklesia* in Greek—not a *"coming together"* on our own initiative, not an *"assembly"* but a *"convocation."* So he first must call. But the call must be answered. Someone has to pick up the phone.

---

von Mainz, zum 65, Geburtstag, ed. O. Semmelroth (Mainz: Matthias-Grünwald-Verlag, 1968) 286–307.

[3]More on this in my *Beyond East and West: Problems in Liturgical Understanding* (Washington D.C.: The Pastoral Press, 1984) 1–12; *The Liturgy of the Hours in East and West: The Origins of the Divine Office and Its Meaning for Today* (Collegeville, Minn.: The Liturgical Press, 1985) 334–46.

4. Liturgy in the narrower sense of the word—actual Christian liturgies, worship services, the liturgical celebration—is one privileged ground of this divine encounter, one theophany or revelation of God's saving presence among us in the world today.

It is by no means the only ground of this encounter, however, for God does not depend on our liturgy to meet and call us to him. But I do not think it needs any proof to say that the New Testament portrays the gatherings of the nascent Church to hear the Word and break the Bread as privileged moments of the presence of the Risen Lord.

If what I have said so far is true, it leads to still further theses:

5. Liturgy is not a thing but a meeting of persons, the celebration of and the expression of an experiential relationship: our relation to God and to one another in Christ through the Spirit. The Holy Spirit, then, is the enabler of Christian worship.

This is a truism, for whatever God does in the Church he does through the Spirit. The failure to explicate the trinitarian and pneumatological dimensions of liturgy can be considered a major defect of some western theologies of worship, a defect sedulously avoided by Edward Kilmartin.[4]

6. Since the basis and source of this grace-filled encounter is the death and resurrection of Jesus, all Christian liturgy plays out this single root metaphor of the paschal mystery as the disclosure, to those who will enter it in faith, of ultimate reality, the final and definitive meaning of all creation and history and life.

For the Christian, Jesus is the image of God, and all other experiences, and the images to which they give rise, are shaped and qualified and reinterpreted in the light of this one, just as the whole experience of Israel was seen as recapitulated in the Exodus-Covenant event. In short, Christian liturgy is an enactment of the paschal mystery of Jesus as the disclosure of God and his plan for us. Col 1:15 calls Jesus "the image of the unseen God," and, for the Greek Fathers at least, liturgy is the image of *that* image.

Christian liturgy has celebrated this root metaphor in Word and sacrament, principally and most primitively in baptism, Eucharist, Sunday, and Easter, but also in matins and vespers and funerals and feasts and, indeed, whenever Christians have gathered in Jesus' name.

---

[4]Edward J. Kilmartin, *Christian Liturgy: Theology and Practice*, vol. 1: *Systematic Theology and Liturgy* (Kansas City: Sheed & Ward, 1988).

7. The actuality, the presentness of it all, is because we are celebrating not a past event, but a permanent present reality, an ongoing call and response, a new life, which we call salvation, that was called into being by those past events.

The events of the past are the cause and mode of this reality's first manifestation or epiphany. But the salvific events of Jesus' earthly life, especially his dying and rising for our salvation, are more than just an epiphany or sign, more than just a *manifestation* of salvation. They are the actual means of that salvation, its very instrumental cause.[5]

These events of the past are past only in the historical mode of their manifestation, that is, as they are perceived within human history by us. For our tradition teaches with the prologue of John that Jesus Christ is not only man but also the eternal Word of God. As such, he is for all eternity that which he has done. Not only is his saving, self-offering eternal; he IS his eternal self-offering, and it is in his presence among us that this sacrifice is eternally present to us.

8. So our liturgy does not celebrate a past event, but a present person, who contains forever all he is and was, and all he has done for us.

That is why the Church can sing in the ancient Latin hymn: "*Iam pascha nostrum Christus est, paschalis idem victima*—For our very pasch is Christ, and he its very victim."

9. Christian liturgy, then, is a living icon, one composed primarily of persons, not signs.

It is a peculiar image, in that it is a human, dynamic one. Its primary components are persons, not things, for we are a constituent part of it. It is not something outside of us which we contemplate, just as the dance has no subsistence apart from the dancers dancing, nor love apart from the lover loving the beloved.

10. Jesus, too, is a constitutive component of the liturgy.

This is seminal: Jesus is not extrinsic to our worship; he is its foundational constituent. He, Paul tells us, is the head of the body, and, to continue the metaphor, just as in any living body, it is only the signals from the head and their reception and execution that makes the celebration a celebration. If one is missing, Jesus' giving or our receiving, there is no celebration.

[5]For a discussion of how this can be, see Brian McNamara, S.J., "*Christus Patiens* in Mass and Sacraments: Higher Perspectives," *Irish Theological Quarterly* 42 (1975) 17–35.

Here, then, we have come full circle. If according to the New Testament, the new worship, the only cult henceforth worthy of the Father, is the self-giving kenosis of his Son, that does not leave us out in the cold.

* * *

11. *Christian liturgy, then, is based on the reality of the Risen Christ, called "liturgie de source" in the felicitous phrase of the Melkite theologian Jean Corbon.*[6]

Because the Risen Jesus is humanity glorified, he is present through his Spirit to every place and age not only as savior, but as saving, not only as Lord, but as priest and sacrifice and victim. Nothing in his being or action is ever past except the historical mode of its manifestation. As the Byzantine Liturgy prays to and of him, "You are the offerer and the offered, the recipient and the gift."

* * *

Of course there is a sense in which every historical event lives on in its effects and its remembering. But in the Catholic/Orthodox tradition, at least, the basis for liturgical anamnesis is not psychological recall, but an active faith encounter with the present saving activity of Christ now. To paraphrase the theology of Vatican II, it is he who preaches his Word, he who calls us to himself, he who binds the wounds of our sin and washes us in the waters of salvation, he who feeds us with his own life, he who is the pillar of fire leading us across the horizon of our own salvation history, lighting our sin-darkened path. He does it in Word and Sacrament—not only there, but certainly there.

One more thesis, then:

12. *If the Bible is the Word of God in the words of men, the liturgy is the saving deeds of God in the actions of those men and women who would live in him.*

Its purpose, to complete once again our circle and return to the Pauline theology of liturgy with which we began, is to turn you and me into the same reality. The purpose of baptism is to make *us* cleansing waters and healing and strengthening oil; the purpose of

[6]Translated as *The Wellspring of Worship* (New York: Paulist Press, 1998).

Eucharist is not to change bread and wine, but to change you and me: through baptism and Eucharist it is *we* who are to become Christ for one another, and a sign to the world that is yet to hear his name.

This is what Christian liturgy is all about because that is what Christianity is all about. So another thesis:

13. *Our Christian liturgy is just the life of Christ in us, both lived and cele-brated. That life is none other than what we call the Holy Spirit.*

This is salvation, our final goal. The only difference between this and what we hope to enjoy at the final fulfillment is that the mirror spoken of in 1 Cor 13:12 will no longer be needed: as Adrien Nocent put it, the veil shall be removed.

All that may sound beautiful, even uplifting. But we have barely touched the theoretical problems concerning just *how* the living, saving Christ is present to us now in the Church, a presence which, as I have said, we believe determines Christian life and worship as something totally new. For God was always present to all ages and all peoples, long before the coming of Jesus. What, then, is new or different about the presence of Jesus in his Church—and hence in its worship? If it means anything, it means Jesus acting on us, saving us, relating to and communicating with us as savior.[7]

* * *

So let me add three more theses:

14. *Basic to all presences of the Risen Christ in his Church is his presence in faith.*[8] *Prior to faith is the presence of the Spirit, however. For faith is rooted in the action of the Spirit, which makes faith possible and through which Christ is present.*

* * *

This does not mean, of course, that the trinitarian God, Father, Son and Spirit, is not and was not always present, working where he will, outside the community. That was true even before the incarnation, before there was any community. But that is not what we mean by Jesus' presence in his Body, the Church, as the glorified redeemer.

[7]See McNamara (n. 5, above), 29 and passim, on God as present to us by acting on us through the instrumentality of Jesus.
[8]Thesis 1 in Langemeyer (n. 2, above) 288ff.

144

This personal encounter is there only when it is believed, is freely received, for it is a relation. In Christianity it takes two to believe just as it takes two to tango: Christ who gives his Spirit, we who receive. For this faith is, of course, also his work. He awakens it in us through the Spirit, as Paul says in 1 Cor 12:3, "No one can say, 'Jesus is the Lord,' except by the Spirit." It is this Spirit which is the first fruits and guarantee of our inheritance, according to 2 Cor 1:22; 5:5; Rom 8:23; Eph 1:14.

* * *

15. *All other modes of Christ's saving presence in the Church are realizations of this basic presence through the Spirit,[9] received in faith.*

* * *

Faith is the basis of the first ministry in the post-resurrection Church. So church office is also rooted in faith: the disciples announce the Word, and are its servant, as eye-witnesses to this faith. That is why not just the *ipsissima verba* of Jesus, but his disciples' word too, is God's word in the New Testament. In the wordplay possible only in German, Langemeyer rightly affirms that God's Word in the New Testament is not only *Wort* but also *Antwort*, not just Word but Answer, not just call but also response, for faith comes to us only because of the apostolic response in faith to the Risen Word of God.[10]

The same is true in the sacraments. The sacramental words that evoke the salvation-history significance of the rite are the Church's words of faith, our *Antwort* to God's *Wort*. As the Vatican II Liturgy Constitution no. 59 says, "Sacraments not only suppose faith, but also strengthen and express faith through words and things: that is why they are called *[fidei sacramenta]* sacraments of faith."[11] And this sacramental faith of the Church is faith in the permanent presence of the Risen Christ which works now, according to his will, through the Spirit, in the sacramental economy. Indeed, it is precisely this permanent saving presence *now* of the Risen Christ that these sacramental ministries make available in Word and Sign. . . .

One final thesis:

[9]Thesis 2 in Langemeyer (n. 2, above) 292ff.
[10]Ibid., 294.
[11]Abbott, *Documents*, 158.

16. The special presence of Christ in the Church's liturgical ministry rests on the fact that liturgy is the celebration in common of Jesus' saving action among us now. As such it is an expression of the faith of the Church.[12]

Sacrament, that is, liturgy, is the existential, common expression of God's self-giving in Christ. It is a theophany, a breaking into the ordinary of an extraordinary manifestation of Christ as being-in-his-Body, the Church. It makes the inner experience of the life of faith transparent, visible. Here too, then, faith is required. Once again, this is not to make the presence subjective, to make God's saving action a hostage to our faith. Christ's presence does not depend on the individual's faith, nor is it caused by faith independently of Christ's Spirit. But it is dependent on the faith of the Church, for without that apostolic *Antwort* it would never have come into being. And it depends on individual faith to be personalized in each of us, for only faith draws back the veil.

* * *

Hence liturgy is not just ritual, not just a cult, not just the worship we offer God. It is first of all God's coming to us in Christ. Nor is it individual, or narcissistic, for it is also a ministry of each one of us to one another. It is only through our faith that Christ can be visibly present to others in the present dispensation. The commonly heard contemporary complaint, "I don't go to church because I don't *get* anything out of it," the summit of a selfish narcissism suitably expressive of our age, shows how little this is understood, this gift of Christ only we can bring to one another by the shining forth of the intensity of our faith in the life of the assembly!

* * *

This has ever been the testimony of Orthodox/Catholic Christendom, East and West: it is through the liturgy that Christ feeds us, and we live. An Eastern expression of it can be savored in one of my favorite anecdotes, the answer given by an old Russian Orthodox village priest to the Western interlocutor who was badgering him, trying to tell him that what was important was conversion, confession, catechetical education, prayer—beside which the overdone

---

[12]A development of Langemeyer, thesis 3, 295ff.

liturgical rites in which his Orthodox tradition was immersed were totally secondary. The Russian priest replied,

"Among you it is indeed only an accessory. Among us Orthodox (and at these words he blessed himself) it is not so. The liturgy is our common prayer, it initiates the faithful into the mystery of Christ better than all your catechism. It passes before our eyes the life of our Christ, the Russian Christ, and that can be understood only in common, at our holy rites, in the mystery of our icons. When one sins, one sins alone. But to understand the mystery of the Risen Christ, neither your books nor your sermons are of any help. For that, one must have lived with the Orthodox Church the Joyous Night (Easter). And he blessed himself again."[13]

But the East has no monopoly on truth. And so the same teaching can be seen equally well, if less dramatically expressed, in what Pius XII said about the liturgical year in his 1947 encyclical *Mediator Dei* (no. 165): ". . . [I]t is not a cold and lifeless representation of the events of the past, or a simple bare record of a former age. It is rather Christ himself who is ever-living in his Church."

And since *we* are that Church in whom Christ lives, the liturgy, as the common celebration of our salvation in him, is the most perfect expression and realization of the spirituality of the Church.[14] If there are different "schools" of spirituality in the East and West, they are but variant local accents of the same spiritual vernacular, the one spirituality of the Church. And the spirituality of the Church is a biblical and liturgical spirituality. The purpose of Christian spirituality is simply to live the life of Christ, to "put on Christ," to live, as Paul says in Gal 2:20, "now, not I, but Christ lives in me." This life is initiated, fed, and renewed in Word and sacrament—in short, in Bible and the liturgy, the "two tables" that feed us, in the felicitous expression of the Latin Fathers, both tables sacraments of Christ's saving presence in his Church. It is in the liturgy that Christ, as the Church's head, acting through the Spirit in the Church's ministry, draws us into his saving paschal mystery. Baptized into the mystery of his

[13]Recounted by Charles Bourgeois, S.J., "Chez les paysans de la Podlachie et du nord-est de la Pologne. Mai 1924–décember 1925," *Études* 191 (1927) 585.

[14]In these final paragraphs I resume what I said in my *Liturgy of the Hours in East and West* (n. 3, above) 346.

death, we rise to new life in him, having "put on Christ." Henceforth, through his Spirit, he dwells in us, prays in us, proclaims to us the Word of his New Covenant and seals it with his sacrifice of the cross, feeds us with his own body and blood, draws us to conversion and penance, glorifies the Father in us. In proclamation and preaching he explains to us his mystery; in rite and song he celebrates it with us; in sacramental grace he gives us the will and strength to live it.

The mystery that is Christ is the center of Christian life, and it is this mystery and nothing else that the Church, through the Spirit, preaches in the Word and renews sacramentally in the liturgy so that we might be drawn into it ever more deeply. When we leave the assembly to return to our mundane tasks, we have only to assimilate what we have experienced, and realize this mystery in our lives: in a word, to become other Christs. For the liturgy is like an active prophecy. Its purpose is to reproduce in our lives what the Church exemplifies for us in its public worship. The spiritual life is just another word for a personal relationship with God, and the liturgy is nothing more than the common expression of the Mystical Body's personal relationship to God, which in turn is simply the relationship of the man Jesus to his Father, given as his Spirit, his gift to us.

The value of such a liturgical spirituality is the unity it effects and manifests between the public ministry and worship of the Church and the no-less-important hidden spiritual life of unceasing prayer and charity carried out in faith and hope by individual members of Christ's Body. The putative tension between public and private, objective and subjective, liturgical and personal piety, is an illusion, a false dichotomy. For in public worship it is precisely this work of spiritual formation that the Church, as the Body of Christ, head and members, carries on.

That's what liturgy does, that's what liturgy means. But unless we encounter this total Christ, head and members, not just Christ in himself, but also in others, in faith, hope, and charity, it will not do or mean what it's supposed to for us.

Gilbert Ostdiek

Mary Collins: Tradition and Contemporary Liturgical Experience in Critical Dialogue

Mary Collins (1935–) is a liturgical theologian whose career has spanned the period of the liturgical renewal since Vatican II. She earned a Ph.D. in Liturgical Studies at The Catholic University of America in 1967, writing her doctoral dissertation under the direction of Kevin Seasoltz on "Presidential Prayer in the Liturgy: Proclamation and Confession of the Christian Mystery." She has been a faculty member at Benedictine College, Atchison, Kansas; the University of Kansas at Lawrence; and The Catholic University of America, where she held the rank of ordinary professor in the Department of Religion and Religious Education. She is currently prioress of the Benedictine community in Atchison, Kansas. She has lectured widely in this country and abroad on various aspects of the theology and practice of the renewed liturgy. She has authored/edited fourteen books, including six volumes in the Concilium series, and has published numerous articles on liturgical theology and practice. She is past president of the North American Academy of Liturgy (NAAL). For ten years she served on the advisory commission of the International Commission on English in the Liturgy (ICEL), and during that time she directed the ICEL Psalter project. She is a seminal and creative thinker who has had a deep impact on the liturgical renewal through teaching, mentoring doctoral students, writing, and lecturing. In recognition of her contributions to liturgical renewal, the NAAL presented to her its Berekah Award in 1993, and the Notre Dame Center for Pastoral Liturgy gave her the Michael Mathis Award in 1995.

She has contributed in a major way to "constructing a more critical liturgical praxis and a more comprehensive liturgical theology." Several convictions ground her approach. First, liturgy is above all an event, not simply text or rubric. Second, liturgy is an event of the assembly gathered here and now. Third, each assembly is a local manifestation of the Church. Accordingly, each local enactment of the liturgy is a realization of the Church's tradition and negotiates the official, received meaning in the particular context of the gathered assembly. And finally, theological reflection on the meaning of the liturgical event must take account not only of the Church's tradition but of the assembly's experience and the ways in which the choices and local enactment of the ritual particularize the meaning liturgy has for it. Critical reflection on the liturgical event must therefore look to the human sciences to incorporate ritual hermeneutics and ritual theory, as she has done in her long-standing study of rites of profession in women's communities. Her writings invariably cite scholars in cultural anthropology (Mary Douglas, Clifford Geertz, and Victor Turner, with whom she did seminar work); ritual studies (Catherine Bell, Ronald Grimes); communications theory (Gregory Bateson); and psychoanalytic tradition (Julia Kristeva). These findings are to be brought into critical dialogue with the tradition in a way that consistently integrates sacramental theology with christology and ecclesiology. Also woven throughout her writings are feminist concerns and the question of appropriate language (to name God in prayer, to name ministry). Such reflections are never purely theoretical; in the end, they must have meaning for the Church's liturgical praxis and spirituality.

FOR FURTHER READING

Contemplative Participation: Sacrosanctum Concilium *Twenty-Five Years Later.* Collegeville, Minn.: The Liturgical Press, 1990; *The New Dictionary of Theology,* co-edited with Joseph A. Komonchak and Dermot Lane. Wilmington, Del.: Michael Glazier, 1987; *Women at Prayer* (1987 Madeleva Lecture in Spirituality, St. Mary's College, Notre Dame, Ind.). Mahwah, N.J.: Paulist Press, 1987; *Worship: Renewal to Practice.* Washington, D.C.: The Pastoral Press, 1987; "On Becoming a Sacramental Church Again." *Open Catholicism: The Tradition at Its Best.* Ed. David Efroymson and John Raines. Collegeville, Minn.: The Liturgical Press, 1997; "Church and Eucharist." *Catholic Theological Society of America Proceedings* 52 (1997) 19–34.

Mary Collins

Critical Questions for Liturgical Theology[1]

As I understand and approach liturgical theology, it is an integrative activity. Liturgy has trinitarian and christological, pneumatological and anthropological, ecclesiological and eschatological components. A classic liturgy will manifest a coherence among all these elements, setting out an integrated vision of the economy of salvation. Certainly the Tridentine liturgy manifested such a synthesis. What Western liturgical theology has done during the recent past regularly spoke to the themes of that synthesis.

We are no longer in that classic moment. Contemporary Western liturgy reflects not a synthesis but our search for one. The goal of this essay is to advance the discussion of the nature of liturgical theology in this historical situation. It does so by looking at classical issues in new ways. Part of the task of liturgical theology will always be descriptive: What is being set out in these texts and rites? I suggest that the contemporary task of liturgical theology is preeminently critical: Is the faith vision being celebrated in the liturgy adequate? Is it congruent with human and ecclesial experience and expectations of the saving grace of Christ? The critical questions have gained in intensity in the past decade. The Church's ritual celebration of its faith and hope takes place today in assemblies which have as many new questions as they have traditional answers about how they share in the saving work of Christ.

* * *

[1]Excerpted from Mary Collins, O.S.B., "Critical Questions for Liturgical Theology," ch. 8, *Worship: Renewal to Practice* (Washington, D.C.: The Pastoral Press, 1987) 115–32. First appeared in *Worship* 53:4 (July 1979) 302–17. Reprinted by permission of the author.

THE CLASSIC STATEMENT

The classic response to the question "what is it that Christian liturgical action expresses" is that liturgy expresses the faith of the Church: *lex orandi lex credendi*. Due to the efforts of nineteenth- and early-twentieth-century scholarly inquiry into patristic liturgy, renewed theological precision was given to the meaning of the classic response. That precision is reflected in the Constitution on the Sacred Liturgy. The liturgy of the Church sets out the mystery of Christ as the paschal mystery—his *transitus* to the Father "for us and for our salvation." Proponents of liturgical prayer have lauded and still laud the liturgy for its objectivity precisely in this regard: liturgical activity focuses on the mystery of salvation revealed in Christ's sacrificial death and resurrection to new life.

Recent liturgical scholarship has provided additional clarification regarding this phenomenon of the objectivity of Christian liturgical prayer. One important recovery of "forgotten truths" was the insistence that the content of the liturgical books—namely, texts and directives for ritual action—does not exhaust the content of the liturgy. Liturgy is above all the particular and actual celebration of a ritual event. Even with this clarification it is possible to advance the thesis of the objectivity of liturgical action. The structuralist perspective brought to bear in ritual studies has provided analytic tools for mining the fundamental structures, not only those borne through texts but also those borne through transactions and exchanges effected between and among persons and ritual symbols. These nontextual structures also constitute objective data in a traditional rite. Scholars can note variants, transpositions, omissions, embellishments of texts and transactions. They can interpret theologically what they uncover structurally. They can do so with confidence that a structuralist methodology can distinguish between basic structures and "structural zeroes." It is clear that there are both objective structures and objective content in the several rites of the Church's liturgy.

The classic statement of liturgical objectivity in content and structure so formulated seems to leave little room or none at all for affirming and interpreting particularity and subjectivity as essential components of the faith of the Church. The variants, transpositions, omissions, and embellishments which reflect choice have generally been ignored or received negative evaluation in liturgical studies. . . . Nevertheless, the data of variants, transpositions, omissions, and embellishments are present in abundance. They are testimony that local, regional, and cultural particularity in expression are every bit as significant for understanding the Church's liturgy and the church's belief as objectivity in content and structure. And perhaps they are more interesting.

EXPANDING THE FOCUS OF LITURGICAL STUDIES

To pursue a line of inquiry on the grounds that it is interesting is not to trivialize the academic enterprise. The argument in favor of studying the interesting rather than the conventional is set out by John Dominic Crossan in *The Dark Interval*.[2] It is an argument in favor of recognizing the human fascination with brinks and borders, edges and limits, with the possibility of the experience of transcendence and the desire to give that experience expression. Since liturgical events are assemblies for the purpose of the engagement of the believing community with the mystery at the heart of its life, one might argue that the structural constants function to facilitate that engagement. The reality and the depth of the engagement desired, achieved, sustained are attended to by the creative choices or "deposits of the spirit." These are the human expressive forms that are testimonials to an active and hopeful faith shaped by available cultural forms and experience. In looking at both of these together we come closer to understanding the phenomenon of liturgical celebration, the event in which the expectation of saving grace is expressed, surrendered to, and appropriated to life. Investigation of living faith is not well served by exclusive attention to issues of objective content and structure. There is a need to look at the whole pattern of structure and choice to discover the faith message of the liturgical medium, and so to uncover the data for descriptive and critical liturgical theology.

Recent sacramental theology supports this orientation, although it does not press the point to any immediate conclusions. Sacramental theology acknowledges that sacraments are always the acts of a particular community, a local church, which is itself a sacrament of the saving mystery.[3] That contention considered in its full significance extends the task of liturgical theology. Insofar as the sacramental action is Christian liturgy, it can be expected to evidence the received tradition with respect both to objective structure and content. Insofar as it

[2] John Dominic Crossan, *The Dark Interval: Towards a Theology of Story* (Niles, Ill.: Argus Communication, 1975) 19–20.

[3] See, for example, Karl Rahner, "The New Image of the Church," *Theological Investigations* (New York: Seabury Press, 1974).

is celebration of the mystery of Christ as that mystery has been culturally perceived and appropriated, the liturgical event will reflect cultural selectivity in its very celebration.

What methods are appropriate for collecting the data of choice? Cultural anthropologist J. van Velsen has distinguished structural analysis from situational analysis of rituals.[4] That distinction can be useful in pursuing the basic question: What is it that Christian liturgical action expresses? Structural analysis will consider all known and possible performances of eucharistic liturgy, for example, and on the basis of all known and possible cases represent the basic structure of that liturgy. The fact of periodic structural deviance will not invalidate the reality of an objective content and structure. In fact, it can heighten the search for understanding. Situational analysis is poststructuralist in its orientations. It does not negate the value of identifying the constants, the objective content and structure. But it does find the variables, the manifestations of choice, more interesting; and so it makes difference the object of inquiry. Situational analysis looks to the concrete particularity of any given ritual performance. What does actually occur occasionally or even consistently by way of variant, transposition, omission, embellishment? Does it point to the actual engagement of the participants, their experience, their appropriation of the meaning as theirs? By pursuing this broadened line of inquiry about choice, the liturgical theologian may advance toward an understanding of the faith expressed in liturgical celebration not as an abstract and universal datum but as a living reality culturally expressed and culture laden.

THE BREAD SIGN: LAYER UPON LAYER OF MEANING

To illustrate the point of the simultaneity of objectivity and subjectivity in liturgical data, the liturgical phenomenon of eucharistic bread is apt matter for exploration. The element of bread in eucharistic action is clearly a constant in the Christian liturgical tradition. It has a constant use: it is the focus of the great thanksgiving prayer of the church and it is distributed and consumed. It is a bearer of deep symbolic meanings at the human, social and religious levels, meanings which have been caught up and extended radically through the action of Jesus and the responsive faith of the church. At a conven-

---

[4] J. Van Velsen, "The Extended-Case Method," *The Craft of Social Anthropology*, ed. Al L. Epstein (London: Tavistock, 1967) 129–49.

154

tional level of doctrinal understanding the bread consistently bears the meaning of sacramental real presence of the risen and crucified Lord, however this presence is explained theologically.[5]

But bread, even eucharistic bread, is not an abstraction nor a generic datum. Bread is a food stuff created from varieties of possible ingredients according to different recipes with a broad range of purposes. Bakers select ingredients according to schemes of use and meaning. There are festive breads and daily breads. What is appropriate for different occasions and uses is determined according to an operative but generally nonconscious system of cultural meanings which may arise, for example, according to a principle of abundance or scarcity or according to a scale of skill in execution.

The phenomenon of eucharistic bread is fundamentally the same: variant possible ingredients, different recipes, distinctive finalities and restricted uses. Moreover, what is judged appropriate bread form and use is also determined according to an operative but nonconscious system of meanings which reflect cultural experience. The need is for that bread sign which can effectively symbolize the sacramental real presence of the Lord—a reality believers hope to experience in their lives. . . .

The matter is nevertheless interesting in liturgical study—interesting in Crossan's sense. As will become apparent, the significance of the bread choice is heightened by setting it in the context of other restrictions on choice related to eucharistic bread use. A convergence of restrictions on choice points to an underlying meaning issue—the stuff of descriptive and critical liturgical theology. Normative decisions about eucharistic bread which intervene to restrict choice and so to classify some bread as illicit are possible pointers to expectations about saving experience and the desire to give that experience or its anticipation expression.

The basic *lex orandi* of eucharistic celebration, bread blessed and shared, has long been and continues to be refined by juridical decisions. Either they are meaningless and arbitrary or they mean something. To reject the notion that the particularity of the bread sign has cognitive significance is to say that the matter is of no real theological consequence. Such a position is belied by the intense engagement of

---

[5]The complex subtlety and variety of early theological explanations is set out in Georg Kretschmar, "Abendmahl" (Alte Kirche) 3/1, *Theologische Realenzyklopädie* (Berlin: Walter de Gruyter, 1977) 1, Lieferung 1:59–89.

the community again and again in history up to the present.[6] Bread style and the protocol related to its handling speak from faith to faith. How is the theologian to uncover the meaning?

If the principle of redundancy is operative ritually, as communication theory indicates is the nature of the case, then the meaning of a particular eucharistic bread form should be reinforced by transactions involving its legitimate use. It is not surprising to note that the historical restrictions placed upon the choice of ingredients and the control of production techniques is replicated in instructions about licit handling and licit consumption in the liturgical assembly. Choice is controlled through distinctions made, presumably for good reason whether conscious or not. In the configuration of licit choices which have accumulated, distinction itself as a fact in the community seems to be a controlling dynamic. That will be considered further below.

When the inquirer begins to follow the leads set out by situation analysis and communication theory, she begins to get a glimpse, in choices about bread, of things christological and ecclesiological. In fact, the issues underlying licit bread choice and use are fundamentally christological and ecclesiological. The very particularity of the bread sign contains information about the ecclesial body of Christ as the manifestation of the real saving presence of the Lord Jesus. The theological meaning is real, even if it is not immediately accessible to historical and structural methods of inquiry. It is theological meaning that is carried by symbolic forms and patterns rather than by basic structure. But it is, nevertheless, meaning which both expresses and shapes the faith of the believers concerning the present experience of salvation.

ECCLESIOLOGICAL AND CHRISTOLOGICAL CONTENT OF LITURGICAL EVENTS

Such an assertion that the bread sign in all its complexity embodies primary theological content needs explication. The basis for that explication comes from the human sciences. Fundamental to the discussion about christological and ecclesiological meanings inherent in the bread sign is acknowledgment of the fact that the content of all rituals is an affirmation about relationships. In the words of Gregory Bateson, ". . . the discourse of nonverbal communication is precisely

[6]An unpublished 1978 research report by J. Frank Henderson, "The Problem of Unleavened Altar Bread Today," recently made available to me by the author, sorts out some of the recurring issues.

concerned with matters of relationships. . . ."[7] Mary Douglas specifies the dynamic of ritual behavior similarly; she says it expresses a relation between the physical self and the social self.[8] Christian liturgical rites, too, speak about relationships, specifically the saving relationships revealed in the paschal mystery.

"Paschal mystery" is a theological formulation which comprehends two salvific moments—the passing of Jesus through death to transforming union with his Father, and the outpouring of the Holy Spirit of the Lord Jesus on those summoned to believe. The people so summoned regularly celebrate the paschal mystery in a ritual way. Intrinsic to the celebration is the comprehension that the mystery in some way extends to and includes the participants personally. . . .

Given the structured movement inherent in the paschal mystery we can expect that the bread, which is a focus of the celebration of the paschal event, will symbolically embody truth about the ecclesial aspect of the paschal mystery. It will do this just as surely as it sets out symbolically the first phase which pertains to the *transitus* of Jesus. The eucharistic element of bread, in other words, intends to express the complexity of the meaning "body of Christ" in its full extension.

How does the bread symbol refer effectively to ecclesial reality and ecclesiological structure, "causing what it signifies" in the traditional formula? I propose that the rite sets out and confirms the way in which the Church is the body of Christ precisely by the scheme of licit forms and licit transactions related to the eucharistic bread. The ecclesial issue focuses on the eucharistic bread because this symbol is the fulcrum of the belief in the reality and the mediation of the saving presence of Christ.

Let us return then to look more closely at the scheme of distinctions regarding what is licit concerning the eucharistic bread sign. Earlier I suggested that distinction itself as a requirement within the community seemed to be a controlling dynamic in the ritual transactions concerning sacramental bread. I would now refine that observation further by suggesting that the issue is not simply distinction but distinction which concerns mediation of the saving grace of Christ. Control or relaxation of control regarding the handling or consumption of the sacramental body of Christ effectively embodies (= is a

[7]Gregory Bateson, *Steps to an Ecology of Mind* (New York: Ballantine Books, 1972) 411–25.

[8]Mary Douglas, *Natural Symbols: Explorations in Cosmology* (New York: Random House Vintage Books, 1973) 93–112.

sacrament of) the Church's understanding of the manner and forms of mediation which are proper manifestation of the risen Christ and are effective in the building up of the ecclesial body of Christ.

* * *

Before attempting to interpret the several parallel developments, it is instructive to look at the kinds of distinctions within the body which emerge, which become the preferred ritual choices in eucharistic action, and ultimately survive as the sole licit choices. Using a formula of equation, we can recognize that the following christological issues were being distinguished and correlated in the church of the third to the fifth centuries:

$$\frac{\text{Christ's divinity}}{\text{Christ's humanity}} = \frac{\text{Christ's majesty}}{\text{Christ's priesthood}} = \frac{\text{Christ's eminence}}{\text{Christ's lowliness}}$$

When the priestly mediatorial role of Christ was deemphasized under the pressure of christological controversy, the presbyterate rose to prominence as priestly mediators. As a result a whole range of ecclesial relationships necessarily underwent readjustment. "Through Christ" came to have a new referent: the priestly office understood as effective power conferred on the *episkopoi* and through them on the *presbyteroi*. As a share in Christ's priesthood, it was sacral in character. It was necessary for it to reflect the eminence and divine authority of Christ from whom it derived.

In order to have some members of the assembly—"in Christ"— signify Christ's eminence, others were required to signify Christ's lowliness. To have some function as sacral mediators, others were required to function as receivers of the divine power. I am suggesting, then, that the formalized distinctions of roles and the absolutized hierarchical ordering in the ecclesial body which gained authority in this era was structured and included as a response to christological heterodoxy. Orthodox christological faith demanded ecclesial expression in the liturgy. . . . .

In the ecclesial body, the counterpoint message of Christ's eminence and power conjoined with lowliness and powerlessness received ritual expression in the ordering of the eucharistic assembly. Divine/human distinctions and functions in Christ were manifested through human/human distinctions and functions in the ecclesial body of Christ gathered for worship. Females were distinguished from males. Female nature was perceived and defined as bodily, carnal, *sarx*—a suitable symbol of lowliness. Male nature was designated a manifestation of spirit, rationality, *logos*—a suitable symbol of eminence. In the theological anthropology of the fathers, the discourse on the issue of male and female is prolix. In liturgy, the same point of male eminence and female lowliness was made by restricting choices about women's participation in eucharistic transactions—the sacramental symbol of the eminence of the risen Christ.[9] Menstruation, pregnancy, childbearing, all unmistakable signs of humanity and human mortality, were for a while the occasion for overt sacramental proscription for females. Subsequently, to the present, these symbols of lowliness function as subliminal bearers of the prohibitions regarding women's suitability for sacral mediation.

If the female expressed lowliness in an androcentric world, the male expressed eminence and so could be the bearer of Christ's sacral priesthood. Yet even within the community of males, distinction was in order. For sacral priesthood to mediate divine grace, human powerlessness and need have to be in evidence. The order of active mediating priests required an order of receptive *laos*. Thus some males in the ritual assembly signify holiness or the source of divine grace; others, deprivation or sinfulness and the need for divine mediation. The classification received confirmation in eucharistic protocol. While all males may signify eminence and are potentially active, only some, the hierarchy, had conferred on them the authority for active eucharistic functions. Others retained receptive or passive ones. Thus we arrive at the body of Christ hierarchically ordered according to the following scheme:

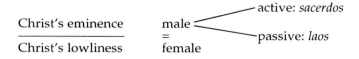

$$\frac{\text{Christ's eminence}}{\text{Christ's lowliness}} = \frac{\text{male}}{\text{female}} \quad \Big\langle \begin{array}{l} \text{active: } sacerdos \\ \text{passive: } laos \end{array}$$

The *sacerdos* came to manifest the eminence of Christ in the ecclesial body by signifying the divine Christ and mediating divine grace

---

[9]Kretschmar (see n. 5, above) suggests antignostic and antimontanist concerns in the second and third centuries are at the origins of earliest explicit controls over women's roles in the eucharistic assembly and in the ecclesial community (see p. 75).

present in the divine eucharistic body. Eventually the circle of relations and appropriate transactions coheres in an integrated pattern of ritual ordering. It does so at the cost of deactivating power present elsewhere in the system.

* * *

What is of interest ritually and theologically is what subverts the pattern of hierarchical ordering, what transcends and confounds the known structures of reality. These subversions, characterized by Crossan as "parabolic," point to the possibility of experience which transcends "world" by undermining it.[10] Some experience presses at the edges and limits of the real with the question: what if things are other than what you know and celebrate as the mystery of the body of Christ? other than what you know and celebrate as the ecclesial showing forth of the divine mystery of saving relationships? Such subversive eruptions are not new; they are constants in the liturgical tradition. Liturgical mediations of divine grace by laymen or women who by definition lacked eminence and divine power are also a part of the historical tradition. They were consistently perceived and repressed as deviations, as distorted expressions of saving mystery.

These ritual considerations finally point us to the present Roman Catholic experience of the saving mystery of Christ. Long-established hieratic ritual forms are in tension with—perhaps already in conflict with and under judgment by—contemporary efforts to conceptualize a nonstratified ecclesiological order, a communal eucharist, and a philosophy of the human person which is not androcentric. But solutions to these theological problems are in turn being shaped by what the community already knows or is currently discovering about divine grace and human mediation. This new awareness is already liturgically evident. It is forcing a displacement of the ritual and ecclesiological categories of eminence and lowliness.

Not surprisingly, this expanded awareness of human mediation of the grace of Christ is contemporaneous with a loosening of traditional eucharistic constraints. Ordained and nonordained, women and men, are again perceived as suitable mediators of eucharistic bread. Once again ordinary (that is, using culturally available ingredients and preparation techniques) bread is reappearing as eucharistic bread. Serious debates occur and treatises circulate about whether all of this is

[10]Crossan, *Dark Interval* 9, 57–62.

licit—that is, whether an expanded scope of "bodily" expression is to be authorized. Issue by issue, the decisions are in favor of a gradual relaxing of constraints about licit choice. What was "always and everywhere by everyone" proscribed is now tenable and permissible.[11]

The symbolic shift in the manifestation of Christ's saving power through lowliness as well as eminence, in effect negating the categories, is not simply a conciliar or postconciliar phenomenon. It is one which preceded and precipitated the more recent developments. The shift diverges from and converges with the breakup of the traditional Western sense of hierarchical social ordering, a breakup which gained political credibility through the French revolution. In any case, the absolute identification of the christological meanings of eminence and lowliness, source and deprivation, with particular classes of persons no longer obtains in the licit ritual handling of the eucharistic bread.

It is commonplace among liberal Catholics to dismiss such liturgical developments as trivial, mere ritualization. The emotional engagement and resistance of conservative believers in the face of such ritual and symbolic issues is in fact much more perceptive. An ordered world is indeed being subverted by such ritual changes. It is not yet clear what "more" is coming, nor whether "more" will be christic or antichristic. From a liturgical perspective it would appear that the eucharistic community has already begun to venture with hope into the unknown "more" of the mystery of saving relationships. What the ecclesial body of Christ already knows in faith to be true, it has begun to explore ritually. This cognition will eventually break through at every level: theological discourse, doctrine, and ecclesiastical order.

WHAT DOES CHRISTIAN LITURGICAL ACTION EXPRESS?

The liturgy of the church expresses the faith of the church. It is a faith which has trinitarian and christological, pneumatological and

[11]Subsequent to the original presentation of this paper the Congregation for the Doctrine of the Faith raised questions in a June 4, 1979, letter to the National Conference of Catholic Bishops about both the liceity and the validity of the growing use of "ordinary" bread for the Church's eucharist. The very raising of the question confirms the point of this essay, that the bread sign is not peripheral but has significant relationship to the Church's doctrinal teaching about salvation. For a canonical reflection on the significance of that letter, see John Huels, "Eucharistic Bread and Wine," *One Table, Many Laws: Essays on Catholic Eucharistic Practice* (Collegeville, Minn.: The Liturgical Press, 1986) 54–62.

anthropological, ecclesiological and eschatological components. The liturgy expresses the faith through a complex world-ordering pattern of ritual symbols, verbal and nonverbal, in the syntax and vocabulary of its prayer and in the scheme of licit transactions associated with the eucharistic species. The liturgy expresses the faith of the church selectively—choosing its themes and emphases from questions of ultimacy put to it by particular cultures. Moreover, it expresses faith in the saving grace of Christ and its mediation to the world in forms that are available within the culture that posed the question.

It is the task of liturgical theology to discern what is being set out in the scheme of licit ritual choices and then to interpret that selective perception of the order of salvation, accounting for what it affirms and what it omits, negates, or rejects as the truth about the present experience of the saving grace of Christ in the church and in the world.

6

What Is the Theological Function
of Liturgical Language and Ritual?

In addition to looking at theological themes in the liturgy, liturgical theologians also study how liturgy "does its work." Liturgy needs both language and ritual in order to do that work. However, language and ritual are not merely "tools" that liturgy uses. We can learn something about the theological nature of liturgy by examining the function they play.

How is language "used" in liturgy? What is the nature of that language? What are the theological implications of the way we use liturgical speech? In a passage that has become foundational for our understanding of these questions, Ramshaw analyzes the nature of "sacred speech" and provides a theological context for liturgical language.

Power also recognizes the importance of language (and I could have chosen a passage that focuses on verbal symbol—"dense" language, irreducible to conceptualization). Instead, we have a passage in which he not only examines contemporary understandings of ritual but both appropriates and critiques them from a theological perspective. Then Chauvet, in a passage not previously available in English, articulates the nature of rituality from a sacramental framework.

Take an act of liturgical worship that is primarily linguistic in nature (for example, the creed, or the psalm), another part of worship that involves a sign/act (the presentation of the gifts or the passing of the peace, for instance), and a third part of worship that involves both words and action (perhaps in your congregation that would be the reading of the Gospel, or the Eucharistic Prayer, or the baptismal act itself). As you read, reflect on what you learn about both the liturgical language and the ritual activity involved in the three acts you have chosen.

Roy A. Reed

Gail Ramshaw: Scholar of Liturgical Language

Gail Ramshaw is one of the preeminent scholars contributing to the conversation about the purposes and nature of liturgy in this country and abroad. She is currently professor of religion at La Salle University in Philadelphia. She is a graduate of Valparaiso University (B.A.), Sarah Lawrence College (M.A.), the University of Wisconsin (Ph.D.), and Union Theological Seminary (M.Div.) She is a member of the North American Academy of Liturgy and *Societas Liturgica.*

No one brings more breadth of knowledge, intelligence, or passion to the study and discussion of liturgy than does Gail Ramshaw. And no one is a more diligent contributor to this study than she. One notices in the body of her work especially four dominant and overlapping motifs: ecumenicity, language, justice, and children.

While deeply rooted in her Lutheran upbringing, her work, especially through participation in professional societies, has been ecumenical in scope and impact. The influence and respect for differing traditions, both Christian and non-Christian, are obvious in her work. I have heard her identify herself as a "Lutheran Catholic," an identity understood and shared in different ways by most scholars whose work involves the theologies and traditions of worship.

Ramshaw understands herself as "a scholar of liturgical language." Her work includes theological/linguistic studies, such as the example in this collection, as well as practical reforms of language, such as the three Lectionary volumes and the Psalter. The pages excerpted here from *Christ in Sacred Speech* are a good illustration of the primary themes of her thought concerning liturgical language, namely metaphor and paradox.

The concern for justice exhibits itself primarily in her writing about feminism, but it would be a mistake to subsume her devotion to justice in the gender issues. Her essay "God's Food" is a consideration of the relation between a Holy Communion and world hunger. Already in 1973 she edited the publication of a symposium of papers on ethics and U.S. foreign policy for the Lutheran Church of America. Her latest book, *Under the Tree of Life*, is a thorough statement of her feminist ideals. No question she is a feminist. She has, however, too much regard for liturgical and theological tradition to be of genuine comfort to either radical feminists or their reactionary despisers.

Her special interest in language for and of children has produced pieces for children's liturgical catechesis, such as *1-2-3 Church, Every Day and Sunday Too,* and *Sunday Morning.* "Celebrating Baptism in Stages," a chapter in volume 2 of *Alternative Futures for Worship* (Collegeville, Minn.: The Liturgical Press, 1987) envisions a solution for the infant baptism/confirmation muddle. Her concern for children is prompted in part by revealing experiences with her own two daughters (see *Worship: Searching for Language,* 136f.).

FOR FURTHER READING

God's Food: The Relationship between Holy Communion and World Hunger. Philadelphia: Division for Parish Services, Lutheran Church in America, 1984; *Christ in Sacred Speech: The Meaning of Liturgical Language.* Philadelphia: Fortress Press, 1986; *Worship: Searching for Language.* Washington, D.C.: The Pastoral Press, 1988; *God Beyond Gender: Feminist Christian God-Language.* Minneapolis: Fortress Press, 1995; *A Metaphorical God: An Abecedary of Images for God.* Chicago: Liturgy Training Publications, 1995; *Reviving Sacred Speech: The Meaning of Liturgical Language.* Akron, Ohio: O.S.L. Publications, 2000.

Gail Ramshaw

The Paradox of "Sacred Speech"[1]

RHETORIC

Speech is an essential ingredient in Christian liturgy. Not by any means the sole ingredient, speech is mated with symbol, and accompanied by music and ritual. For liturgy to be liturgy, this complex occurs within the assembly before God. Those Christians who thought that speech constituted the entire liturgical event suffered through painfully barren worship, for even a longer and longer sermon cannot replace symbol, music, and ritual. But for worship to be Christian, symbol, music, and ritual must be focused by specific speech: speech to God, about Christ, about the event, about the assembly.

Speech is composed of words, yet it is more than words. Words have individual entries in a dictionary, but even though some words have many denotations and even more connotations, we sometimes fool ourselves by believing that the dictionary can tell us a word's definitive meaning. Speech is communication, words in combination, address exchanged. In speech each word bears on each other word. Within the context of speech we discover which of the many possible meanings of each word is appropriate. Thus it is more accurate to think of liturgy as speech than as words, for in the liturgy words find their meaning in the context of the sentence, the hymn, the prayer, the whole rite, and the assembly. The words themselves—words like "heaven," "grace," "offer"—are diamonds in their many facets. Theological dictionaries exhaust themselves giving the Hebrew, Greek,

[1]Excerpted from Gail Ramshaw, "Liturgical Language as Speech," ch. 1, and "The Paradox of 'Sacred Speech,'" ch. 3, *Christ in Sacred Speech: The Meaning of Liturgical Language* (Philadelphia: Fortress Press, 1986) 1–10, 23–26. Reprinted by permission of the author.

Syriac, and Latin roots, the biblical use, and the theological definition of the key words in the Christian vocabulary. As well, there are the secular meaning and the contemporary consolation. Yet in the liturgy these multivalent words are set beside other complex words, and the speech that results from the interrelationships between these words calls us into lively scrutiny and living faith.

The speech of our liturgy derives from the incantatory chants and ecstatic exclamations of earlier religions.[2] The very rhythmic power of the communal song transformed the consciousness of the participants and, it was hoped, called forth the attention and perhaps the mercy of divinity. In ancient religious chant it was not that certain words effected certain conditions, like in medieval magic. Rather, the people's participation in powerful speech was strong enough to alter their perception of the universe and perhaps the universe itself. Contemporary Christian hymns, chants, mantras, and choral responses, as well as the sung liturgy, are a rationalist concession to ancient orgiastic rhythms. Yet even our staid contemporary music and rhythm alter religious speech, and while here we study words on a page, the incantatory power of holy words when sung full voiced in the assembly constitutes a dimension this examination of speech can hardly touch.

The speech of the liturgy is not primarily doctrinal speech. The liturgy is not constructed out of a systematic theology, although a systematic theology of sorts can be constructed from the liturgy. Indeed, like Cyril of Jerusalem in the fourth century, several theologians in our time have heeded the often-cited principle, "The rule of prayer establishes the rule of faith," and have built their theological systems out of the liturgy.[3] But doctrine and systematic theology are third-order language, abstract philosophical speculation that organizes thought into consistent and logical categories. Such third-order language is written for the rational mind to absorb; its syntax is not meant for communal recitation, and it need not be intelligible to the

[2]Gerardus van der Leeuw, "Beautiful Words," pt. 3 of *Sacred and Profane Beauty,* trans. David E. Green (Nashville: Abingdon Press, 1963) 115–18.

[3]Cyril of Jerusalem, *Lectures on the Christian Sacraments,* ed. F. L. Cross (Crestwood, N.Y.: St. Vladimir's Seminary Press, 1977). See also Aidan Kavanagh, *On Liturgical Theology* (New York: Pueblo Publishing Co., 1984); Robert W. Jenson, *Visible Words* (Philadelphia: Fortress Press, 1978); Alexander Schmemann, *Introduction to Liturgical Theology,* trans. Asheleigh E. Moorhouse (Portland, Me.: American Orthodox Press, 1966); Geoffrey Wainwright, *Doxology* (New York: Oxford Univ. Press, 1980).

ear. Instead, liturgical speech is a combination of first- and second-order language. First-order language, the exclamations of human communication, we find in exchanges like "The Lord be with you." Second-order language, the narratives recording human exchange, we find in the lessons. The creed is the closest thing in the liturgy to doctrinal speech. It was a late addition to the liturgy, and optional besides. More important, within the liturgy this third-order language functions not as intellectual abstraction but as communal exclamation: We believe!

Nor is liturgical speech primarily poetic language. Poetry is subjective; it exists in its own right for itself. Poetry does not need any outside point of reference—the original audience, for instance—to be legitimate. In fact, even if there is an outside point of reference, the greater the poetry, the less significant this reference point. It does not matter to whom Shakespeare addressed his sonnets, and the biblical sources for Dante's *Divine Comedy* or Milton's *Paradise Lost* do not account for the greatness of the poems. A poem needs no "meaning" apart from its inexplicable esthetic effect. On the other hand, Christian liturgy is not written by a single self-reflective consciousness. Liturgy must have reference beyond its own beauty. So it is that committees working on liturgical revision have not been well served by contemporary poets, that poems inserted into the liturgy as prayers or responses are risky business. So too, hymns composed by demonstrably great Christian poets may require liturgical revision. No, liturgy is not poetry.

Nor is liturgical speech colloquial. We have learned this lesson during ten years of flimsy dialogue like "May the Lord get through to you." Not even in the secular world do we elect current conversational tone when the communal situation is socially significant. Colloquial speech is dictated by individual feeling; it changes rapidly in a fast-moving culture. The presider's cheery greeting, "Good morning!" may be offensive to those suffering recent loss. In such a case the colloquial speech has fragmented rather than united the assembly. Liturgical speech ought to be vernacular, but vernacular is not the same as colloquial. The formal conventions of a marriage rite ought to be altered by the vernacular to reflect women's rights, but that is quite different from the couple's colloquially extemporizing immature reflections on love. No, the liturgy is not colloquial speech.

Although not colloquial, Christian liturgical speech at its best is vernacular. Christian speech is not a Sanskrit, a wholly other language required and reserved for sacred purposes. To the extent that Christians rely on transliterations and archaisms in liturgical speech, our incarnational theology is in trouble. Christianity has from its inception struggled to translate the parent languages of Hebrew and Aramaic into the vernacular. Paul wrote in Greek. Theology was systematized in Latin. Reformation insights were articulated in German, French, and English. Christian speech is vernacular with a twist: the language of faith is a dialogue between our contemporary experience in its vernacular dress and the gospel as written in the Scriptures and repeated in the tradition.[4] We must use common speech to proclaim good news that is outside our common experience. The recasting of liturgical speech or the fine tuning of a eucharistic prayer is a momentous task: one must know the gospel, the tradition, and the contemporary situation, and must hold them together in liturgical language.

If liturgical speech is not dogmatic prose, poetic monologue, or colloquial conversation, then what is it? The category of rhetoric will serve well. Sometimes, of course, "rhetoric" has a pejorative connotation, the lies of Hitler having given the skill a bad name, the folksiness of television having displaced the classic art. Instead let us recall rhetoric as the ancient Greek art of using formal language eloquently in order to persuade. For liturgy does intend to persuade—to praise God, to remind God of our need, to plead for mercy, to remind ourselves of our faith, to call one another into faithful living. The persuasive character of worship is clearly seen in Pentecostal services, where the preacher exhorts God and the people in expansive tones and the congregation cries out its amens. But all worship has its roots in persuasive rhetoric. Jewish liturgy reiterates the praise of God and calls down God's justice on the world. As the liturgy of John Chrysostom says, "Again and again in peace let us pray to the Lord." The adoption in the west of formulations of court address for the Christian prayer of the day also indicates a sense of prayer as effectual speech of persuasion.

* * *

In the art of speaking effectively, one chooses words thoughtfully. It is not that one matches words to discrete meanings, for words have

---

[4]Gerhard Ebeling, *Introduction to a Theological Theory of Language*, trans. R. A. Wilson (London: William Collins Sons, 1973) 191.

their denotation and connotation in combination with other words—all the more reason that word choice is a difficult task of discrimination. Words in rhetorical speech require a gravity of acceptability, yet they cannot be so ponderous as to sink underground. The vocabulary in religion deserves special consideration, for religions are, among other things, traditions of words, words translated from original languages, words with a long history of meaning and devotion. Thorough analysis of Christian liturgy requires fluency in Hebrew, Greek, Latin, in the languages of the European and English reformers, and with contemporary novelists and poets. What were and are the meanings and the feelings of these words? This is the first consideration for the critic of rhetorical speech.

In the art of speaking effectively, one judges imagery. Which images assist in eloquent speech, and which do not? What are the sources of the most effective imagery? Rhetorical speech will have little use for imagery grounded solely in personal experience, since for its communal purpose rhetoric must rely on common sources for imagery. C. G. Jung suggests that the images most powerful in human consciousness are not innovations but are ancient mythic and religious symbols shared by all humankind.[5] If Jung is correct, archetypes like light and water are significant even for those who have not read the Bible and Milton. Let us hope that Jung is right.

Rhetoric is also the art of shaping syntax carefully. The lines we so often hear quoted from Winston Churchill—"Never in the field of human conflict was so much owed by so many to so few," "I have nothing to offer but blood, toil, tears, and sweat"—are masterpieces of syntax. Syntax concerns itself with design, balance, and euphony; with the placement of words, the amount of tension in the lines, and the tone of the phrase. Superb syntax approaches beauty. . . .

Finally, the art of speaking effectively involves the matter of structure. Generally, rhetoric is not extempore. It is ordered and crafted into a form that is balanced and appropriately weighted. Rhetoric takes time to speak and to hear, and over that period of time the structure of the prose becomes a set piece of effective eloquence.

* * *

[5]C. G. Jung, *Psychology and Religion* (New Haven: Yale Univ. Press, 1938) 49.

METAPHOR

This study of liturgical language seeks to inquire into meaning. What does the speech of the liturgy "mean"? . . . Increasingly in the twentieth century, philosophers of language view human speech with a poet's eyes. It is as if these students of symbolic expression followed C. G. Jung, who began as a psychiatrist and ended a mystic. But not only mystics and poets subscribe to this school of metaphor: Paul Ricoeur's massive synthetic studies have given the consideration of metaphor all the intellectual weight it may previously have lacked.[6] . . . Thus metaphor was long thought to be pleasant though unnecessary substitution of an image for an idea, the claw foot on the chair leg. Ah, but even in the common noun "leg," we have metaphor. Metaphor makes new mental reality. By seeing something old or new in terms of something else, metaphor changes everyone's perception from that time forward.

More than a few junior-high-school teachers have done us no favor by defining a metaphor as nothing other than a simile without "like" or "as." Metaphor, far from being merely a decorative figure of speech, is the fundamental unit of creative thought. In metaphor the mind expands in a fresh way, imagining the new and renovating the old. Metaphor does not label: it connects in a revolutionary way. Metaphor is not merely an image, the look-alike, the reflection in the mirror. Rather, metaphor forms a comparison where none previously existed. Metaphor alters perception by superimposing disparate images. A metaphor has been called "an affair between a predicate with a past and an object that yields while protesting."[7] The two images are logically incompatible. What shall we call the four sticks holding up the chair seat? How about "legs"? We speak scarcely a single sentence without relying on the metaphoric quality of language. Hidden inside our prosaic talk about chair legs is an ancient personification of the simple chair, a metaphor of lively limbs on dead wood. Such an openness to a history of transposed and superimposed meaning is most apparent in poetry. Not surprisingly it is the poets and novelists who keep speech continually birthing for the next generation. In George Orwell's *1984*, complete governmental control of language in Newspeak is possible only because creative writing has been eliminated from the culture.

[6]Paul Ricoeur, *The Symbolism of Evil*, trans. Emerson Buchanan (New York: Harper & Row, 1967), and idem, *The Rule of Metaphor*.

[7]Nelson Goodman, *Languages of Art* (Indianapolis: Bobbs-Merrill, 1968) 69.

The school of metaphor seeks to understand where the metaphors originate, how the connections were made, what kind of reality results, and what the relationship is between the universe of speech and the universe outside speech. This approach to human speech is increasingly significant in theology and liturgy.[8] . . .

LITURGY AS METAPHORIC RHETORIC

We have arrived at the category for liturgical speech: metaphoric rhetoric. The liturgy is rhetoric, communal speech of formal eloquence. The liturgy is metaphoric, its words, phrases, and sentences functioning within a creative tradition as the symbols of our faith. Thus, to analyze the meaning of liturgical speech we must ask questions of rhetorical purpose and of metaphoric meaning.

Textbooks of rhetoric urge writers never to mix metaphors. That is, one does not begin the sentence galloping on a charger and conclude the sentence by running out of gas. One metaphor should be safely in port before another is launched. But in liturgical speech metaphors mix freely.[9] In the phrase "Jesus Christ is Lord, to the glory of God, the Father," the metaphors line up next to one another so fast that for most people they march by undifferentiated from one another. Jesus is the given name Joshua; Christ recalls the Hebrew plea for the Messiah; the metaphor of Lord is Christianity's most complex, applying the Hebrew name for God to the risen Jesus; glory can be explicated differently with help from Exodus or from John; and the metaphor of father has innumerable interpretations. The rhetoric of Christian liturgy relies not on metaphoric purity, but on the mingling of metaphors. The exegesis of the liturgy is much more complicated than the explication of a poem by George Herbert, in which the cleverness of the metaphysical conceit lies in the sustained adherence to a single dominant metaphor. In Christian liturgy the metaphors are myriad.

In liturgical speech both metaphor and rhetoric must serve a hospitable unity of the assembly. The symbolic language strives to be, like a rainbow, symbolic in a primordial way. Of course, liturgical

[8]See, for example, Sallie McFague, *Metaphorical Theology* (Philadelphia: Fortress Press, 1982); Norman Perrin, *Jesus and the Language of the Kingdom* (Philadelphia: Fortress Press, 1976); David N. Power, *Unsearchable Riches* (New York: Pueblo Publishing Co., 1984); Phyllis Trible, *God and the Rhetoric of Sexuality* (Philadelphia: Fortress Press, 1978); Amos Niven Wilder, *Theopoetic* (Philadelphia: Fortress Press, 1976).

[9]Daniel Stevick, "The Language of Prayer," *Worship* 52 (1978) 547.

speech, like T. S. Eliot's *Waste Land,* also calls out for footnotes, and this study will provide some such annotation. But if the liturgical speech is not on the deepest level symbolically accessible, the glosses will do little good. The unity of the assembly is served in the first place by the human metaphors below glosses: water, bread, wine. In the same way the rhetorical character of liturgical speech must serve the hospitable unity of the assembly. . . . Christian contemplative mysticism is not a rejection of words but a journey through words, up the path of speech, on towards God. But this word became flesh. God took on the metaphor of a first-century Judean male, so that when we speak of Jesus, we speak, as in all metaphor, simultaneously of two different things at once: the life of a Jewish man and the being of God. On Holy Cross Day, the festival on which, incongruously, we revere the despised cross, we recall John's Gospel: "And I, when I am lifted up from the earth, will draw the whole world to myself" (John 12:32). On first hearing we are delighted by John's rhetorical skill. But the metaphor is astonishing. Jesus draws us upward to God by drawing us towards himself, as he is lifted up to God by being lifted up onto the cross. Rhetorical eloquence, abounding metaphor, such is liturgical speech.

* * *

YES-NO-YES

Liturgy is informed by both the mystics and the theologians. In the liturgy we sing metaphoric songs, rely on music, art, and symbol to express the inexpressible, and admit the inadequacy of our language. . . . How is this admittedly meager language affirmed as truth? What is the meaning of sacred speech?

The hermeneutical method for the study of liturgy is yes-no-yes. Because our words are sacred, we say yes to liturgical language. Because we revere the language as holy, we take off our shoes and kneel down. We affirm its truth and its meaning for our lives, devoutly responding with a yes. But step two is required by our linguistic sophistication. Our liturgical language is mere human language. It is only speech, words in English or Hebrew or Greek. These words cannot contain divinity or convey the essential being of God. Our words are pitifully meager: step two is a disillusioned no. But our sacred speech is the language of faith, our tradition of grace. We are the community that continues to receive God's life through these words. These words are salvation for us. Step three is our faithful response to the admittedly hidden God, a hearty yes to the sacred speech given us.

Let us first consider step one, the reception of the speech as sacred. Baptized into the death of Christ, we receive this language as our basic vocabulary. Helpless as either a kicking infant or a dying adult, we exist before the mystery of God. Like the *tohuwabohu* of Gen 1:2, that formless void of created matter, we confront God, the I AM of all time and space. And we kneel. We acknowledge the difference between who we are and who God is, and we receive the sign of the cross on our forehead. Abba, we pray. Thanks be to God, we say after the lessons. Amen, we say upon receiving the body of Christ.

But then we apply to liturgical language the hermeneutical skills of the biblical scholar. We establish as best we can the original text. We attempt to construct the original situation, the better to understand the original theological meaning. We study the tradition of translation and trace the history of meaning. We see our sacred speech evolving in new languages, meeting religious needs of altered cultural settings. We inquire into its meaning in contemporary America, aware that words constantly change in significance and that symbols acquire new connotations. We apply this historical-critical method to, say, the image of God as rock. What was the original Hebrew image? How was it used in the narratives and in the psalms? How did the rabbis expound on it? How does the Jewish symbolic meaning relate to other ancient mythological rocks? What happens to that Jewish symbol in the incarnation? What about Jesus as rock, Peter as rock, the Church as rock, Golgotha as rock, Jerusalem as rock, Rome as rock, doctrine as rock? Only after all this study can we expound the many meanings in the morning psalm (Psalm 95), "Let us shout for joy to the rock of our salvation." Pages could be written on the metaphor of the rock. Yet compared with sacred speech like "Jesus is Lord" or "Christ is arisen," the metaphor of the rock is child's play. We have much work to do in tracing the meaning of our sacred speech.

This critical task often leads us to say no. The Majorca storytellers begin their tales with the phrase *Aixo era y no era*, "It was and it was not."[10] Even if the realization makes us insecure, even if we would like to be fundamentalists, we must admit that the language is not

[10]Paul Ricoeur, *The Rule of Metaphor*, trans. Robert Czerny (Toronto: Univ. of Toronto Press, 1977) 224.

the full truth for which we had hoped. Critical biblical scholarship will not allow us to "believe in" the text. We know too much: God did not dictate the Scriptures or our latest liturgical text. As well, contemporary philosophers of language call us into honesty about the legitimacy of our truth claims. Our only response is meager indeed: to talk enthusiastically about metaphor! Yet even we must admit that metaphor is a naming that is not. God a rock? The modern cynic cites the fact that urban dwellers have not enough meaningful experience of rocks—except those behind glass at a museum—for the image to work appropriately. Even as an archetypal image of solid ground and stable protection in the wilderness, rock is extremely limited as image for the being of God. Far from bearing easy resemblance to God, rock may seem particularly antithetical to divinity. A rock is not alive, it has no consciousness, it is not free, it crumbles with time. And where was this rock during the Holocaust? No, God is not a rock.

Yet, finally to be the community that meets weekly to praise God with Christian sacred speech, we take the third step. Yes, this is the language we use to name truth. This is the tradition of religious language turned on its head by the death of Jesus. We are the people who received God's grace through Hebrew, Aramaic, Greek, Latin, German, English. We pronounce God's name as LORD, and we claim that Jesus is Lord. Step two was, with Anselm, faith seeking understanding: "I desire in some measure to understand thy truth, which my heart believes and loves. For I do not seek to understand in order to believe, but I believe in order to understand."[11] But step three recalls Tertullian: "It is to be believed because it is absurd."[12] Belief is, after all, not knowledge. It is consciousness beneath and beyond knowledge. It is acceptance of a tradition of grace in spite of the no forced upon us by the limitations of language. To claim that worshipers "believe in the Bible" means that they take to themselves the biblical metaphors for God, for the human self, and for human community, and so form themselves into an assembly around Christ. The psalms were recited in the concentration camps. Aquinas, abandoning his *Summa*, struck by silence, still celebrated the liturgy. The con-

[11]Anselm, "Proslogion," in a *Scholastic Miscellany: Anselm to Ockham*, Library of Christian Classics 10, ed. and trans. Eugene R. Fairweather (Philadelphia: Westminster Press, 1961) 73.

[12]Tertullian, "On the Flesh of Christ," in The Ante-Nicene Fathers, vol. 3, ed. Alexander Robert and James Donaldson (Grand Rapids: Wm. B. Eerdmans, 1978) 525.

temporary philosopher, having grappled with Friedrich Nietzsche, sings a *Te Deum*, in fervent hope that through this sacred speech the real God is worshiped. Like the women at the tomb, there was first their devout adoration of God, second their disillusionment at the cross. But the third step propels them into a final yes, a belief in God and a faith in the resurrection that recasts their old categories, leaps over their doubt, and assembles them into the body of believers around bread and wine.

The final yes is both hard and easy. It is difficult to affirm liturgical language as sacred speech after the painful honesty of step two. It is hard to push always toward the balance so that no single interpretation distorts the truth of the metaphor. It is complicated, being true to contemporary experience while claiming to be formed by ancient symbols and traditional vocabulary. Yet such faith is also easy. It is the final resignation into God, the last abandonment of the critical task. It is at the end allowing the waters of baptism to wash us into God's life. It is conceding the paltriness of both our scholarship and our doubt. Such faith is easy in that it is a gift from God, the gift we call grace.

The gospel narrative of the temptation of Jesus has given us this method. The tempter knows well the Hebrew poems: the beloved metaphors promise that God's Messiah will feed the poor in the desert, will gather into his justice all the world's authority, and appearing suddenly in the temple, will perfect a priesthood for the LORD. The tempter asks Jesus to say yes to these metaphors of salvation. But no, Jesus cannot take them on, then, literally answering the tempter's teasing and our prayers' pleading. But finally, yes: as Jesus goes on through his ministry and onto the cross he becomes food for the poor, life in our desert, justice for the nations, king of the universe, bearer of the New Covenant, purifier of the holy ones. Yes, no, yes: Christ in sacred speech.

R. Kevin Seasoltz

David N. Power: Searcher for the Riches of God

Born in Dublin, Ireland, in 1932, David Noel Power received his early education from the Christian Brothers. He entered the Oblates of Mary Immaculate and was professed in 1950. Sent to Rome for his seminary formation, he was ordained a presbyter in 1956. Back in Ireland, he taught dogmatic theology at the Oblate Scholasticate for seven years, then returned to Rome for doctoral studies at the Pontifical Institute Sant' Anselmo. He was awarded the doctorate in 1968 with a dissertation published under the title *Ministers of Christ and His Church*. Through Herman Schmidt, S.J., the director of his dissertation and a professor at the Gregorian University, Power became an editor of the international theological review *Concilium*, with which he was associated for many years.

Returning to Ireland, Power became superior and director of formation at the Oblate house in Piltown and also taught systematic theology at Milltown Institute of Philosophy and Theology in Dublin. In 1971 he returned to Rome as director of studies, then superior and director of formation at the Oblate International Scholasticate, lecturing at the same time in sacramental theology at the Gregorian University, the Angelicum, and Regina Mundi.

In 1977 Power joined the faculty at The Catholic University of America in Washington, D.C. He served as president of the North American Academy of Liturgy in 1987–1988 and received the Academy's *Berakah* award in 1991. His pastoral and academic career has been marked by a deep concern for social justice for the poor and marginalized in both the Church and the world.

David Power is a systematic theologian who has applied his expertise to the analysis and critical evaluation of the Church's worship.

Almost all his publications, which range over a broad field, look to liturgy as a source for theology. Hermeneutics has been a driving theme in much of his academic work. This is evident in the selection that follows. Sensitive to the context in which liturgical texts were originally formulated as well as the context in which his own interpretation takes place, Power has paid special attention to the role of language in liturgy as a means of understanding how God's self-communication comes about in the celebration of sacraments. Almost all of his writings move from liturgy to the worship of God, since his overriding concern is that thanksgiving and praise due to a gracious and merciful God.

FOR FURTHER READING

Ministers of Christ and His Church: Theology of the Priesthood. London: Geoffrey Chapman Publishing Co., 1969; *Christian Priest: Elder and Prophet.* London: Sheed & Ward, 1973; *Unsearchable Riches: The Symbolic Nature of Liturgy.* Collegeville: The Liturgical Press, A Pueblo Book, 1984; *Gifts That Differ: Lay Ministries Established and Unestablished.* Collegeville: The Liturgical Press, A Pueblo Book, 2nd ed., 1985. *The Sacrifice We Offer: The Tridentine Dogma and Its Reinterpretation.* Edinburgh: T. & T. Clark Limited, 1987; *Eucharistic Ministry: Revitalizing the Tradition.* New York: Crossroad, 1992; *Sacrament: The Language of God's Giving.* New York: Crossroad, A Herder & Herder Book, 1999.

David N. Power

Ritual and Verbal Image[1]

Some recent philosophers stress the linguisticality of understanding and reality.[2] Being stands forth in language, and it is only through language that we participate in Being. There is no access to knowledge of things, just as there is no access to self-knowledge, except through language. While language serves discursive, practical, and theoretical purposes, its primary nature is symbolic or presentational. It represents things in their relationships to one another. This is why ordinary, everyday language, what we use in naming things and in the predications we make of them, already offers insight into the poetic nature of human dwelling. Simple words—jug, water, wine, bread—hold together earth and sky, times past and times future, humanity's boundedness to earth and its desire for a fulfillment that breaks this boundedness. . . .

Although this power of language is to be kept in mind, its relation to the bodily must be explored. The symbolic has been described already as the transformation of experience and the bringing of experience to formal expression so that it may be understood and given new projection, with new virtual possibilities of being and action. In fact, ordinary words are not the most rudimentary expressions of ex-

---

[1]Excerpted from David N. Power, "Ritual and Verbal Image," ch. 4, *Unsearchable Riches: The Symbolic Nature of Liturgy* (Collegeville, Minn.: The Liturgical Press/Pueblo Publishing Co., 1984) 83–99. Reprinted by permission.

[2]Hans-Georg Gadamer, "Man and Language" and "The Nature of Things and the Language of Things," *Philosophical Hermeneutics* (Berkeley: Univ. of California Press, 1977) 59–68, 69–81; Paul Ricoeur, "A Philosophical Journey: From Existentialism to the Philosophy of Language," *Philosophy Today* 17 (1973) 88–96.

perience, even if they do serve in a culture as a key to its interpretation. Experience has a structure that is prior to linguisticality, one that can be investigated through reference to play and ritual.[3]

RITUAL

In the body and through the body, human persons find and express themselves in relation to environment, to other persons, to society, and to history. In and through the body they have the initial experiences associated with the sacred, experiences formulated interpretatively in some bodily ritual. Before any of these relationships are brought to language, they are given in some rudimentary form through bodily experience. The initial appropriation of relations to others and to self is in bodily reaction, gesture, and disposition. "Initial" does not have simply a chronological sense—attempts to write the prehistory of human expression have little success—but indicates that throughout life and in all forms of social interaction the bodily remains the fundamental mode whereby experience is received and given structure and articulation.

In his book *Homo Ludens*, Johan Huizinga explored the relationship between play and ritual, and for some years this relationship was the topic of several works.[4] Play expresses a perception of body and cosmos and is an instinctive form of self-expression and interaction that is unreflected, undistanced, and therefore not interested in presenting intelligible form. Play moves quickly to the point of *game*, however, where rules and patterns are decided, so that play takes place within the compass and according to the patterns determined. One can see children engaged in wild and exuberant play, but soon enough some toddler emerges to set rules, assign parts, and demand repetition. As such, a game is not for spectators, but tries and tests players and allows them to play out structures of being and, in playing, to appropriate them. When a game is played before an audience, the trend is to engage the audience in it.

Ritual provides a greater degree of abstraction than does a game, since its rules, rhythms, and repetitions are more definite and demand

---

[3]Hans-Georg Gadamer, *Truth and Method* (New York: Crossroad, 1982) 94–105; Johan Huizinga, *Homo Ludens: A Study of the Play-Element in Culture* (Boston: Beacon Press, 1955); Gibson Winter, *Liberating Creation: Foundations of Social Ethics* (New York: Crossroad, 1981) 10–19.

[4]For example, Harvey Cox, *The Feast of Fools* (Cambridge, Mass.: Harvard Univ. Press, 1969).

a more exact observance. Historical, anthropological, and sociological investigations point to ritual as formalized play. It marks the key moments of seasons and life, it manages order and chaos in times of change, and it is one of the necessities of social ordering and behavior. Sometimes what is called "primitive" ritual is associated with magic, since observers think that the intention of such ritual is to influence the powers that control life. This is not exact, however, for ritual is more an expression of harmony with, perception into, and conformity with the patterns of bios and cosmos.[5]

* * *

One school of the history of religions, that associated most particularly with Mircea Eliade,[6] exhibits a primary interest in the bodily ritual that relates body and cosmos. Cosmic rituals—which celebrate the manifestation of the holy or the divine in the movements of night and day and in the flow of the seasons, or which commemorate hierophanies in sacred places or the presence of sacred power in such things as trees or rivers—bind humanity's destiny with respect for nature, a sense of awe before it, and a necessary oneness with it and with the powers that control it. When this sense of harmony and awe, which is expressed in bodily rites and attitudes, vanishes as it has in contemporary Western society (as recalled in the analysis of crisis presented by Gibson Winter), then conflicts, chaos, and exploitation ensue. Some look to ritual to revive these sentiments. Behind the interest in cosmic rites and symbols sometimes lies the persuasion that the divine, even in Judeo-Christian religion, is manifested in this form of revelation.

* * *

Another approach to the bodily element in ritual looks to studies that analyze religious symbol in virtue of a set of basic bodily experiences, taking these as cues to the entire range of the human.[7] These ex-

[5]Suzanne K. Langer, *Philosophy in a New Key: A Study in the Symbolism of Reason, Rite, and Art,* 3rd ed. (Cambridge, Mass.: Harvard Univ. Press, 1978) 144–70.

[6]Mircea Eliade is at present engaged in writing a history of religious ideas. Two volumes have appeared: *A History of Religious Ideas,* trans. Willard R. Trask, 2 vols. (Chicago: Univ. of Chicago Press, 1978, 1981).

[7]Gilbert Durand, *Les structures anthropologiques de l'imaginaire. Introduction à l'archétypologie géneral* (Paris: Bordas, 1969); *L'Imagination symbolique* (Paris:

periences are presented as the basis for ritual action and symbolic imagination. Thus three acts—remote action, copulation, and digestion—become reference points for understanding the symbolic and, more particularly, a range of symbolic actions. Ritual action does not use these actions in their normal rendering, but imitates them in a variety of ways, such as to present their meaningfulness and the meaningfulness of actions referable to them. In that sense, their imitation presents what the philosophers would call the structure of human experience before it is brought to language.[8]

In remote action, one acts toward persons or things in virtue of a separate and distinct personal identity. This includes actions such as moving away from, looking at, listening to, and touching. Whether the ritual actions derived from this type of bodily expression signify individuation or alienation, it is bodily or personal individuality that is signified. Except in cases of ritual sex, copulation is not a ritual action, but it does serve as the analogue for a second group of rites which somehow imitate this fundamental human experience of sexual union. Such rites are initiation ceremonies, sacrifice in certain of its features, and sacred dance as interacted rhythm, all of which carry a meaning of bonding persons together, or bonding persons with things and otherly realities, even while keeping their separateness intact. The third basic bodily function, digestion, provides the analogue for rituals that signify intimacy and mystical union. What is signified is fusion, two becoming one, where distinction is not felt or attended to, as when food is assimilated into the stomach. Although copulation is sometimes used as an image in mystical language, this is simply due to cultural traditions that assimilate it to the digestive in order to express the union to which sexual union aspires rather than that which it attains. After copulation, people are again apart, even though they feel bound to one another. Digestion is experienced as a more complete assimilation (although it is an image which allows for an ironic twist, as when James Joyce associates it with defecation). Even when a classification of this sort is adopted as an avenue of insight into the shaping of experience by ritual, it must be remembered that rites and their signification interplay with one another. Some rites carry patterns of two or more of these categories. For example,

Presses Universitaires, 1968); B. R. Brinkman, "On Sacramental Man," *The Heythrop Journal* 13 (1972) 371–401; 14 (1973) 5–39, 162–89, 280–306, 396–416.

[8]Paul Ricoeur, "Metaphor and Symbol," *Interpretation Theory: Discourse and the Surplus of Meaning* (Fort Worth: Texas Christian Univ. Press, 1976) 60–65.

the ordering of a ritual meal, with its allotment of roles and places, indicates separation and distinction, but it is also a binding action of covenant and a symbol of communion as one body. Baptismal immersion is an assimilation of personal identity and a journey (ascending from the pool), as it is an action of initiation into a covenant group and a fusion of identities expressed in the images of descent into the earth or return to the womb. Most important to remember from this classification is that ritual represents and imitates the most fundamental bodily experiences, which are separate identity, coming together in mutual bond, and fusing identities to the point of blurred distinction.

SOME PARTICULAR RITUALS

Three types of religious ritual that relate to the cosmic and the bodily have received special attention and are increasingly invoked as paradigms for understanding Christian liturgy. The value of this insight and the nuances with which it is to be accepted are worth attention. These three types of ritual are rites of taboo and purification, rites of passage, and mimetic rites.

Rites of Purification and Taboo

The establishment of taboos, and the purification rites made necessary by their infringement, is a basic way for a society to mark out the field of the sacred and designate the vital forces and powers that it feels the need to identify with and serve in ordering its life and projecting its vision of reality.[9] Today people are often horrified when they hear of the old Catholic practices of a mother's purification after childbirth or penances imposed on spouses who received communion the morning after having sexual relations. Taboo is an odious word to modern ears, and the practices mentioned may be deemed to reflect both superstition and sexual guilt or disdain. Today people may be less censorious, but still benignly amused, when they are told of the rigorous silence that once had to be kept in places of worship. Talking in church has since become a sign of liberation, and approaching communion after a night of extramarital sexual enjoyment is seen almost as a compliment to God.

It can hardly be questioned that superstition, misplaced guilt, and ecclesiastical efforts to dominate people by controlling their intimate lives had something to do with these and similar rituals. It would be

[9]Mary Douglas, *Purity and Danger: An Analysis of Concepts of Pollution and Taboo* (London: Routledge & Kegan Paul, 1966).

a mistake, however, to see this as their main source and reason. A woman's seclusion from social contact after childbirth, practiced in so many societies, did not express a sense of wrongdoing or of guilt in sex and childbearing. Rather, it expressed awe and fear in face of the life-force or sacred power with which one is united in sex and in giving life. One contracts impurity by showing disregard for this, and one who has been in touch with the sacred must undergo rites of purification before others dare to resume contact with that person. A mother and her newborn were deemed to be in a sacred space which others dare not approach. The mother and child had to reenter the realm of the profane before others could resume normal relations with them.

All rites of taboo and purification have a similar character. They may be outmoded and impatient of use today, but the sense of things expressed in them needs to be integrated in some new way into our vision of reality. Turning the "churching" of mothers into a prayer of thanksgiving is not adequate, unless the rite expresses awe in the face of new life and the generative force which is intrinsic to the woman-man relationship. Demythologization (and in this case de-patriarchalization) must be a part of appropriating the meaning of such traditional rites, but appropriation in some form is necessary to the bodily and cosmic roots of the psyche and of the sense of the holy.

Rites of Passage

Rites of passage, the second type of religious ritual, owe their most significant study and classification to the work of Arnold Van Gennep.[10] Such rites are of three kinds: those which deal with the passage of the seasons and its significance for a human community; those which assist individuals and groups to move through the great passages of human life, namely, birth, adolescence, marriage, and death; and those which affect the passages or movements which must be faced by society as a whole, such as moving from one pasture to another for nomadic groups, the beginning and end of wars, or the transfer of ruling power. Van Gennep related all of these rites to socialization and discerned in all of them a common pattern. He divided the pattern into three stages: separation, liminality, and reentry or reintegration.

[10]Arnold Van Gennep, *The Rites of Passage* (Chicago: Univ. of Chicago Press, 1960); see Luis Maldonado and David Power, eds., *Liturgy and Human Passage*, Concilium 112 (New York: Seabury Press, 1979); Power, "The Odyssey of Man in Christ," Concilium 112, 100–11.

The pattern is exemplified most easily in the set of rites affecting an individual's change in social status and responsibility, whether through a life-passage or through induction into office. To move into the new position and encounter the holy powers which watch over and animate the society, the person must first be separated from the community in ceremonies which represent a cutting off from old relationships and renouncing former behavioral patterns. The person then spends a period of time in a stage of liminality or marginality, where he or she is forced to experience the core of the self and communion with others, as presented in the fundamental myths of the society and in ways which wipe away any trace of social status or dignity. Then by the final rites of reentry, the person returns to the community and assumes a new status and responsibility. It is interesting that in traditional societies, rites of passage are also performed for the dead since the dead are considered to remain members of the society, having a part to play in its life but in a new social position.

Sometimes this kind of anthropological paradigm is invoked by sacramental theologians. . . . [I]t serves as a useful model to explain the catechumenate, especially the catechumens' marginality, their learning of the beliefs and stories of the Christian community, and the final aggregation to the community in the sacraments of the paschal night. . . .

Mimetic Rites

The third category of rites mentioned is mimetic rites. This category overlaps with the previous two. The designation *mimetic* comes from the nature of these rites as an imitation or representation of something else, for example, the story of the gods, the fundamental myths of the society, or cosmic and life cycle rhythms. Naturally enough, the parallel with Christian liturgy rests on the idea that Christian sacrament is an imitation or representation of the mysteries of Christ.

Several remarks need to be made about comparisons of Christian liturgy with any of these rites. First, while Christian liturgy has shown a historical proclivity to adopt some of the patterns apparent in these rituals, the Church has never been at ease with the tendency. Current studies on popular religion in the history of Christianity talk about the religion of the four seasons, meaning the four seasons of the year and the four seasons of human life, (birth, adolescence, marriage, and death). Without a doubt, history shows the Church coming to terms with the felt need to mark these points of life, so that sacraments are attached to seasons of life and feasts to seasons of the year. The controversies over the relation of baptism to birth, over the link between confirmation and growing up, and over the concurrence between valid marriage and sacramental marriage are well known in both historical and pastoral theology. The attachment of Christmas to the winter solstice, the celebration of ember days, the importance attached in many places to the feasts of John the Baptist, the Annunciation, and the Assumption are historical facts and represent an ecclesiastical compromise with natural religious instincts. Whatever the links officially established or tolerated, it must be remembered that Christian liturgy is a celebration of historical event and personal conversion through grace and faith, so that intrinsically its rites bear no relation to the cycles of season and life, except inasmuch as they adopt some of their symbolism.[11] Indeed, there is an experience of power represented in cosmic and bodily symbolism, and Christian liturgy adverts to this in the interests of wholeness. Yet, what it celebrates is divine freedom and gratuity and the grace that comes to humanity thereby, prevailing over all contrary forces.

This brings us to the second observation, which affirms the immense difference between the historical religion and rites of Judaism and Christianity, on the one hand, and cosmic religion and its rites, on the other. The place of bodily ritual—with its evocation of deep human experience, its relations to cosmos and body and the unconscious—in Jewish and Christian worship can be understood only in the turn to the word, the commemoration of the historical events in which God is revealed, and the antiritual bias, all of which are intrinsic and vital to the development of this form of worship.[12] The encounter with power and with vital forces that is expressed in the rites recalled briefly from the history of religions is not denied, but is integrated into a faith that celebrates God's free and gracious entry into human history. This means a move from images of the divine that are primarily cosmic or heroic to those expressive of love's gratuity, images joined to the promises of liberation that emerge from the events of

---

[11] Anscar Chupungco, *The Cosmic Elements of Christian Passover* (Rome: San Anselmo, 1977); "Liturgical Feasts and the Seasons of the Year," Concilium 142 (New York: Seabury Press, 1981) 31–36.

[12] Louis-Marie Chauvet, "La ritualité Chrétienne dans le cercle infernal du symbole," *La Maison-Dieu* 133:1 (1978) 31–77.

divine intervention in history. In other words, what is expressed is God's "nonidentity" with what is symbolized in the cosmic and in the bodily manifestations of the sacred. The Jewish and Christian people are promised freedom in the face of the powers thus manifested, not a freedom that ignores humanity's need for harmony with the bodily and the cosmic, but one that with confidence in God's Spirit allows them a creative rather than a servile participation in the building of humanity's future.

Images of cosmos and body, representative of the power and life that they reveal and of the initial structuring of human experience, do carry over into liturgy. In that sense they offer intuition of a structure which needs to be integrated into personal and social experience. The images and symbols are a constant reminder of finitude, of the forces to be integrated, and of the risk of either flouting these forces or becoming enslaved to them. The graciousness of God promises a liberation that cannot come from cosmic religion, however, and this is what is symbolized and celebrated.

* * *

A final remark on this evocation of cosmic and bodily ritual concerns the kind of ritual most prominent in Christian liturgy. Christian ritual is somewhat parabolic, so that it constitutes a disclosure of divine presence very different from cosmic religion. In fact, though cosmic images are found in Christian liturgical symbolism (Easter abounds in them), its rituals do not of their nature evoke either seasonal or human cycles. The bodily things that Christian liturgy incorporates are more ordinary, more daily, more domestic. They are the life of every day, not the drama or heroism of wrestling with the chaos of passage. The things used are simple: bread, wine, water, and oil. The actions are homely, nurturing, and caring, such as breaking bread, pouring wine, bathing, touching, and salving with oil. Inasmuch as liturgy has been associated with more social purposes and has taken on all the burden of religious desire in civic society, it has absorbed more of the cyclic. Yet, the parabolic and prophetic qualities of its core symbols demand to be eventually freed from all such associations. These very simple items and actions are to be held in great awe and respect for what they reveal by their nature. They lose their meaning in the liturgy when they are instrumentalized, either as means of grace, expressions of an institutionally bound notion of the divine, or as a means of establishing community order, such as happens when the cup is not freely given to all participants in the Eucharist. Bread and wine or the touch of a hand, in their very simplicity, hold together "earth, sky, gods, and mortals."[13] They point more to the daily and domestic, rather than to the extraordinary, as the place where being and human dwelling show forth, where things and humanity together come to be. As the focus of the hermeneutic of traditional texts is on everyday language as the key to understanding, so the focus of sacramental understanding is on these daily and domestic things.

The bodily element is indeed essential to Christian worship, for Christians do not celebrate some pseudo-mystical cult, and many of the images of cosmic religion are retained in it. Bodily actions and cosmic images are incorporated in such a way, however, that they refer to fellowship in Jesus Christ, rather than to participation in a mythical reality or cosmic rhythms. As practiced in a variety of religions, a meal has certainly acquired many cultic connections as sacrifice and godly feast, but the eating and drinking that are the heart of the Christian Eucharist are modest and sober, taking their meaning from domestic meals rather than from cultic meals. Indeed, the New Testament literature does not use cultic language for the church's acts of worship, but transfers this kind of language to the people themselves or to the death of Christ. It is in holiness, obedience, and willing testimony to God's love, and in the hope rooted in this, that all worship is fulfilled and thus changed radically. The Eucharist is a celebration and an act of worship because of the people who celebrate it in faith. If those participating do not live the gospel fellowship in earnest, their act is more a profanation than a proclamation of the Lord's death.

Similar remarks could be made about water immersion. This rite was not invented by early Christians, but was adopted by them as a rite of entry into the community. However, the reference to the cross of Christ and to faith in him determined its meaning. It is then an act of incorporation by faith into Jesus' death rather than a rite of ritual purification or mythical initiation.

That this "antiritual" type of celebration should constitute the core of Christian worship is significant for what it says about the Christian's relation to society. A close relationship exists between how people perform in the body and how they relate to the social body.

---

[13]The expression is taken from Martin Heidegger, "The Thing," *Poetry, Language, Thought* (New York: Harper & Row, 1975) 173.

Sociologists study religious cults in terms of what they say about the sect's relation to society.[14] In this century, a greater distinction must be made between acts of Christian worship and those rituals, formal or informal, whereby members of the churches effect their relations to the body social and politic. Normally, socialization is the same for Christians as for others, insofar as they accept society's outlook on reality and its values. In their own worship, they express what type of community or fellowship they are among themselves, as well as the values to which they contribute by reason of their faith in Christ. This can actually give them a certain freedom in the face of social and cultural pressures. The bodily mode of Christian worship, as it has been described here, and not only the verbal, can enhance the prophetic role that a Christian community plays in society.

[14]Roger Bastide, *The African Religions of Brazil: Towards a Sociology of the Interpretation of Civilizations* (Baltimore: Johns Hopkins Univ. Press, 1978); Mary Douglas, *Natural Symbols: Explorations in Cosmology* (New York: Pantheon, 1970) 65–81.

Susan K. Wood

Louis-Marie Chauvet: Interpreter of Symbolic Mediation

Louis-Marie Chauvet, a priest and professor of sacramental theology at the Institut Catholique de Paris since 1973, was born into an agricultural family in the Vendée, south of Nantes, in 1942. His theological formation includes the Faculty of Theology of Angers (1960–67), the Institut Supérieur de liturgie de Paris (1967–69), a year in Germany for his first doctorate, writing a thesis entitled "John Calvin's Doctrine of Penance," which he submitted to the Sorbonne (Paris I) in 1972. He defended his final doctoral thesis, which became the book *Symbol and Sacrament* in 1986.

As a priest, he ministers in the parish at Eaubonne. He is responsible for the formation of the laity and serves in the diocesan liturgical office in the diocese of Pontoise. He reports: "My theological work has always been strongly tied to pastoral experience in the field." He describes his sacramental project as reconciling Christians with socio-historical, bodily, and institutional mediations.

Chauvet's primary contribution to liturgical theology is his critique of the scholastic metaphysics of causality, which he finds necessarily tied to the idea of production and augmentation, and his rethinking of sacramental theology in postmodern terms. He proposes symbolic mediation as an alternative to the scholastic metaphysical explanation of the sacraments and turns to Heidegger and contemporary language theory as philosophical alternatives. While he agrees that one cannot simply translate Heidegger into theological categories, Chauvet argues that the theological equivalent is found in the kenotic hymn in Philippians 2 and a theology of the cross in 1 Corinthians.

His fundamental insight is that the presence or the absence of God is mediated through symbol in an analogous way to how the power and glory of God is present in Christ's self-emptying or in the vulnerability of the cross. The sacramental mediates Christ's presence within the experience of his absence.

Chauvet develops his sacramental theology in conversation with the human sciences. He calls on data from linguistics, anthropology, psychology, and philosophy to shed new light on sacramental mediation. He rearticulates the meaning of sacramentality in postmodern terms through categories of contemporary philosophy placed in conversation with Scripture and tradition. His synthetic work, *Symbol and Sacrament*, essentially a systematic theology conceived in sacramental terms, expands upon his study of sacrament in a reconsideration of the faith and doctrine of the church through the lens of sacramentality. He discusses what it means to believe in Jesus Christ if such a belief is structured sacramentally. He concludes from a study of Luke 24 that it means to consent to the presence of the absence of Christ and thereby embrace the mediation of the sacramental.

In the following excerpt from an article on rituality and theology, Chauvet establishes the necessity of rituality and the sacramental. He begins by exploring the significance of Thomas Aquinas' dictum that "sacraments are in the nature of a sign," which immediately leads him to an examination of the contribution of anthropology to theology.

FOR FURTHER READING
Symbol and Sacrament: A Sacramental Reinterpretation of Christian Existence.
Trans. Patrick Madigan and Madeleine Beaumont. Collegeville, Minn.: The
Liturgical Press, A Pueblo Book, 1995; *Les sacrements: Parole de Dieu au risque du corps.* Paris: Les editions ouvrières, 1993; *Du symbolique au symbole: Essai sur les sacrements.* Paris: Edition du Cerf, 1979.

Louis-Marie Chauvet

Rituality and Theology[1]

We could have avoided many gridlocks if we had adhered to this "first law" of sacramentality: since the sacrament is "in the nature of a sign" and since sacramental discourse has the ritual practice of the Church as its object, there is no other way of expressing the divine *res* [reality] offered there than beginning where the Church begins in celebrating it, in fidelity to the Word. From this perspective it is impossible to treat the eucharistic presence of the Lord "in itself," that is, independently of the elements instituted by Christ (bread and wine—or realities whose essence is intrinsically constituted by their relation to human beings), or independently of the words recited (notably the *hyper,* this relational "for" which requires us to think of presence as an *adesse* [act of being for] and not as a simple *esse* [act of being] of a subsistent being),[2] or gestures (those of giving and breaking, which, as embodied words, make visible the intentionality of the proclaimed word). In addition, more broadly, there are the prayers of epiclesis and anamnesis which enclose these elements and which are the referent of the institution narrative. Finally, the whole of the eucharistic prayer is itself situated within the dynamic structure of the celebration, notably the constitution of the assembly as Church and the reception of the Scriptures as Word.

Likewise, the serious taking into account of the liturgical *we*—which made Lombard say that a priest cut off from the Church could not

---

[1]Excerpted from Louis-Marie Chauvet, "Ritualité et Theologie," *Recherche de Science Religieuse* 78, no. 4 (1990) 535–64, and translated for this volume by Susan K. Wood.

[2]Trans. note: This refers to the prayer of eucharistic consecration, "my body which will be given up *for* you," or "It [blood] will be shed *for* you."

validly celebrate Mass since he could not say *offerimus quasi ex persona ecclesiae* [we offer as in the person of the Church] in the anamnesis[3]—would have contributed to balancing a theology of the priesthood which too unilaterally inflates the importance of the priest at the expense of the Church. This would also have avoided separating the institution narrative, where it would be forbidden to speak only *in persona Christi* [in the person of Christ] (Thomas),[4] from the whole of the prayers of the Mass where the priest speaks *in persona ecclesiae* [in the person of the Church].

CONTEMPORARY REDISCOVERIES

1. The problematic just outlined here has become familiar today. Vatican II, with the theological movement which preceded it, has, as we know, emphasized the sacraments as signs more than as causes or means of salvation, without in any way denying this aspect of them. We know as well the fortunate pastoral results of this emphasis: the reforms following the Constitution on the Liturgy have paid great attention to the "signifying" quality of signs (vernacular language, celebration facing the people, fewer but more expressive gestures, etc.). On the other hand, the Copernican revolution within ecclesiology has had equally important repercussions in the liturgy: the *sacramenta ecclesiae* [sacraments of the Church] are those of the local Church understood not only as the diocese, but also, in certain texts,[5] as the celebrating assembly where the Church of Christ is wholly realized in its particularity.[6] Since the gestures of faith which the assembly makes in the name of Christ are directly perceived and lived very concretely as sacraments of the Church, we must pay particular attention to their quality, an attention which was largely missing formerly. This research into quality is on a par with the rediscovery of the symbolic richness of the ancient liturgies to which we have returned through adaptations judged to be suitable (perhaps too much so, from a pastoral point of view . . .).

2. *Pastoral* concerns have not, of course, been a stranger to all this theological movement. A certain uneasiness has existed with regard to

[3]P. Lombard, Sent. 4, d. 13. See B. D. Marliangeas, *Clés pour une théologie du ministère. In persona Christi, in persona Ecclesiae* (Paris: Beauchesne, 1978) 55–60.
[4]*ST* 3, 82, 7, ad 3; 78, 1 ad 4.
[5]*Lumen gentium* 26; see 28. *Sacrosanctum concilium* 41.
[6]Thus H. Legrand comments that "each eucharistic assembly is truly the Church of God." *Initiation à la pratique de la théologie* 3 (Paris: Cerf, 1983) 166.

the liturgy as with the sacramental theory which supported it. One criticized it for being too "reifying," "exacting," "individualistic." Such jargon was certainly not conceptually rigorous; in addition, it was largely unjust regarding the theory. It did not exhibit any less desire for a new type of theological language in which the "lived" daily experience of the faithful would be taken into account in its relationship with the liturgy and the sacraments and in which the Church would take precedence over individuals within the theological discussion.

In this way we saw the liturgical renewal promote a whole series of new emphases. Rather than an excessive attention given to the *ex opere operato*,[7] we asked first that the signs be "expressive." Rather than a discourse which seemed to excessively reify grace or graces conferred "the moment when" the sacrament was received, we understood this discourse to be connected with the whole of a believer's existence which was already permeated with a certain "sacramentality." Rather than representations and behavior that appeared too individualistic, we recalled that the sacramental event is always first and foremost of the Church. We strongly exploited the theme of the "sacramentality" of the Church by applying it most often to the celebrating community. Does this community have pastoral concern for the welcome of immigrants? Is it concretely "formational" of the faith of young people? Does it sufficiently attend to accompanying them? Is it an active party in promoting reconciliation between rival groups in the community? Is it a counter-cultural sign when it celebrates baptism as welcome into the Church, or confirmation, or the sacrament of reconciliation? What baptism and what Eucharist for which Church? The questions were posed in these nearly political terms.

This type of pastoral questioning did not lack ambiguity. Didn't the desire to tie the sacrament too closely to "life" run the risk of reducing the mystery? Didn't it make the sacramental celebration some kind of "reward" for having lived "rightly" (according to what criteria?)? Doesn't insisting too strongly that the community be the living sign of what one celebrates set up a disastrous elitism for the Church and does not that forget that Christ came "not only for the just, but for the sinners"? All this could lend itself to a kind of neo-pelagianism on the level of Christian anthropology, to sectarianism on the ecclesiological level, to Malthusianism on the level of pastoral legislation. The

---

[7]Trans. note: Literally, "from the work worked." This expression refers to the religious efficaciousness of sacramental action deriving from the action of Christ in the sacraments.

questioning evoked here contributed to the restoration of a greatly needed evangelical and missionary dimension to pastoral and sacramental liturgics from which we greatly benefit today. All this presupposed a pastoral theology attentive to the quality of the signs of the celebration. Because these signs can be assumed to be Christian only by way of a (re)initiation into them, this reinitiation process is a necessary route for most Christians.

3. Furthermore, these theological rediscoveries and these new pastoral emphases occurred nearly at the same time that the research of the human sciences began to draw the attention of theologians, that is, during the sixties and seventies. Through their work on rituality, ethnologists discovered that there was in ritual a mode of expression and even a specific "play on language" originating from archaic depths, arising from particular laws and exercising vital symbolic effects in the social, institutional, and psychic spheres. Linguistics, from its perspective, led them towards an awareness of the extreme variety of language acts (or quasi language, if one understands by that such nonverbal modalities of speech as gesture and posture) in the liturgy. . . .

Simultaneously, the *philosophy of language* solicited a great interest. What type of relation does language create between a subject and the real? Of what is it the referent? Is language simply an instrument, probably the most precious of all, that the human being (logically supposed to preexist language) would have at his disposition? Isn't it rather contemporaneous with the subject? Doesn't it furnish, somehow, the "matrix," the mediation at the heart of which the subject constitutes himself and acts as subject? Isn't language always already considered in its own domain, that is, in the symbolic domain of culture? And if this is so does it fundamentally do anything else, in speaking, other than respond? Respond to the socio-cultural and traditional "Other" which inhabits it from the material womb? Respond to the parental figures which, weaving the unconscious of each person, continue to haunt him or her? Respond, finally, perhaps, to the "silent word of being" (Heidegger)? In any case, what is more symbolically efficacious than language as language? Before being the labeling of beings and an instrument of knowledge, it is communication between subjects and the mediation of recognition. A fatal process from a psychological point of view—a process which not infrequently ends in physical death by suicide—is at work in every human being to whom no word of recognition is addressed through the intermediary of discourse (or who believes that no such word is addressed). *"A human being does not live by bread alone, but by the word . . ."*

Theology in general, and sacramental theology in particular, have been able to benefit greatly from ethnological, linguistic, and sociological studies and from the new questions which gave rise to them. If the object of sacramental discourse is for all practical purposes that of ritual language at the heart of which is the grace of salvation given by God and received through faith, if then, in other words, the *res sacramenti* [sacrament] does not occur other than through the concrete mediation of the *sacramentum* [the sign] and according to the mode of expression proper to this type of particular language which is rituality, how would the discourse of the *intellectus fidei* [understanding of the faith] have been able to avoid welcoming the new resources which anthropology and the philosophy of language offered it, even if a certain number of these resources remain problematic? Along the same lines, it was necessary to forge a new path in sacramental theology, a path evidently characterized by a priority given to signs or, perhaps better, to the constitutive symbols of celebration. In any case, rituality appeared more than ever as an obligatory element of sacramental discourse.

On the other hand, even if everyone agrees on this obligatory element, the question of its place in the properly theological process remains debatable. For example, Gisel asks whether one must proceed "from the symbolic to the symbol" or "from the symbol to the symbolic."[8] In reality, the apparently simple question which the author poses is twofold: (a) Is it appropriate to proceed from the symbolic order, that is, from what structures the humanity of a person, towards the symbol as it is defined in a Christian way in the sacraments? The question at this level bears on the passage from the anthropological to the theological. (b) From another perspective, is it appropriate to proceed from the symbolic order proper to the Church towards the sacramental symbol? That is, is it appropriate to proceed from a broad idea of the "sacramental" applied to the sacramentality of the

---

[8]P. Gisel, "Du symbolique au symbole ou du symbole au symbolique? Remarques intempestives," *Les sacrements de Dieu,* Revue des sciences religieuses (1987) 197–210. The author makes reference to L. M. Chauvet, *Du symbolique au symbole. Essai sur les sacrements* (Paris: Cerf, 1979). I'm sorry that the author at this time was not aware of my last work which had appeared a little earlier (see the following note).

Church, and even more broadly still but not independent of this, from an idea of the "sacramental" applied to a certain sacramentality of creation, towards a sacrament in the proper sense? We will keep this twofold question in mind in what follows.

FROM THE ANTHROPOLOGICAL TO THE THEOLOGICAL?

Theological discourse proceeds thus: it always engages the discourse prior to it, either reinforcing it or contesting it. The anthropological option of *Symbol and Sacrament*[9] was surely determined by the desire, frequently expressed in the seventies, to react against a theological discourse, which, somehow too sure of itself and its proper principles, did not sufficiently honor the desire to embed itself *also* in the new knowledge and the new questions received from the human sciences mentioned earlier. The intention is undoubtedly good, but where is Christian theology leading? Gisel fears that the choice of the path which leads from anthropology towards theology, a choice made in the legitimate desire and even, according to some, the salutary desire to react against a too-frequent sacramental "extrinsicism" within classical theology, will lead too directly from the realm of human existence to the realm of faith, to an at least partial blurring of Christian distinctiveness and, finally, to a new apologetic where the "Christian" flourishes too conveniently on the terrain of the "human." Consequently, one would have a beautiful example of the ideological function of theology. The risk is apparent and not only, or even primarily, from the side of sacramentality; it poses above all a risk to Christology.[10] The sacramental symbols would be unthinkable as being simply the accomplishment of the great symbolic rituals where the desire of a person to enter into communication with God is expressed. In other words, they are not the simple encoding of the hopes of humanity. For, if an accomplishment of the human is within them, it is by way of a disengagement, since, for the Christian, the human is determined by the primacy of the Christological and the difference introduced by eschatology. The relationship of anthropology to theology is necessarily mediated within Christianity by way of Christology. There are three terms and not two.

[9] L. M. Chauvet, *Symbol and Sacrament: A Sacramental Reinterpretation of Christian Existence,* trans. Patrick Madigan and Madeleine Beaumont (Collegeville, Minn.: The Liturgical Press, A Pueblo Book, 1995).

[10] J. Doré, "Foi en Dieu et identité chrétienne," in J. Doré, (dir.), *Sur l'identité chrétienne* (Paris: Descleé, 1990) 171–216.

Therefore, by respecting these three areas, and within them the primacy of the Christological, the path which goes from the anthropological to the theological (a path which departs "from below," but which within any hypothesis is tenably Christian only if, as in Christology, it intersects at a given moment with the path "from above") has the double advantage of giving to the sacrament a density simultaneously both anthropological and historical.

7

What Is the Role of the Word in Liturgy?

The experience of liturgy includes symbols, sacraments, icons, metaphors—all of which contain multiple layers of meaning. A number of the articles you've read deal with the rich textures of meaning in sacramental ritual. We often talk about liturgy as involving Word and Sacrament. Thus in this chapter we turn our attention to the role of the Word in liturgy.

Before we try to answer this question, you may want me to clarify what I mean by "the Word." Am I talking about Jesus Christ, the Word made flesh? or about the Word of Scripture, our sacred text? or is my concern with the "proclamation of the Word" in preaching? Just what can we expect these writers to be talking about?

A brief look at this chapter's contents will give you a clue regarding my answer. When I talk about the Word in liturgy, I am talking about all of the above, and even more. "Word" is one of those concepts in liturgy that seems to have inexhaustible layers of meaning.

Once again, however, we are asking our question from a theological perspective. Brunner's article is a real "find," providing us with a summary of his life's work in terms of the larger context of our question. Lathrop, in an article that is a precursor to his more recent work on the juxtaposition of opposites in the liturgy, helps us uncover the depth dynamics within liturgy. For a theology of proclamation, I turn to Hilkert, whose sacramental understanding of preaching will speak to Protestants as well as Roman Catholics. Finally, Hoon reminds us of the incarnational foundations of Christian worship. Word and Sacrament turn out to be more than components of liturgy, but dynamics underlying all our worship in Christ's name.

Fritz West

Peter Brunner: Worship at the Dawn of the New Age

Peter Brunner was born in Germany in 1900. After serving in the German army during the final months of World War I, he studied theology and philosophy in Germany, the United States, and France. An early opponent of the Nationalist Socialist Party, Brunner's university career was nipped in the bud when Hitler came to power in 1933. He became active in the Confessing Church and worked as a pastor and teacher until the fall of the Nazi regime—despite time spent in Dachau, a ban on his preaching, and the closing of his school. In 1947 Brunner accepted a post in systematic theology from the University of Heidelberg, where he taught until his retirement in 1968. Firmly grounded in Lutheran confessional theology, he was above all a teacher of the Church, active in liturgical revision, theological discussions, and ecumenical dialogue. Brunner wrote on various aspects of the life of the Church, *Worship in the Name of Jesus* being his crowning achievement. He died in 1981.

For Brunner, worship is an eschatological activity that takes place in the transition in salvation history when the old age is passing and the new age dawning. In the crucifixion and resurrection Jesus Christ has initiated the new age. Now, between his ascension and return, the Church gathers in hope, able to sing the angelic praises but not yet with a full throat. So situated on the edge of the new, Brunner regards worship to be a moment of decision and anticipation. It throws the individual into an "eschatological crisis," in which the decision must be made whether to open the heart and let Jesus in or harden it and close him out.

In Brunner's view, the worship of the Church entails a duality conveyed in the single German word, *Gottesdienst:* the service God renders to us and the service we offer to God. Ultimately the service God renders us is salvation, incarnate in Jesus Christ and made present by the power of the Spirit in the saving Word and the revealing meal. In response, the Church serves God in prayer, which, like Jacob's ladder, leads to the gates of heaven where a glimpse can be caught of the glorious new age. Therefore bear in mind, dear reader, that, in English translations of Brunner's writings, phrases like "divine service," "service of God," and "service of worship" are various translations of the German word *Gottesdienst,* a single concept with dual aspects.

The following essay, "Divine Service in the Church," summarizes a theology of worship that Brunner first published in German as an extended article in the "Handbuch" *Leitourgia* and subsequently as *Worship in the Name of Jesus.* In that theology Brunner systematized reflections occasioned by his work in the 1940s on liturgical revision in the German Lutheran Church. This essay is a translation of a lecture Brunner delivered on July 30, 1952, in Hanover to the second General Assembly of the Lutheran World Federation.

FOR FURTHER READING

Luther in the 20th Century. Decorah, Iowa: Luther College Press, 1961; *Worship in the Name of Jesus.* St. Louis, Mo.: Concordia Publishing House, 1968; *The Ministry and the Ministry of Women.* St. Louis: Concordia Publishing House, 1971; *Pro Ecclesia Reformanda.* Göttingen: Vandenhoeck und Ruprecht, 1977; *Evangelium, Sakramente, Amt und die Einheit der Kirch: die okumenishe Tragweite der Confessio Augustana.* Göttingen: Vandenhoeck und Ruprecht, 1982.

Peter Brunner

Divine Service in the Church[1]

When Holy Scripture says, "Serve the Lord," it means that our whole life should be spent in continuous service of God. But we, the disciples of Jesus, cannot serve the Lord without assembling in his name in order to hear the Word of God, to celebrate the Lord's Supper, and to offer prayer, praise and thanksgiving. The service of God, which involves our whole life, has as its living center the Service of Worship by the assembled congregation.

* * *

The Cross of Jesus and his resurrection mark the beginning of the "last things." The Cross of Jesus and his resurrection are the point where two aeons meet. The Cross and resurrection of Jesus lift, as it were, the old aeon from its hinges and burst open the door for the new aeon to come to us. The Holy Spirit is the first-fruits of God's new world to come. The Service of Worship held by the Church presupposes this turn of the aeons; each Service contains this turning point; in its Service the "last things" begin. Divine Service—like the Spirit, like the Church—is an eschatological phenomenon. In Service we stand at the farthest edge of history; we are near the return of Christ. The Lord is at hand. The Kingdom of God is near. The resurrection of the dead is nigh. It is in this atmosphere of the end of all things that the Church celebrates its approaching Service.

[1]Excerpted from Peter Brunner, "Divine Service in the Church," *Scottish Journal of Theology* 7 (1954) 270–83. A lecture delivered at the Lutheran World Federation Assembly, Hanover, 1952, trans. J. Bodensieck and A. T. Mackay. Republished by permission of T&T Clark, Ltd. Publishers, Edinburgh, Scotland.

But the Lord has not appeared as yet. The bodies of the dead have not yet been raised. We are still pilgrims. We still live in the transitional period between the Lord's ascension and his return. We conduct Service *in this transition*. It determines the nature of our Service. Divine Service resembles the tabernacle of the Israelites traveling through the desert, who behold already from afar the city in which there will no longer be any temple and God will be all in all. In the "Exodus" from the land of death, on the journey over to the heavenly Jerusalem, the Church celebrates its Service.

In the life of the individual, Divine Service also represents a transition. Before you can fully participate in it, something must happen to you. Certainly, long before you were born, Jesus received you as a member of his body, took your guilt upon himself, and redeemed your life. But now, since you have been born, the things which were realities in him must become realities also in your present bodily existence. This is accomplished by baptism. Your baptism means that you, as a being with physical existence, have an *actual share in Jesus' death*. By your baptism you were incorporated into the sacrificial body of the crucified and exalted Lord. Only after passing through the waters of baptism and joining the eschatological people of God as a member of the body of Jesus, a member of the *Ecclesia,* can your service of God commence. Baptism is the foundation of Divine Service.

When you passed through the baptismal door, Gospel and Baptism gave you all that pertains to salvation. But salvation may be lost, squandered, or abandoned. You need to watch over it, especially in seasons of temptation and of assailment; you will have to struggle valiantly in order to preserve it. But the only way to preserve our salvation is by a continual return to baptism, i.e., by *abiding* within the body of the crucified and exalted Lord. To this end we have been given the preaching of the Word and the Lord's Supper.

* * *

The Church's Service of Worship is surrounded by the angels' worship in heaven. Angels are individual beings like us, except that they are beyond the possibility of temptation and assailment. They devote their total existence exclusively to the uninterrupted praise of God. Their adoration, praise and testimony form, as it were, the sounding board reflecting and re-echoing God's nature and deeds.

Divine Service in the Church is surrounded by the worship which the so-called mute creation offers to God. Creation is "mute" only in the sense that we are unable to hear its voice. Even now, all creation is continuously at work, praising the Creator who called it into being by his creative Word. The "groaning of creation, earnestly expecting the liberty of the glory of the children of God," is only a thin veil covering for the present moment the eschatological jubilation which will break forth and join the chorus of the heavenly hosts when all things are made new. When that great day comes, we shall hear the voice of the cosmos, from most sublime heights to lowest depths, as it ascribes blessing, glory and honor unto him that sitteth on the throne and unto the Lamb.

Divine Service occupies a place *between* the angels' worship and nature's worship. The worshiping Church lifts its eyes to the heights above, where the angels worship, but it also is ready to join in the songs of the cosmos. These three, the angels' service above, the Church's Service here on earth and the Service rendered by the cosmos, are directed toward one and the same goal; they are converging lines, as it were, and will ultimately merge on the last day in one grand, all-inclusive Service of Worship.

Thus the Church's Service is conducted in a period of transition which may be regarded from three points of view: soteriologically, as between Christ's ascension and his glorious return; anthropologically, as between man's baptismal death and his physical death; cosmologically, as between the superhuman creation in heaven above and the subhuman creatures here on earth. . . . Expressed differently, the point at which the Church conducts its Service of Worship witnesses a three-fold eschatological movement: firstly, there is the transformation of this perishing world into the Kingdom of God; secondly, the transition of the justified sinner from a life filled with temptation and assailment to final and complete union with Christ in the resurrection; thirdly, the transformation which bestows upon the entire cosmos the liberty of the children of God and raises the children of God to the heights where the hosts of heaven sing God's eternal praise. This threefold transition with its eschatological implications determines and limits the nature of the Church's Service of Worship.

What actually takes place in Church Service, is an eschatological mystery. What we hear and see are human words, human actions, and poor, earthly signs. But in, with, and under these human words God himself is speaking. In, with, and under these human actions he himself is acting. In, with, and under the bread and the wine in the Holy Supper the body and blood of our Redeemer are really present.

In, with, and under the words of human persons, a Spirit-wrought word will rise through all the reaches of the universe to the throne of God and converse with God in the Spirit. In, with, and under these words and actions of men, there shines the reflection of the glory of God, magnifying the Lord. In, with, and under human and earthly elements—God himself, the Lord himself, the Spirit himself! This is what makes Church Service an eschatological mystery.

Divine Service has two aspects: God speaks to us in his holy Word, and we in turn may speak to him in prayer and praise. Christ remains in the midst of us as he that serves; in his Word and in his Supper he gives himself to us. And we in turn may freely serve him, the Lord of lords and King of kings. God serves us. The service is *sacramentum*. We may serve him. The service becomes *sacrificium* at God's pleasure. These two phases interpenetrate. . . .

God's service to us is the basis for our service to God. His Word enjoins us to answer; His gift of himself, to give ourselves to him. Let us, therefore, consider on the one hand how God serves us through the proclamation of the Word and through the Sacrament, and on the other hand, how we may serve him through prayer, confession, and praise.

The proclamation of the Word includes more than the sermon. Preaching serves the Scripture that has been read. The congregation also proclaims the gospel in the form of psalms and hymns and songs of praise. In the words of absolution we have the heart and center of the gospel.

The Word is proclaimed by order of the risen Lord. The preaching of the gospel has within itself the authority of him who said, "All power is given unto me in heaven and on earth." When the Apostolic gospel is proclaimed, Jesus Christ comes to his assembled congregation as its contemporary Lord. Where he is present, there also His words and deeds become present and contemporary. What Jesus has done for our sakes, cannot any longer be confined within the limits of time and space. . . . Jesus' victory on the Cross is part of this sovereign eschatological kingdom and now, by the gospel, baptism, and the Lord's Supper, becomes contemporary with us, tangibly and truly present. Gospel, baptism, and Communion are, as it were, the arms with which Jesus' Cross and Jesus' victory reach out for us; the hands with which He gives Himself to us. In the Word of the Cross the soteriological event of Christ's crucifixion is made contemporary by virtue of its sovereign eschatological freedom. In the word of reconciliation the event of reconciliation occurs. Through the proclamation of the gospel the things which Jesus accomplished for our sake, become actually present before us, just as food and drink set on a table for a man to take and touch and eat.

The spoken gospel, therefore, is no empty word. It is filled to overflowing with the superabundant blessings of salvation. It is a creative Word. It creates whatever it says. It is the open hand with which God distributes the treasures of forgiveness, life, and salvation. . . .

Since this Word contains the fullness of eschatological salvation, all those who hear it face the eschatological crisis. The gospel would save, and not condemn. In the power of Jesus' victory it bursts the locks of our hearts and enters into the very center of our existence. Now we face the crisis where the decision is made whether we allow Jesus the Savior to accomplish his saving purpose in us and accept it in faith, or whether—unfathomable mystery!—we harden our hearts and reject the work of the Spirit. Faith means life everlasting; obdurate unbelief, eternal death. The Word of God is full power, but it never "overpowers" or violates a human being. . . .

The Gospel is preached to all . . . the unbaptized as well as the baptized. The preaching service is a public service open to everybody. The Lord's Supper, however, is a service where only the baptized members of the Church participate and the doors to the outside are closed. The Lord's Supper is the special gift of Jesus for those who have crossed the waters of baptism; it is the specific means of grace for the already constituted congregation of his followers. The most distinctive part of the Service of Worship is the Lord's Supper.

The Lord's Supper which we celebrate, was instituted by Jesus. To deny this means to discard the Sacrament. The sacramental reality of this meal flows forth from the authority of its being instituted by Jesus and from the authority of his work of institution. The Supper which Jesus celebrated with his disciples in the night in which he was betrayed has the power within itself to initiate a series of celebrations which go beyond this particular hour and this particular group of disciples and at each of which that original meal again becomes present, to inaugurate a series of identical suppers in which the original meal is ever and again re-enacted. The same Lord who on the night of his betrayal acted and spoke in the fullness of messianic authority, now acts and speaks with the same divine authority every time his congregation celebrates the Holy Supper in his memory; and thereby he constitutes it as his Supper.

208

The sacramental reality of the Lord's Supper is like a large circle; from its center shining rays emanate in all directions and extend to every part of the area within the circle, filling the entire area with the deep meaning of the Holy Supper.

The Lord's Supper is Gospel proclaimed by word and action. Whatever we have said concerning preaching also applies here. The Lord's Supper, however, has several distinctive features. The Lord's Supper is the form of a symbolic action, endowed with eschatological content, in which Jesus' act of salvation in the power of its eschatological freedom becomes present. That unique eschatological act of salvation which is concentrated in the Cross of Jesus becomes present in the Lord's Supper by an actual re-presentation. Jesus allows his disciples to share in the atoning power of his death which is already mysteriously present within the Word and the symbol of the action. What happens when we celebrate the Lord's Supper today, is the representation of Jesus' total work of salvation. In terms of the comparison used above, this re-presentation is the area of the circle, but not yet its very center.

The innermost center is created and revealed by the words which Christ spoke concerning the bread and the cup: "This is my body broken for you. . . . This is my blood of the new covenant shed for you unto the remission of sins." These words do not interpret an action or a symbol. They state what the food is that is used in this action. The relation which Jesus establishes between bread and body and between wine and blood is "not analogy but identity" (Lohmeyer). The bread remains bread, and the wine remains wine. But by virtue of Jesus' word of institution this bread is his body given to the death for us, and this wine is his blood shed for us.

* * *

Forgiveness of sins and life eternal are given us in the Lord's Supper in such a way that they are included in the sacrificial Body of Jesus which is really present in the Eucharistic food. The treasure chest—the sacrificial Body—and the treasure—forgiveness of sins—are here united and identical. Nothing stands between the Cross and forgiveness. The gift and the giver are one, the sacrifice and its effect are one.

The Lord's Supper bursts open all the bolts and fetters of this perishing world of death. Clothed in the garments of salvation we ourselves are placed within the doorway which has been opened by

Christ's sacrificial death and leads directly into God's world to come. The Lord's Supper takes on the character of an eschatological festival of joy. . . . While we celebrate the Lord's Supper here below we are close to that other supper that will be celebrated when the great multitude in heaven cries aloud, "The marriage of the Lamb is come!" We celebrate the Lord's Supper on the threshold of that other feast. In the Lord's Supper the presence of the other feast is only thinly veiled; in this feast the congregation already hears the voice of the Lord saying, "Behold, I come quickly," and the response of the Spirit and the bride, "Come, Amen. Come, Lord Jesus." It is there, where this dialogue takes place, where Bride and Bridegroom are near the final threshold, waiting for each other, that the Church of Jesus Christ celebrates the Supper of her Lord.

* * *

We are certain that in the Gospel and in the Lord's Supper God offers to us the gifts of salvation. He serves us. Whether we serve him is open to question. Our Divine Service is service of God only when we pass through the eschatological crisis in such a way that we accept in faith the proffered blessings of salvation. Unless God awakens us by his Holy Spirit, we are unable to worship him in Spirit and in truth. We cannot grasp with our intellect but only gratefully confess that the eschatological crisis does not in all cases result in hardening of the heart and unbelief but that also the blessed miracle of faith takes place. Worship is a fruit of such faith. Worship is "new obedience." Because of this, our worship in this life will always be imperfect. The new man's obedience and the old Adam's disobedience are warring against each other, like spirit and flesh. Therefore our worship will only be service to God when we through baptism possess our life, when we daily die with him and through dying live with him.

Since Divine Service is our "new obedience," it is not governed by the coercion of the law. Our worship is characterized by a spontaneousness which is produced solely by the Holy Spirit. This Service does not resemble a violent struggle but rather the unselfconscious happy play of the child. The Service is rendered not with murmuring, but with gladness.

The fundamental form of Service to God is prayer. The mysterious character of Divine Service may be most plainly observed in prayer. We do not know how to pray as we ought. Our prayers are but the vessel to be used by another One. What matters is that this other

One, the Spirit, enters into our words and that he himself in, with, and under our words makes intercession for us before God with groanings which cannot be uttered.

* * *

Prayer reaches its culmination in the adoration and praise of God. We cease to supplicate and entreat when we praise God. The praise of God rises above thanksgiving also. Praise of God reflects the very glory of God. Praise expresses itself in exultant hymns of adoration. When we praise God—though we are still pilgrims on earth—we have a foretaste of the Service rendered above by the hosts of heaven before God's throne.

To prayer is added confession. The confession offered by the congregation assembled to worship God is their immediate reaction to having met the living God in his living Word. This encounter forces us onto our knees. The confession is of sin. Sinners who confess receive grace. This encounter raises us up and lays the *credo* on our lips. The creed adds the congregation's Amen to God's message. The confession becomes one of faith. When confessing her faith the Church is reminded of the fact that she is still engaged in battle against the world. As a witness to her faith the confession is the last word which the Church can utter as she is arraigned by the world. Beyond this can come only witness by martyrdom.

The confession has no design or purpose or any ulterior motive; it announces simply with the inner compulsion of the Spirit what is, what God has done for us. The confession takes on the character of an offering of thanks and praise. The confession is the public, thankful acknowledgment of salvation as planned by the Father, accomplished by the Son, and bestowed on us by the Spirit. It is jubilant praise of those who are saved. It resembles the Church's hymns of triumphant joy.

Both prayer and confession reach their climax in glorifying the Triune God; "Glory be to the Father and to the Son and to the Holy Ghost! Glory to God in the highest! Glory be to Thee, O Lord! Hosannah, praised be He that cometh." These are acclamations. Here the congregation offers homage to its King. These exclamations make manifest the dominion of this Lord; they are means of the epiphany of this dominion. At the end of time every knee shall bow and every tongue shall confess that Jesus Christ is Lord, but the congregation of the Lord renders this homage voluntarily, now. As the Church worships, the last things begin to assume shape. The Service celebrated in the city to come casts its radiance upon the Service of the pilgrim Church. This indicates that the Church's Service of Worship has a relation to the earthly *polis*. The very act of conducting a Church Service is a fact of political significance. When the assembled congregation ascribes all glory to God, it rejects any deification of earthly political powers of rulers. Whenever political rulers snatch after the glory of God and seek to adorn themselves with divine dignity, then the mere fact that the Church keeps on conducting Services of Worship is equivalent to a political challenge and act of war. The battle between Christ and Antichrist will go on until the end of this world, and then the Church's doxologies will turn into the cosmic song of praise when the tongues of all beings in heaven, on earth, and under the earth shall confess that Jesus Christ is Lord, to the glory of God.

This acclamation is excelled only by the hymns of praise and adoration. Here the Church reaches the limit of what it says of God to God. In prayer, confession, and ascription there still are tangible traces of the eschatological struggle, but the hymn of praise presupposes the end of all struggle. It is the hymn of victory. It shares in the new song of those made perfect. In its hymns of praise the Church on earth joins with all the angels and archangels, with principalities and powers and all the company of heaven. In this last word which the creature may say of God before God, his whole existence is for God alone without other intention, purpose or aim, and his particular nature lies completely in being, and in needing to be nothing else but the perfect mirror of God's glory. Now takes place what is the first, the last and the eternal purpose of all creaturely being; so to receive God's glory that it may be mirrored by the creature and shine out to fill the universe and that God may be all in all.

Joyce Ann Zimmerman

Gordon W. Lathrop: Word Meets Ritual

Gordon W. Lathrop was born in California in 1939 and was ordained on August 3, 1969, in St. Paul Lutheran Church in Agoura Hills, California. It was that same year that he was awarded the Doctor of Theology degree (cum laude) from the Catholic University of Nijmegen, The Netherlands. His dissertation was entitled "Who Shall Describe His Origin? Tradition and Redaction in Mark 6:1-6" and was written under the direction of B. M. F. van Iersel; the chair of his examining committee was well-known theologian Edward Schillebeeckx, whose hermeneutical influence can be seen throughout Lathrop's work. He is currently the Charles A. Schieren Professor of Practical Theology at The Lutheran Theological Seminary at Philadelphia.

Both pastor and professor, Lathrop studied Sacred Scripture and entered liturgy through that door, as had so many other renowned liturgists; no wonder he has retained an undying interest in the Word! Further, he studied at a Catholic institution; it is not surprising to find an ecumenical sensitivity in his work. But most importantly, his pastoral and academic interests led Lathrop at a rather early time in the liturgical foment in the wake of Vatican II to bring into balance and equal partnership two elements of worship that had been largely out of balance for more than four centuries after the Reformation: Word and ritual (sacrament). He was able to turn these interests to the practical needs of the Lutheran Church when he got involved in several projects at the early stages of generating the *Lutheran Book of Worship,* namely, by contributing materials for its baptism, Eucharist, and Holy Week sections.

The article that follows was Lathrop's vice-presidential address given in 1984 to the North American Academy of Liturgy. Given that date, barely a decade after the close of the council, his was a cutting-edge challenge to his liturgical colleagues. The focus of his presentation—calling for a "rebirth of images" that both reflected and thrust forward the interest in liturgy and language (especially symbol and metaphor), a recovery of lament that took seriously liturgy's engagement with lived Christian experience, and the centrality of Jesus Christ that reminded his hearers that it is the story of the living, proclaiming, crucified Jesus Christ of the Scriptures that is to be solemnized in the very *ordo* of the liturgy—was a blueprint for academic and pastoral activity that has been carried out by liturgists for the two decades since.

Virtually all of Lathrop's work since his vice-presidential address has in one way or another carried out this vision. Both his contributions to the Proclamation series and his *Lectionary for the Christian People* are consistent with his interest in language and the Word, and the way that plays itself out in ritual celebration. More than mere pastoral aids, these works marry the academic and pastoral, worship with living. His two latest works on liturgical theology and liturgical ecclesiology are as much biblical theology as works in liturgics, strongly witnessing to his continuing interest in Word and ritual. No doubt, Lathrop's work parallels and continues today in a new re-birthing of images and language the work of liturgical renewal begun already with Luther and his *Deutsche Messe* and landmark German translation of the Bible. Lathrop surely is a faithful disciple!

FOR FURTHER READING

Holy People: A Liturgical Ecclesiology. Minneapolis: Fortress Press, 1999; *Readings for the Assembly*. 3 vols. Cycles A, B, C, with Gail Ramshaw. Minneapolis: Augsburg Fortress, 1996; *Holy Things: A Liturgical Theology*. Minneapolis: Fortress Press, 1993; "At Least Two Words: The Liturgy as Proclamation." *The Landscape of Praise: Readings in Liturgical Renewal*. Ed. Blair Gilmer Meeks, 183–85. Valley Forge, Pa.: Trinity Press International, 1996; "The Institution Narrative." *New Eucharistic Prayers: An Ecumenical Study of Their Development and Structure*. Ed. Frank C. Senn, 139–45. New York/Mahwah: Paulist Press, 1987.

Gordon W. Lathrop

A Rebirth of Images: On the Use
of the Bible in Liturgy[1]

In his *Liturgical Piety* Louis Bouyer expressed the hope that what
he called the "third phase" of the liturgical movement would be
marked by a synthesis of Maria Laach with Klosterneuberg, of Odo
Casel with Pius Parsch.[2] What he hoped for was the joining of liturgical research and "the mystery of Christian worship" with biblical
mystagogy and the living word of God.

* * *

To some extent, Bouyer's third phase, the synthesis of Maria Laach
and Klosterneuberg, of research and biblical piety, has been achieved
today. It is there in the *Centre de Pastorale Liturgique* in Paris and in
the Constitution on the Sacred Liturgy's discussion of the "rich fare"
of the Scripture and in the resultant lectionary now enjoying significant success in all of our churches and in that evangelical liturgical
movement which takes seriously its own heritage of the assembly
around the Scripture proclaimed.

But there is another sense in which Bouyer's third phase is still in
abeyance, still waiting for realization. There has, after all, intervened
between Bouyer's writing and our present time the growing reception of critical biblical studies in all of our communions. With that reception has come an abandonment of the old senses of the Scripture

[1]Excerpted from Gordon W. Lathrop, "A Rebirth of Images," *Worship* 58,
no. 4 (July 1984) 291–304. Reprinted by permission of the author.
[2]Louis Bouyer, *Liturgical Piety* (Notre Dame, Ind.: Univ. of Notre Dame
Press, 1955) 66-67.

and, willy-nilly, of any easy application of liturgical typology. For all of us there is a new sense of the modern responsibility of the preacher who must work through the text with critical tools in order to preach well. That preacher follows the given texts with ease, especially when they are taken *lectio continua* from a certain book ("this is the year of Matthew," we say) but with no clear idea or even a slight embarrassment about their liturgical function.

I have no argument with criticism. But biblical scholars are freshly aware that criticism, marked as it is by what Paul Ricoeur calls the hermeneutics of suspicion, must be joined with what he calls the hermeneutics of recollection, the "surprising" at the roots of the primary meaning of a symbol.[3] One must press through criticism to arrive at the "second naiveté." Thus biblical scholarship is newly interested in the pattern and language and symbolic function of whole books and, indeed, the whole canon. A new situation has arisen in the very biblical studies which have drawn our attention.

Perhaps, then, this is a fruitful time for us to inquire again about the Scripture and the liturgy, about Bouyer's third phase. And perhaps this Academy, this gathering of those who bear central responsibility for the synthesis of Maria Laach with Klosterneuberg, is a good place to begin the inquiry. I want to propose three ideas which build on each other: the biblical word in the liturgy engages us in *a rebirth of images,* in a *recovery of lament,* and in a new appropriation of *the centrality of Jesus Christ* to the assembly. All three of these ideas are intended as reflection on the actual use of biblical texts and images in the Christian liturgy.

A REBIRTH OF IMAGES

The Bible read in the assembly or used as the source of liturgical texts is not understood profoundly enough, not understood according to the Bible's own pattern, if it is thought to be exhausted simply in the presentation of biblical images or the telling of Bible stories, as if presenting a static image were what the gathering was about. We do not gather, for example, simply to hear the story of the manna. No, the Bible in the assembly is about the images *shifted* or, in a phrase borrowed from Austin Farrer's commentary on the Apocalypse, images *reborn. . . .* A rebirth of images was there at the outset

[3]Cf. Paul Ricoeur, *The Rule of Metaphor* (Toronto: Univ. of Toronto Press, 1981) 318; *Freud and Philosophy* (New Haven, Conn.: Yale Univ. Press, 1970) 20–36.

of the Christian movement: "the bread which I will give for the life of the world is my flesh" (John 6:51). Much of Christian history can be seen as continued work on the grammar of that primary rebirth.

The liturgy uses images *shifted,* images *reborn,* and in doing so it follows the Bible itself. One thinks, for example, about the Song of the Sea (Exod 15:1-21): the historic event at the heart of Israel's life is made to bear mythic meaning; the event of the escape of some slaves is told in such a way as if it were about the conquest of the primal chaos and the bringing to birth of a new creation. That one event comes to have significance for the many, for all times and places, by being told in mythic terms.[4] The biblical narrative itself, then, has involved a powerful shift as Canaanite religious language is made to speak of historic, narrative event. Or one thinks of the way parables function in much of Scripture: the mythic tree of Ezekiel 17, the tree in which the birds of the air all nest, the world tree, becomes the mustard bush of Mark 4:30-32. The image is reborn. Or one thinks simply of the biblical use of metaphor, the application of the alien name: the people who follow Jesus are called "holy ones" and "priests"; the crucified is called "temple"; God is called "rock," "fire," and "king." These names are inappropriate and yet they are inappropriate in the right direction. They are accurate misnaming. The very use of the names is itself a shift of images.

The liturgy employs images in just this way, as images shifting, images reborn. The liturgy is also interested in sea, in tree, in priests, in fire, or in a hundred other powerful images in the biblical text. Sometimes it evokes those images by narrative and by name. Sometimes it calls them up by the strong sign value of the things at the center of our gathering, attended by biblical narrative attached to the signs. But the liturgy is not then done with the images. Rather, a revelatory twist occurs. We look up and see that the images of sea, tree, priests, fire are being used in a radically new way in the liturgy. This assembled people, people we know, they are the holy priests. This bread and this wine, they are the fruits of the wonderful, mustard bush, mythic tree. Or this font, it is the sea from which we are rescued, while God is making the whole world new. The liturgy is interested in a shift of images that itself becomes revelatory.

[4]Cf. F. M. Cross, "The Song of the Sea and Canaanite Myth," H. Braunand and others, *God and Christ, Journal for Theology and Church* 5 (New York: Harper, 1968) 1–25.

Now images, when they are used at all, mean to gather us into themselves, to carry us. "Their story," says George Herbert about the Hebrews, "pens and sets us all down."[5] By all the old stories and images, we and what we are, our human need, our human situation, are meant to be gathered up and drawn in. . . . But, when we are gathered into images that are reborn, we ourselves, in our projected hopes, are brought to crisis. The needs and hopes we, out of our need and out of our religious tradition, sing toward the expected God are not nearly enough, not right at all when they encounter the unexpected one and the unexpected event, the possibility of God and God's grace.[6] With the crisis in the images there comes a crisis in ourselves. So liturgy makes use of a shift of images as a little paradigm of conversion, of *metanoia*, of coming to faith. In this light, *typology* is seen not so much as a key to salvation history but as a liturgical figure of speech which is itself revelatory, as a name for the shift of images which occurs in the assembly, calling us to conversion and faith. So the liturgy uses images reborn, images shifted, and in doing so follows the Bible's own use.

The Bible's own use, however, is followed in yet another way. These images used in the liturgy are arranged in successions, in skeins, which make the reinterpretation even clearer. In doing this the liturgy does what the Scripture does. Ephraim says, "the first rushed out and kissed me, and led me onto the next." Thus the Song of the Sea of Exodus 15 might lead us on to read the Song of the Arm of the Lord in Isaiah 51:9-11, and to discern that one of the ways the prophet says that the God of the Exodus has become the God of the return from their exile is by recasting the imagery of the conquest at sea. Now the arm of the Lord, which slew the ancient dragon and mastered the ancient chaos, which made a new world by bringing the people through the sea, is besought to be the source of the people's return from exile by doing a new thing, making a path through the desert and not just a path through the sea. Mythic creation and exodus and return from exile are made into a succession of reborn images. . . .

The liturgy uses images in just this way: a skein of images reborn. We sing the Song of the Sea at the Easter Vigil, in the midst of a whole

5"The Bunch of Grapes," *George Herbert*, ed. John N. Wall, Jr. (New York: Paulist Press, 1981) 250.
6Cf. Edward Schillebeeckx, *Tussentijds verhaal over twee Jezus boeken* (Blomendaal: H. Nelissen, 1978) 32–33.

218

series of lessons which lead us to the font. The God who is victor at sea, making a people and making a world new, is the God of each of these accounts of deliverance and, at last, is the God of the font. There, in that sea, a people is delivered to become God's dwelling place. Similarly, every Sunday at the Lord's Supper we replicate the pattern of the gospels themselves, their use of the skein of signs or stories leading to the cross. We read a text from the gospel, not in order to recapture the time when independent tradition units circulated in the Christian communities, but in order to set the pericope we read next to the passion and resurrection of Christ held forth now in the Supper. Hence reading the individual pericopes and then celebrating the Supper presents us with a skein of images reinterpreting images which is the very pattern of the gospel books themselves. . . . A similar skein is found every Sunday in the sanctus which takes the Song of the Cherubim from Isaiah 6 and sets it next to a verse from Psalm 118, reunderstood in the sense of the Jerusalem entry account in the Synoptic Gospels. Once again, by that very juxtaposition of image to image, a rebirth occurs at the eucharistic event: the holy God seen in the temple, the pilgrims coming, the coming of Christ, this table—these are all made a chain. Thus the liturgy functions with the same skein that it has learned from the Bible itself.

One way of understanding what Alexander Schmemann called the *ordo* of Christian worship, its core shape—at its origin the pattern formed by the "eighth day" juxtaposed to the cycle of Jewish daily prayer in the whole week[7]—might be to say that it is the juxtaposition of a skein of images to Jesus Christ. The *ordo* of Christian worship is then the very patterning of images as images reborn. . . .

We have a need for a liturgical aesthetics which knows how the images in the liturgy, the signs and their sequence, the visual signs and their accompanying narratives and words, may draw us into the depth of the event and the depth of ourselves and, at the same time, lead us into the *ordo*, into the pattern of faith. We are in need of clarity, simplicity, and gravity in acted and spoken signs. And we are in need of those signs brought to crisis and rebirth.

A RECOVERY OF LAMENT

There is an important second thing to be said. The images in the Scripture seem to have arisen in their greatest strength and their

[7]Alexander Schmemann, *Introduction to Liturgical Theology* (New York: St. Vladimir's, 1975) 45–51.

greatest concentration at times of greatest disappointment. The books whose fabric is made most fully of images—Zechariah, for example, or the Apocalypse—are books written in the midst of disappointment and pain. The God of the Exodus did indeed need to become the God of the return from exile, and the Song of the Arm of the Lord in Isaiah 51 means to celebrate that. But the God of the return from exile had to become the God of the rebuilding, too, the God of the people returned to the city. In Haggai 2, a writing more or less contemporary with Zechariah, one finds what is almost an apology for the little, poor temple the returned are able to put up. "Do you think this is the temple?" the prophet seems to say. "It is not enough of a temple." Either by its smallness or by its history of compromise this temple is not finally the Great Temple of the Lord. Thus the image of the *temple,* so powerful in both Haggai and Zechariah, becomes an image of a thing lamented and a thing hoped for. Strong image is image for lament. It is also *then* image for hope and for prayer because of the confidence that the image carries the promise of God: God will be what God has been.

* * *

While we speak a great deal about the presence of God in God's word, there is another sense in which the word of God *stands* for God and so *is not God,* and we must also be aware of that. The Bible which is full of the presence of God is also full of God's absence. The Bible is a book of thirst, of disappointment. I cannot read Isaiah 9 at Christmas and not hear the old oracle, probably originally spoken at either the birth or the coronation of some ancient Judean king, as a painful story. The boot of the tramping warrior and the garment rolled in blood were somehow to be countered by this king, who could be called by the august and hopeful epithets: Wonderful Counselor, Mighty God, Everlasting Father, Prince of Peace. And it did not happen. The oracle is a disappointed story, gathering to itself echoes of other such disappointed hopes through the ages. The Bible is a book full of the thirst for God and of the absence of God, and the places in the Bible that are most profoundly full of images for God's work are frequently places most profoundly full of need, of lament, of disappointment. Nonetheless, that the images were used at all, used to speak and contain the painful need, this was itself a gift, an act of lively faith, an engendering of hope.

* * *

Mystagogy into the book and the assembly must be mystagogy into the disappointment and pain and prayer which is in the book. It must be an opening to let that in, to become thirsty with the biblical thirsty ones. It is a biblical, liturgical goal to let lament into the center of our assemblies. Nothing else is appropriate for the twentieth century.

David Power spoke last year to the Academy about worship in the time "between the holocausts" as worship which must be permanently marked by lament and by some sense of God's presence in the midst of lament.[8] The Bible in the liturgy has, in fact, kept alive the underside of history, the unofficial history, the history of suffering and loss, throughout ages. Simply keeping alive this remembrance of suffering resists all official triumphalism and may even become a matrix for radical, new social action.[9] Remembrance of suffering, remembrance of the underside of history, are at the heart of what the Bible and the liturgy are about.

* * *

We have considered the shift or rebirth of images in the use of the liturgy. The point here is this: almost the principal shift in the liturgical use of biblical images is the shift from thanksgiving to lament, found so clearly in Nehemiah 9. The liturgy recites the images before God's face with great confidence, proclaiming them as the deeds of God. It then shifts them in hope to cover our needs, to speak out our thirst together with all the needy and thirsty ones who have no images available to them for their needs. It follows from this that it is right for the agenda for our liturgical work to have included the recovery of intercessions, in the prayer of the people and in the anaphora itself, and to have included a new understanding of liturgy as something other than univocal ceremony, rather as embracing both joy and sorrow, thanksgiving and lament, praise and beseeching. The recovery of the eschatalogical "not-yet" may be the true characteristic of celebration in our time. So it is that work with the images in the assembly is not a dabbling with superficial poetry, but the hopeful use of the words and signs that stand for our present need and place us in honesty, together with the needy people of the world and with the remembrance of the holocausts of our century, before God's face.

[8] David N. Power, "Liturgy, Memory, and the Absence of God," *Worship* 57 (1983) 326–29.

[9] Cf. J. B. Metz, "The Future in the Memory of Suffering," *New Questions on God*, Concilium 76 (1972) 9–25.

Thereby we come to the central and most important point: the greatest shift which we make in the liturgy or the greatest rebirth of an image, the greatest revelatory metaphor or the most accurate misnaming, the greatest inheritor of the whole skein of images and the whole of the *ordo,* the greatest disappointment and yet the greatest words of hope are summed up in the name *Jesus Christ.* For Jesus is not the Messiah in any way that that image was originally meant to function. He is a crucified man, one among multitudes of those so cruelly executed at that time, crucified at the hands of the Roman authorities for charges that still remain not entirely clear. Coming to trust that there is in him the Messianic for us all—that is the point of all the images and of all the readings, of all the use of the Bible in the liturgy, and, I dare say, of all our work.

* * *

We act out that central shift, that christological meaning of the Scripture, when in the liturgy we solemnize the readings. We carry the book into the midst of the people as if the book itself were a sign of the presence of the eschatological *basileus,* of the great eschatological king. Or we read the sacred reading as if it were like the reading of the ancient Babylonian *Enuma Elish,* read at New Year to create the world anew by the sounding of the holy words. Or we read with everyone hushed, listening, and at least in the order of the sentences and their rhetoric there is a "quasimagic" which makes the world seem an ordered place.[10] But when we hear the content of the lesson, it may speak not of order, but of chaos and of hope for life. At its depth it says essentially: "This man is slain, this man is crucified for you." And thereby we come to the central image-rebirth present in the liturgy, paradigmatic of all the image shifts and, in its jarring quality, paradigmatic of the *metanoia* which is at the heart of faith.

The new thing of God's grace is always spoken in the language of the old, but it is nonetheless an utterly new thing. The liturgical shift of images means to say that Jesus Christ the crucified is at the heart of all the images of the Scripture and is their fulfillment, that this crucified man among the crucified ones of the world, among the little and suffering ones, is the source of life created new by God, is himself the

---

[10]Cf. Northrop Frye, *The Great Code* (New York: Harcourt Brace Jovanovich, 1982) 6, 11.

eschatological *basileus*—giving that old idea a radically new content—and is himself the word that gives new order to our disordered word.

Hearing this central shift of images is always hearing an invitation to faith, to being with those whom he is with—the little ones—and to mercy for ourselves and all the stuff of ourselves which is gathered up by the images and by the hope for God which the liturgy expresses. There is no king, no order to the world, indeed no God for me but this crucified man. And then all the world is new: my neighbor and myself and all the skein and fabric of the world.

* * *

Thus we sing the Song of the Sea at the font in order to declare, in a shift of images, that the sea is this font, and that all the deliverances of the many texts are focused here. We sing it also to say that these persons being baptized cry out with the needy of the world for deliverance and life, making the song a lament like Psalm 74. But we sing it especially as *the* rebirth of images and as the depths of lament, of Jesus Christ. We sing it because this font is the place for baptism into the death of Christ and because that death (and the baptism which signs and carries and speaks that death so that we may live) is the conquest of the chaotic sea and the making of a new world, a people won and that people made the eternal dwelling place for God. Such is the point not only of the Song of the Sea but of all liturgy, all readings, all images, all the successions and skeins. . . . [A]ll human suffering, historically researched or currently evoked, belongs appropriately to the text used of Jesus Christ. The sufferings of the crucified cannot be separated from human suffering. The New Testament use of the psalm is accurate. Lament opens on to the trust that for all humanity the *messianic*, the presence of God and of life, is found, to our utter surprise, in this little, crucified one among the little, needy ones of the world.

To read the texts as coming to their fullness in him is to find the letter becoming spirit, the letter itself dying—in the shift of images, in lament and hope for God, in the breaking open to meaning in Christ-amidst-our-need—the letter dying that there may be life. But one always begins with the letter, as it is. The Spirit is the life-giving Spirit flowing from the side of the crucified, Jesus Christ. Without that Spirit the word read among us may only be a sign of hope for the Word of God, Luther's "prattling and rattling" of words.[11]

[11]Martin Luther, "Concerning the Order of Public Worship, 1523," *Luther's Works*, American edition, vol. 35 (Philadelphia: Fortress Press, 1965) 14.

We may receive the christological-liturgical use of the Scriptures in our own work with vigor, finding there new joy in the life-giving power of the Scriptures broken open amidst actual human need.

* * *

One last image: the volume *Jewish Liturgy* contains a remarkable and painful photograph of Hannukah celebrated at the Westerbork transit camp in Holland in 1942.[12] The lampstand being lighted is, of course, as in the rebirth of images on any Hannukah night, the temple lampstand itself lit at the feast of unfailing oil. In the terms of the *haftarah* of the feast, Zechariah 2:14–4:7, it is indeed the sign of the very eye of God. But this is Westerbork, on the way to the death camps. Where is the light, the oil, the all-seeing merciful eye of God?

If, in Christian communities, we sing that Jesus Christ is the light of the world, it must be that thereby we gather up the truth of that lament into the truth of our song.

---

[12]*Jewish Liturgy*, ed. R. Posner and others (Jerusalem: Keter, 1975) 194.

Jill Y. Crainshaw

Mary Catherine Hilkert: Naming God's Presence in Human Experience

For the early Church, to acquire "wisdom" meant recognizing God's presence in both the mundane and difficult realities of human living. In the worship patterns of Christianity's earliest faith communities, all of the details of people's everyday existence were gathered together with God's Word, and new understandings of life-determining significance were revealed. In their gatherings, as they broke ordinary bread baked by ordinary human hands, Christ was made present among them.

Mary Catherine Hilkert, a Dominican scholar who is associate professor of theology at Notre Dame University, articulates an understanding reflective of the early Church, namely that the faith community is the place both for the application and the generation of theological knowledge. Working within her framework as a systematic theologian, Hilkert seeks to reestablish the integral relationship between systematics and homiletics, disciplines whose fragmentation she attributes to the dichotomy established by the modern university between research and practice.

To accomplish a retrieval of the vital connections between theology and preaching, she argues that there is a pre-reflective presence of ultimacy or grace in the depths of human experience; preaching, within the context of liturgy, names that presence as God. Systematic theology's role in this "naming of God's grace" is primarily that of critical reflection, as a solid theological foundation for preaching is continually shaped and reshaped.

Hilkert's work makes several contributions to liturgical theology. First, in her understanding, preaching is a sacramental act. The actions and objects of human living are transparent to God's grace, and proclaiming God's Word in the midst of the faith community operates to make explicit that redemptive reality. Second, central to this act of naming God's grace is the liturgical context. The liturgical context of proclamation provides both implicit and explicit connections between the human story and the Gospel. In other words, liturgy is emphasized as the horizon where the Word of God touches the concrete lives of those within the worshiping community.

Finally, in articulating a theology of preaching that locates God's revelation at the depths of human experience, she joins the voices of others within the liturgical renewal movement in pointing to the primacy of the Church's prayer in establishing the Church's doctrine. In this, she also draws attention to the praxis dimension of preaching and of liturgy as a whole; naming God's grace involves both speaking words of hope and justice and "making those words concrete realities."

Hilkert earned a doctorate in systematic theology from The Catholic University of America in 1984. Prior to joining the faculty at Notre Dame, she served as associate professor of systematic theology at the Aquinas Institute of Theology in St. Louis, Missouri. The following article reflects the argument she develops in *Naming Grace: Preaching and the Sacramental Imagination*, published in 1997. In that work she outlines a sacramental understanding of preaching that reflects the work of Karl Rahner and Edward Schillebeeckx. When God's Word is proclaimed, Hilkert emphasizes, we join with those who have gone before us in the faith in sharing the Gospel story so that God's presence in the breaking of the bread, in the ordinariness of human experience, is revealed.

In addition to serving on the editorial boards of *Spirituality Today* and *Theology Digest,* Hilkert has contributed several helpful articles and books.

FOR FURTHER READING
The Praxis of Experience: An Introduction to the Theology of Edward Schillebeeckx.
Ed. with Robert Schreiter. New York: Harper & Row, 1989; "Preaching and Theology: Re-Thinking the Relationship." *Worship* 65 (September 1991) 398–409; "Revelation and Proclamation: Shifting Paradigms." *Journal of Ecumenical Studies* 29 (Winter 1992) 1–23; *Naming Grace: Preaching and the Sacramental Imagination.* New York: The Continuum Publishing Co., 1997.

Mary Catherine Hilkert

Naming Grace: A Theology of Proclamation[1]

Peter's preaching following the cure of the blind beggar in Acts 3 is often cited as a classic example of early Christian preaching.[2] Relocating that model sermon (Acts 3:12-26) in the broader context of the chapter suggests a new angle for reflection on the mystery of preaching. Rather than beginning with the power of the proclaimed word, we might begin with the power of grace found in the depths of human experience and describe preaching as the art of naming grace.

What are the elements of a theology of preaching which emerge from the third chapter of Acts? As the passage opens, Peter and John are going to the temple to pray. They stop and recognize a crippled beggar on the fringes of society. All of that is part of their preparation for preaching, their formation as preachers. The hearer of the word is a beggar, one who expects something. The preachers themselves have nothing to give except the name of Jesus. Trusting the power of that name, Peter speaks a word of healing, but his preaching is not just in word. He "took him by the right hand and raised him up, and immediately his feet and ankles were made strong" (Acts 3:7). In other words, before Peter as preacher announces salvation (in this case, healing) in word, that salvation has already been made tangible. The disciples of Jesus have already proclaimed the power of the resurrection in healing touch, in the community's attention to the needs of the world. The result of this "preaching is praxis" is the very kind of conversion

[1]Excerpted from Mary Catherine Hilkert, "Naming Grace: A Theology of Proclamation," *Worship* 60, no. 5 (September 1986) 434–49. Reprinted by permission of the author.
[2]See C. H. Dodd, *The Apostolic Preaching and Its Developments* (New York: Harper & Row, 1962) 20–24.

that is the goal of all preaching—the freedom of the spirit and the restoration of human wholeness which overflows in joy and praise.

Only then, after the preaching in deed, does Peter preach what we usually identify as his sermon. He starts with the concrete event they have just witnessed: "People of Israel, why do you wonder at this? Why do you stare as though by our own power or piety we had made him walk?" (Acts 3:12). First Peter names the experience of what has happened in our midst and only then does he speak the name of God. That's the art of any ministry of the word: to name God neither too soon nor too late. As preacher, Peter names the power that has been operative in the depths of the human experience they have witnessed; he names God.

At the same time, the preacher names the deepest truth of the human situation which includes a word of judgment: "The God of Abraham and of Isaac and of Jacob, the God of our ancestors, glorified his servant Jesus, whom you delivered up and denied in the presence of Pilate, when he had decided to release him. But you denied the Holy and Righteous One, and asked for a murderer to be granted to you, and killed the Author of life, whom God raised from the dead" (Acts 3:13-15). Christian conversion, which is the goal of all preaching, always involves a twofold movement: the turn toward God (and therefore toward our deepest truth) and the turn from sin (from the ways in which we have been "people of the lie").

The passage also reveals the deepest identity of preachers as witnesses to the resurrection who give testimony with their lives, not only with their words. Preachers do not simply retell a story from the past—not even the story of Jesus' being raised from the dead; rather, preachers point to the power of the resurrection here and now in concrete human lives. "*This* beggar, *whom you see and know* has been made strong by faith in the name of Jesus" (Acts 3:16). The final word of the preaching event is not a word of judgment. Neither does the preacher leave the community in their temporary awe and amazement. Rather, the preaching is an invitation to repent and follow, a word of hope centered on what God can and will do for humanity. It is a word which empowers the conversion it demands.

The Chilling of the Word. When we reflect on our own experiences of preaching, from either side of the pulpit, we know how rarely it happens like that. . . . Why this "chilling of the word"? As Pope Paul VI remarked in his 1975 apostolic exhortation On Evangelization in the Modern World: "In our day, what has happened to that hidden energy of the good news which is able to have such a powerful effect on the human conscience? To what extent and in what way is that evangelical force capable of really transforming the people of this country?"[3] One factor contributing to the blocking of the power of the good news may be precisely our theology of preaching, our understanding of what is going on in the preaching event. Even more fundamentally, the problem may be that we have failed to grasp the implications of the mystery of the incarnation: God has been revealed in human history. Could it be that we try to preach grace without locating it in the depths of human experience? At stake here is not only a theology of preaching but the more foundational question of a theology of revelation.

THE LOCUS OF REVELATION: SHAKING PREACHING'S FOUNDATIONS

Most fully developed theologies of preaching have been constructed either in terms of a biblical theology of the word or from Lutheran or Reformed theological perspectives which emphasize the transcendence of God's word and the radical effect of sin on the human condition.

* * *

It is precisely at this point that a contribution to the growing ecumenical discussion of the theology of preaching might be made from a Catholic perspective which views grace as active in and through humanity and describes revelation in sacramental terms. Grounded in the conviction that sin never completely destroyed the created goodness of humanity, the Catholic response to the debate initiated by Emil Brunner as to whether there is a "point of contact for preaching the gospel of grace"[4] is clearly affirmative. The Catholic tradition has emphasized that grace builds on nature and that grace effects a real inner transformation of the human person. Karl Rahner has taken the insight even further in his claim that human beings always stand within the call to grace; God's offer of self-communication in love constitutes a fundamental orientation of human existence (the supernatural existential). Human persons are actually constituted as "hearers of the word"; humanity has been fashioned as "openness for the incarnation."

[3]Paul VI, apostolic exhortation *Evangelii Nuntiandi* (December 8, 1975) no. 4.
[4]Emil Brunner, *Man in Revolt* (Philadelphia: Westminster Press, 1947) 527–41.

Because human beings remain body-spirit, however, grace as the spiritual mystery at the heart of reality needs to be manifested in concrete, historical, visible ways. God's presence is mediated in and through creation and human history, but that mystery remains hidden or "anonymous" unless it is brought to word. The prophetic word and the sacraments (Augustine's "visible words") allow the depth dimension of reality (grace) to be recognized and celebrated.

Whether from a Thomistic perspective of creation and analogical ways of "naming God" or from the perspective of contemporary symbolic theories of revelation which describe the experience of grace as the depth dimension of ordinary human experience,[5] Catholic spirituality and theology have traditionally emphasized the continuity, rather than the discontinuity, between nature and grace, creation and revelation.

* * *

What kind of theology of proclamation might emerge from a more Catholic understanding of grace and a sacramental theology of revelation such as *Dei Verbum* describes: the mystery of God's self-communication in love which occurs in and through creation and human history, a mystery recognized and named in salvation history and culminating in Jesus Christ?

Any Christian theology of preaching will center on Jesus Christ as Word of God. Most frequently, however, theologies of preaching then move to a biblical theology of the word and the unique power of God's word. What if, instead, we were to focus on the incarnation—the mystery that God's fullest word has been spoken in history, in a human being, in human experience?

Surely it is true that there is a dynamic power in the biblical *dabar Yahweh*, that God's word cannot be separated from God's actions, that the word of God is creative, bringing about what it says. Clearly the word of God is a promise which carries real power:

[5]See Avery Dulles, "The Symbolic Structure of Revelation," *Theological Studies* 41 (March 1980) 51–73. Although this approach (shared by Karl Rahner) is often described in Catholic terms as a sacramental theology of revelation, theories of revelation as symbolic disclosure have been developed by such diverse writers as Paul Tillich, Paul Ricoeur, Mircea Eliade, Langdon Gilkey, Ray Hart, John Macquarrie, Louis Dupre, and Gregory Baum. For further bibliographical references see Dulles' article as well as his *Modes of Revelation* (New York: Doubleday, 1983).

"For just as from the heavens the rain and snow come down, and do not return there till they have watered the earth, making it fertile and fruitful, giving seed to the one who sows and bread to the one who eats, so shall my word be that goes forth from my mouth; it shall not return to me void, but shall do my will, achieving the end for which I sent it" (Isa 55:10-11).

Surely it is true that the word of God has the power to touch hearts and to challenge and change us: "the word of God is living and active, sharper than any two-edged sword, piercing to the division of soul and spirit, of joints and marrow and discerning the thoughts and intentions of the heart" (Heb 4:12). But what are the implications of believing that *that* word has become flesh in Jesus of Nazareth, that God is now to be discovered enfleshed in human history?

* * *

Perhaps we can take a clue from contemporary christology and try to understand the mystery of the word "from below" rather than "from above." Rather than beginning with the power of God's word as something totally other and beyond our experience, why not begin with the revelation of God which is to be discovered in the midst of—at the depths of—what is human. Can we reflect on the mystery of preaching as the naming of grace in human experience?

If we are to describe preaching in that way, it's important to recall three things: (1) we are talking about human experience in its depth dimension, (2) for most people in our world, the experience of God may very well be a "contrast experience," and (3) human experience is interpreted experience.

Human experience in its depths. Naming the presence of God in human experience requires pressing to the limits of human existence where both the threat of radical human finitude and experiences of overwhelming meaning raise the fundamentally religious question of the "ground of our being." At the boundaries of human life "signals of transcendence" emerge within human experience. Secular language breaks its limits in trying to express "the other dimension" or the "surplus of meaning" disclosed from the depths of human experience.[6] Here language ultimately becomes religious or we must

[6]See Paul Ricoeur, "Naming God," *Union Seminary Quarterly Review* 34 (1979) 215–27, and "Biblical Hermeneutics," *Semeia* 4 (1975) 107–48; David Tracy, *Blessed Rage for Order* (New York: Seabury Press, 1975) 91–131; Louis

remain silent. Thus one of the contemplative tasks of the preacher (and the preaching community) is to reflect on human experience in order to identify in faith the ultimate foundation of the mystery of human life—the God who often remains hidden. That proclamation presumes, of course, that the preacher is in touch with the human struggle and that he or she, like Jesus, has faced the darkness in hope.

Just as prophets like Hosea, Ezekiel, and Jeremiah were formed for their preaching through the profound, and usually painful, human experience of whatever aspect of God's word they were called to preach, so too those who pray to become ministers of the word are asking to be baptized in the experience from which that word emerged. In order to become effective preachers we are asking that nothing human remain foreign to us so that we can know what it means to say that all of humanity has been taken into God and redeemed in the incarnation.

* * *

Contrast experience. One of the problems of speaking of discovering God in human experience today is that we are more conscious than ever in our global village that not everyone's experience overflows with a surplus of meaning that can be described only in religious language. On the contrary, for the majority of humanity, the basic experience of life is an experience of suffering—or at least survival. How then can we talk of God as revealed at the depths of human experience?

Here Edward Schillebeeckx has made a valuable contribution to a theology of revelation with the notion of "contrast experience."[7] He suggests that, while the immediate experience of two-thirds of humanity is that of suffering and the apparent absence of God, a still deeper mystery is revealed in their response to that suffering—responses of protest, hope, and sheer endurance. Human beings are able to cling to life against all odds, to cling to God in the face of ap-

---

Dupre, *The Other Dimension* (New York: Seabury Press, 1979); Langdon Gilkey, *Naming the Whirlwind: The Renewal of God-Language* (Indianapolis: Bobbs-Merrill, 1969). For an approach which emphasizes cognitive reflection in faith and a dialectical, rather than a direct disclosure of the experience of grace as the basis for naming God at the limits of human experience, see Edward Schillebeeckx, *The Understanding of Faith* (London: Sheed & Ward, 1974) 78–101, and *Christ: The Experience of Jesus as Lord,* trans. John Bowden (New York: Seabury Press, 1980) 29–79.

[7]See Schillebeeckx, *Christ,* 897, n. 158. Cf. *God the Future of Man,* trans. N. D. Smith (New York: Sheed & Ward, 1968) 136–38, 154–61, 191–99, and *Understanding of Faith,* trans. N. D. Smith (London: Sheed & Ward, 1974) 91–101.

parent abandonment. That kind of human resistance and hope can be sustained only by a deeper spirit of life—the very Spirit of God within humanity. It is the Spirit who creates life out of nothingness, who raises the dead to life. Because the suffering of this world share in a daily way in the crucifixion, they have a unique experience of the mystery of God at the limits of their human experience. This is at the heart of what it means to claim that the poor or the crucified of this world have a privileged hearing of the word. Preachers need to hear that word, too, if they are to speak an authentic word.[8]

Experience interpreted by faith. Finally we cannot talk of revelation occurring in human experience without recalling that human experience is interpreted. We do not have raw human experience apart from some framework for understanding or perceiving. We interpret our lives in the context of traditions—the traditions of our personal histories, of our family histories, of our culture. We may modify, change, or even reject those traditions based on new experiences which do not seem to fit, but initially we stand within the tradition. We are formed in the context of meanings which have been handed on to us. We are given language; we do not create it.

In speaking then of recognizing God or grace at the depths or limits of human experience, we are talking within the framework of a faith tradition which alerts us to a deeper dimension in our experience and gives us a language to name that dimension. We stand within the living tradition of the Christian community. Those who have gone before us in faith have handed on their story, their framework for understanding and living human life. It is the story of Jesus as recounted in the Scriptures, remembered, lived and celebrated in the community, and retold uniquely in every age and culture.

* * *

Proclaiming grace in word and deed. Ultimately preaching is a matter of handing on the Christian story in such a way that the experience of grace—God's presence in ordinary human life—is communicated. In the broadest sense, preaching is the retelling of the story of Jesus

[8]Further, Gustavo Gutiérrez remarks, the liberating power and truth of the gospel will not be effectively proclaimed until the poor are among those who proclaim the gospel. He warns, however, that "then we shall have a gospel no longer 'presentable' in society. It will not sound nice and it will not smell good." *The Power of the Poor in History,* trans. Robert R. Barr (Maryknoll: Orbis Books, 1983) 22.

in word and deed. Retelling the story requires that the Christian community both make grace (salvation) more of a reality in this concrete moment in history and name the power which makes that possible, the power of God. Proclamation in word flows from, as well as nourishes, proclamation in deed. That is the point of the 1971 Bishop's Synod claim that "Activity on behalf of justice is a constitutive part of preaching the gospel."[9]

Here we have the model of Jesus' own preaching. He announced the reign of God—the compassion of God for all—in word and deed. He forgave sins not only by words of forgiveness but by eating with sinners. He announced the healing mercy of God by touching lepers. He taught community by celebrating with his disciples. He challenged preconceived social roles by talking with and loving Samaritans, women, tax collectors, prostitutes. How did Jesus tell the story of God—name grace? He shared ordinary human experience and named it as "of God."

So, too, contemporary preachers can announce compassion, healing, mercy, and hope only if the community and the preacher are involved in making those words concrete realities. Ultimately, it is this living of the gospel life in fidelity to the gifts of the Spirit bestowed in baptism and confirmation that is the source of the power and authority to preach the gospel.[10] The Spirit active in the life of one who lives the gospel impels the disciple to speak of the source and power of that gospel life.

If this story of Jesus is a living tradition, a universal story true for every age and culture, it has to be retold anew in every period of history, recaptured in new experience and expression. Never before has the Christian story been heard or proclaimed in the way we will hear or announce it from our own unique moment in history and cultural

[9]"Justice in the World," Statement of the 1979 Synod of Bishops (Washington, D.C.: United States Catholic Conference, 1972) 34.

[10]For a discussion of baptism as the ultimate foundation for the preaching ministry—whether exercised by ordained or by non-ordained members of the community—see Mary Collins, "The Baptismal Roots of the Preaching Ministry," *Preaching and the Non-Ordained* (Collegeville, Minn.: The Liturgical Press, 1983) 111–33. In the same volume Edward Schillebeeckx argues that the *vita apostolica,* rather than a purely juridical mission, provides the authentic basis for the proclamation of the gospel in the Christian community ("The Right of Every Christian to Speak in the Light of Evangelical Experience 'In the Midst of Brothers and Sisters,'" 11–39). The disputed question remains that of how this charismatic authority to preach is mediated and confirmed by the church.

context. What new dimensions of the story unfold when it is retold by women, by Nicaraguan peasants, by prisoners, by married Christians, by refugees or communities that have declared sanctuary? How is the word of God heard and proclaimed in South Africa, in the experience of American black Christians, Hispanic communities, the Vietnamese, Native Americans? How is the story retold in a world facing potential nuclear holocaust? Our experience, our perspective, affects what we hear in the text. The Spirit is active in our new experience, affects what we hear in the text. The Spirit is active in our new experience, stirring up what might be called "new memories of Jesus,"[11] new possibilities of the meaning of his life, his words, his death and resurrection. If we do not hand on the tradition by telling the story of salvation from the context of our own experience, no one else can or will.

On the other hand, while our experience opens up new dimensions in the story of Jesus, that story as preserved in the biblical texts also challenges and confronts contemporary experience. The Spirit who calls forth new experiences and new memories in the community is the Spirit of Jesus—the crucified and risen one. We cannot simply re-fashion Jesus in our own image. Rather, the gospels and the history of Jesus limit and focus our retelling of the story. We are confronted by the text, and by the very reality of Jesus who is the source of the experience recorded in the text. Here is the truth of Paul's concern that we preach God's word and not our own, that it is the gospel of Jesus Christ which we have received that we hand on, not "some other gospel." Here is the other side of what it means to dwell in the word.

The preacher and the Scriptures: an ongoing story. Clearly the preacher needs to be rooted in the Scriptures, not only in the content of the Scriptures (the Christian story) but also in the process of the Scriptures (the story-in-the-making—the development of the tradition), because the preacher is called to continue that process of the transmission of a living tradition. The Hebrew Scriptures, for example, emerged from the faith of the Jewish people. God's word, they claimed, had been "spoken" in their concrete human history. They proclaimed that God was active in their liberation from slavery, in desert wanderings, in the conquest of a foreign land, in wars and exiles, in political struggles. . . . In claiming their ancestors' history and faith as their own tradition, the

---

[11]For a brief discussion of the relationship between the Spirit and the re-membrance of the community (pneuma and anamnesis) in terms of new *memoria Jesu* see Schillebeeckx, *Christ* 641–42, and *Jesus: An Experiment in Christology,* trans. Hubert Hoskins (New York: Seabury Press, 1979) 46–48.

tribes of Israel experienced their own history as another moment in that ongoing covenant relationship. The same process was at work in the gospels and the Christian Scriptures as a whole. Jesus' life and meaning was reinterpreted in light of the resurrection and the concrete contexts of different communities of faith.

Preaching involves that same contemplative and prophetic gift of making connections between the story of God's fidelity in the past and God's continuing fidelity in this new moment. It is not a matter of simply retelling the story of the past, no matter how creatively. On the contrary, the promises and tradition of the past take on a new meaning and need to be reinterpreted in light of present experience. The story continues—as *our* story. Hence the challenge of Isaiah is one that preachers need to take to heart: "Behold I am doing a new thing. Can you not perceive it?" (Isa 43:19).

The "new thing" God is doing, however, is being done in and through the community. The experience of grace is a communal experience. Hence the word of faith which the preacher proclaims is ultimately the community's word. The preacher speaks in the name of the community and speaks the deepest beliefs of the community. This may involve a word of challenge, but one that is based on the challenge that the gospel is for each of us and all of us.

* * *

In the black community, the ultimate criterion for acceptance of a new pastor has been expressed in the question: "Can the reverend tell the story?"[12] No one asks whether it is the story of Jesus or the people's story; they know that ultimately it is the same story. Telling the story of grace active in and through humanity requires preachers who resemble the paralyzed grandfather in Martin Buber's Hasidic tale: "My grandfather was paralyzed. One day he was asked to tell about something that happened with his teacher—the great Baalschem. Then he told how the saintly Baalschem used to leap about and dance while he was at prayers. As he went on with the story my grandfather stood up; he was so carried away that he had to show how the master had done it, and started to caper about and dance. From that moment on he was cured. That is how stories should be told."[13]

[12]James H. Cone, "The Story Context of Black Theology," *Theology Today* 32 (1975–76) 147.
[13]Martin Buber, *Werke,* vol. 3 (Munich: 1963) 71.

Thomas A. Rand

Paul Waitman Hoon: The Word as Incarnational Event

Paul Hoon, pastor, theologian, and teacher, was born in Chicago in 1910. With undergraduate studies at Yale and seminary training at Union, he was ordained in 1933, becoming the fourth generation of Methodist clergy in his family. He pastored churches in New York, Connecticut, and Pennsylvania during twenty years of parish ministry. Studying with John Baillie at the University of Edinburgh, he earned a doctorate in systematic theology in 1936. His thesis explored soteriology in John Wesley's writings and was greatly influenced by the Wesleyan scholar Newton Flew at Cambridge and Rudolf Otto at Marburg. Called from the local church, he was named to the first Henry Sloane Coffin Chair of Pastoral Ministry at Union Theological Seminary, from 1953 to 1975.

His primary contribution to liturgical theology is his elaboration of the christological foundation of worship. By exploring the relation between theology and liturgy, the dialectic of liturgy and life, the language of worship, and the nature of liturgical action, he consistently draws our attention to the theology and practice of christology revealed in the New Testament gospel and manifested in the life of the Church. For him, Christian worship is grounded in the reality of the action of God toward humanity in Jesus Christ and in the human responsive action through Jesus Christ. This reality he calls "Word," understood as both the living person and Event of Jesus Christ, through which God's very ontology is communicated and shared with humankind.

In the excerpt that follows, Hoon explores liturgical action as christological expression, that is, how Christ reveals himself in the sacraments, the Word among us.

FOR FURTHER READING

The Integrity of Worship: Ecumenical and Pastoral Studies in Liturgical Theology. Nashville: Abingdon Press, 1971; "Theology, Death, and the Funeral Liturgy." *Union Seminary Quarterly Review* 31 (Spring 1976) 169–81; "Some Theological Guidelines for Liturgical Renewal." *Andover Newton Quarterly* 11 (January 1971) 150–59; "Liturgy or Gamesmanship?" *Religion in Life* 38. No. 4 (winter 1969) 482–97; "Subjectivity and Objectivity in Public Worship." *Union Seminary Quarterly Review* 19 (March 1964) 199–212.

Paul Waitman Hoon

Liturgical Action in Light of the Word[1]

* * *

[O]n the one hand, the ground of liturgical action is always an ontological ground in that action rises from Christ's mystical presence in his people. On the other hand, Christ's being is "being in action." The presence of Christ is declared in the action of Christ, and in this sense the ground of liturgical action is event as well.

The paradigm for the mind's reflection in this sense must always be some such image as that with which St. Luke pictures Christ in relation to the disciples at Emmaus after the resurrection: through Christ's *action* in taking, blessing, breaking, and giving the bread, his *being* is known and his *life* is received. *In fractione panis eum cognoverunt:* "they recognized him"—not in the bread, not in conversation before he broke the bread, not in the table bearing the bread, but—"*in the breaking* of the bread" (Luke 24:30-32, 35 *KJV*). Divine "being" is known in human "breaking." The presence of the Word is the act of the Word.

But liturgical theology is drawn to such an image not only because of the Emmaus incident in itself. Even more, this image summarizes the meaning of the total Christ-Event liturgically understood. The action of Jesus Christ in taking, blessing, breaking, and giving the bread at Emmaus only epitomizes all other actions through which the mind of the Church knows Jesus Christ as Life. Thus it is said that the disciples *re*-cognized, not merely "cognized" him, as it were. They knew

[1]Paul Waitman Hoon, "Liturgical Action in Light of the Word," in ch. 8, "The Nature of Liturgical Action, part 2: The Context of Church and Word," *The Integrity of Worship: Ecumenical and Pastoral Studies in Liturgical Theology* (Nashville and New York: Abingdon Press, 1971) 342–53. Reprinted by permission of the author.

him again only as they had known him before. His liturgical action at the table at Emmaus was one with the liturgical action of his life. Of virtually any action Jesus performed, it could be said that he made himself present in what he did. In reading from the prophet Isaiah in the synagogue in Nazareth, in conversing with a Samaritan woman at the well, in teaching and preaching from the mountainside, in healing a demoniac, in cleansing the temple, in washing the disciples' feet, in bearing his cross and dying his death—in all these a liturgy was done and an epiphany took place. The liturgical action of breaking the bread at Emmaus is but Christ's signature to the liturgy of his life; and in that liturgy, ontology and event are finally one.

For the mind's reflection upon worship as for the experience of worship itself, this insight underlies everything else, first in the sense that Christ's liturgy is the ground of our liturgy and that his liturgical action precedes ours. From the mystery of his presence acting toward us derives our ability to act. In the poetic language of the Emmaus story: only because he breaks the bread and acts can we act. Or in the drier language of theology: liturgical action inheres in prevenient grace. Or in the philosophical language of the schools: Christ's liturgy is both the "final" and the "efficient" cause of our action. Or in the metaphorical language of Judaism: through the living priesthood of Jesus Christ we are able to act as priests. Or in the language of pneumatology: we do not know how to worship as we ought, but the Spirit makes intercession for us. But however it be said, it is Jesus Christ who liturgically holds the service. He is the true Celebrant, and our action is grounded in his. This is to say, we can think theologically on the question of liturgical action only in the same manner in which we engage in the action of worship itself: through Jesus Christ our Lord.

Restated as a conceptual principle, this insight requires, first, that action be thought of as sacramental, but "sacramental" understood not as referring to a particular rite but to the initiatory action of divine grace coming to us from outside as well as within our existence. In this sense, the term "sacramental" is to be referred to the liturgy of Jesus Christ as that in which the Divine as other than man yet gives itself in service to man; and worship possesses integrity only as its action is sacramental in the sense that it provides for Christ's offering himself to us before we offer ourselves to him. It is this fundamental truth which the Church especially needs to remember as it undertakes to rethink action in our day, a truth which under varying thought-forms and in different categories we have affirmed again and again . . . in asserting the priority of impression to expression, in yoking "irrelevance" with "relevance" as essential to liturgical integrity, in understanding objectivity as the ground of subjectivity, in borrowing from art the principle of vitality, restating it christologically and saying that we know the Word to be Act when its action moves us with the movement of God. Ultimately, these are only different ways of stating that truth which the apostle far more simply and profoundly laid down as the deepest truth of the Gospel for liturgy as for all else: we love because God first loved us.

However, the sacramental nature of action needs to be thought of not only conceptually but functionally as well. And functionally—as we have said—the action of the Word can only take place through man's action. The congregation is the field of Christ's action, and his action becomes real only through what man does. Thus, we have said, the congregation are priests to one another. Or in Luther's bolder metaphor: they are "Christs to one another." Functionally, their action is mimetic action in the sense that they reach into the liturgical event of Jesus Christ and reenact it to one another. In this sense, congregational action goes beyond the formula with which we commonly describe it: revelation and response. In its deepest meaning it is revelation itself. To cite Lutheran categories . . . described earlier: divine action occurs "in," "with," and "under" human action. Alternatively, we may say that through the congregation's action the "mystery" of Christ takes place. Or again, through the congregation's action a miracle occurs whereby past, present, and future time is transcended and what we can do no better than to speak of as "eternity" becomes eschatologically present. In a word: through the action of ordinary, weak, sinful, flesh-and-blood people, nothing less than the action of incarnation again takes place.

8

How Do Liturgical Theologians Engage Cultural Diversity?

Liturgical theologians cannot do their work today without engaging cultural diversity. We have become sensitized to the rich fabric of particularity in liturgical celebrations, which provide the context for the dominant patterns we have tended to study. We have begun to recognize that the official liturgies of "dominant" groups are themselves culturally conditioned.

In the introduction to the second chapter, I encouraged you to reflect on these questions: From whose perspective are we asking our questions? Whose voices will we be hearing? Whose voices are we likely not to hear?

Those questions were an attempt to help us recognize, early on, that the theologians included in this reader tend to be from a rather limited part of the world. I hope that increasingly the literature in the field will reflect diversity, and that some of you will be the writers whose work will be included in future readers. Your contributions will enable our understanding to be broadened, deepened, and enriched.

We begin with an excerpt from Chupungco, whose work in this area has had such far-reaching influence. Be aware that the terminology keeps changing (inculturation is a more satisfactory term than adaptation at the moment, but better terminology will undoubtedly emerge). In any event, Chupungco calls attention to incarnational theology as basic here.

The articles by González and Trulear are substantive contributions to liturgical theology in their own right and could have appeared in other chapters as well. They are not only examples of liturgical theologizing within particular cultural contexts. Although they do an excellent job of that, they also provide us with important theological insights into the nature of liturgy itself.

Lorraine S. Brugh

Anscar J. Chupungco: The Praxis of Liturgical Inculturation

Anscar Chupungco's life is a demonstration in cultural border crossings. Chupungco is a Roman Catholic Filipino citizen who teaches at the Pontifical Liturgical Institute in Rome, Italy, and Notre Dame University in South Bend, Indiana. He is also frequently at World Council of Churches gatherings around the globe. He has written extensively in the area of worship and culture. His writings are found in numerous Roman Catholic publications and in Lutheran World Federation study documents on worship and culture. Just as his life manifests the practice of cultural pluralism, his writings reflect the theory of crossing cultural borders. His writings in liturgical theology date from 1969 and continue at the end of the twentieth century. He is an interpreter of Vatican II's reforms for local liturgical practice.

Chupungco was born a Filipino citizen in 1939. He became a Benedictine monk and was ordained a presbyter in Manila in 1965. From this point, his life began a series of cultural changes. He undertook doctoral study at the Pontifical Liturgical Institute in Rome and received his degree in sacred liturgy in 1969. His doctoral dissertation is titled "The Cosmic Elements of Christian Passover."

Chupungco believes "the basic fact that all liturgical rites are vested in culture, that no liturgy is celebrated in a cultural vacuum."[1] This idea leads in two different but related directions. First, no one liturgical form is completely free of cultural influence. Even New Testament practices were shaped by Hellenistic and Middle Eastern customs. It is not possible to experience any culture-free liturgy. Second,

---

[1] Anscar J. Chupungco, "Liturgy and the Components of Culture," *Worship and Culture in Dialogue* (Geneva, Switzerland: Lutheran World Federation, 1994) 153.

245

any culture can find expression for its worship through its own culture. It is not necessary to import another's culture in order to have an authentic expression of Christian liturgy.

Chupungco credits others with developing the use of terms like adaptation, inculturation, acculturation, and contextualization in describing the relation between the Christian message and a particular culture. It is Chupungco, however, who develops and explores the idea of liturgical inculturation for Christian worship. Beginning with his 1976 book, *Towards a Filipino Liturgy,* he describes "the process of inserting the texts and rites of the liturgy into the framework of the local culture."[2]

Perhaps more than any other liturgical theologian, Chupungco has pushed the study of Christian liturgy toward an honest recognition of its cultural limits and perspectives. At the same time, he has opened up for Christian liturgy an infinite variety of cultural expressions, through its contact in a local, cultural setting. He validates each local context as a setting for Word and Sacrament, and then demonstrates how elements of culture can be expressions of Christian liturgy.

FOR FURTHER READING

Towards a Filipino Liturgy. Quezon City, Philippines, 1976; *Cultural Adaptation of the Liturgy.* New York: Paulist Press, 1982; *Liturgical Inculturation.* Collegeville, Minn.: The Liturgical Press, 1992; *Liturgies of the Future: The Process and Methods of Inculturation.* New York: Paulist Press, 1989; "Baptism in the Early Church and Its Cultural Settings," "Eucharist in the Early Church and Its Cultural Settings," "Liturgical Music and Its Early Cultural Settings," "Liturgy and the Components of Culture." *Worship and Culture in Dialogue.* Geneva, Switzerland: Lutheran World Federation, 1994; *Handbook for Liturgical Studies: Introduction to the Liturgy.* Ed. Anscar J. Chupungco. Collegeville, Minn.: The Liturgical Press, 1997.

---

[2]For a more complete discussion, see Anscar J. Chupungco, *Liturgical Inculturation: Sacramentals, Religiosity, and Catechesis* (Collegeville, Minn.: The Liturgical Press, 1992).

Anscar J. Chupungco

The Theological Principle of Adaptation[1]

It has been said that what we need in the Third World is not so much liturgical adaptation as a good translation of texts and better music. This is not the place to engage in polemics nor is there any need to make an issue of it. One who reads the signs of the times will not even debate on the prudence of sailing with the current. In Asia it may be the only way to survive and be relevant. The disastrous Chinese Rites controversy has taught the Church in Asia that "unbending soldiers get no victories." When the signs of the times indicate that a country wishes to preserve its family and national traditions or to return to them, the Church will do well to follow in the same train or else face the embarrassment of an overstaying alien. In matters which are not essential to the Gospel the Church can learn from the wisdom of a Chinese aphorism: "The stiffest tree is the readiest for the axe; the strong and mighty topple from their place; the soft and yielding rise above them all."[2]

But expedience is not the sole nor the principal reason for adaptation. The main reason must be sought in the nature of the Church as the prolongation in time and space of the incarnation of the Word of God.[3] In the final analysis, the mystery of the incarnation is the theological

[1]Anscar J. Chupungco, ch. 3, "The Theological Principle of Adaptation," *Cultural Adaptation of the Liturgy* (New York: Paulist Press, 1982) 58–62. Reprinted by permission.

[2]Anscar J. Chupungco, *Towards a Filipino Liturgy* (Manila, 1976) 45.

[3]C. Vagaggini, *Il senso teologico della liturgia* (Rome: Edizioni Paoline, 1965) 290–97; Y. Raguin, "Indigenization of the Church," *Teaching All Nations* 6 (1969) 151–68; I. Omaecheverria, "The Dogma of the Incarnation and the Adaptation of the Church to Various Peoples," *Omnis Terra* 73 (1976) 277–83.

principle of adaptation. The Word of God, in assuming the condition of man, except sin, bound himself to the history, culture, traditions and religion of his own people. The Word was made flesh, that is to say, he became a Jew, a member of the chosen people. In the words of St. Paul, "From their flesh and blood came Christ who is above all, God for ever blessed" (Rom 9:5). More pointedly he writes, "When the appointed time came, God sent his Son, born of a woman, born subject to the law" (Gal 4:4). The Word of God, in other words, assumed not only what pertained to the human race, but also what was proper to the Jewish race. He inherited its natural traits, its genius, its spiritual endowments and its peculiar mode of self-expression. He was a Jew in every way, except in sin. The historicity of the incarnation demanded that he identify himself with his own people in heart and mind, in flesh and blood.

Far from limiting the sphere of the incarnation, such a vision guarantees the universality of Christ and his Gospel. The fact that the Word became a Jew gives us the assurance that in his resurrected state he can, even today, incarnate himself in different races and cultures through the faith of the Church and the celebration of his mystery. Because he identified himself with the people of Israel to whom God entrusted the promise of salvation, the incarnate Word can identify himself with the rest of humanity whom God called to take part in the promise made to Abraham.[4] The Christ of faith is the universal Christ, the man for others, because he was an historical Christ.

The once-for-all character of the incarnation is the key to the understanding of the Church's role in the work of salvation.[5] Through the Church, the non-repeatable historical event becomes actual, and Christ continues to be actively present in the world. The extent of the Church's incarnation in various races and cultures will be the extent of Christ's universality. The incarnation is an historical event, but its mystery lives on whenever the Church assumes the social and cultural conditions of the people among whom she dwells. Adaptation is thus not an option, but a theological imperative arising

---

[4]Pastoral Constitution on the Church in the Modern World, *GS* 58, "For God, revealing himself to his people to the extent of a full manifestation of himself in his Incarnate Son, has spoken according to the culture proper to different ages."

[5]D. Amelorpavadass, *Towards Indigenization of the Liturgy* (Bangalore: St. Paul Press, 1971) 14–20; O. Dominguez, "Ecclesial Indigenization: Vital Prerequisite for Catholicism," *Omnis Terra* 73 (1976) 285–89.

from incarnational exigency. The Church must incarnate herself in every race, as Christ incarnated himself in the Jewish race. *[Ad gentes]* AG 10 declares that "the Church must become part of all these groups for the same motive which led Christ to bind himself, in virtue of his incarnation, to the definite social and cultural conditions of those human beings among whom he dwelt."[6] The procedure proposed by the Council is one of integration, after the example of Christ who "entangled" himself with a particular people. This means that the Church cannot remain a stranger to the people with whom she lives; she must be adopted by it. This pluralistic view will not hurt the universality of the Church; on the contrary, it will foster it. For there can be no truly universal Church without truly local Churches. These, says AG 22, will have their own place in the ecclesial communion only if they adorn themselves with their own traditions and define their own identity as local churches. Underlying this statement is the Council's vision of catholic unity, borrowed and adapted from patristic theology, which speaks of the recapitulation of all things in Christ.[7] In the significant words of AG 22, "Particular traditions, together with the individual patrimony of each family of nations, can be illumined by the light of the Gospel, and then be taken up into Catholic unity."

Incarnation brings about mutual enrichment to the people who receive the faith and to the Church who incarnates herself. The local churches (AG focuses its attention on "young churches") must imitate the plan of the incarnation of the Word of God, so that, rooted in Christ and built upon the foundation of the apostles, they may "take to themselves in a wonderful exchange all the riches of the nations which were given to Christ as an inheritance." The *admirabile commercium* of the incarnation, whereby the Creator of the human race took to himself the nature of man and enriched it with the gift of divine nature, is the model that the Council proposes to the young churches.[8] With deep respect the Council acknowledges the presence of God in the cultures and endowments of various nations and encourages the

---

[6]S. Brechter, "Decree on the Church's Missionary Activity," *Commentary on the Documents of Vatican II*, ed. Herbert Vorgrimler (New York: Herder & Herder, 1967) 87–181.

[7]Reference is made to LG 13 where this citation is given: cf. St. Irenaeus, *Adv. haer.* III, 16, 6; III, 22, 1–3: PG 7, 925 C-926 A and 955 C-958.

[8]J. Daniélou, "Vatican II et les nouvelles Eglises," *Revue du Clergé Africain*, 24 (1969) 203–12.

churches to adorn themselves with the traditions of their people, with their wisdom and learning, with their arts and sciences, unto the glory of the Creator, the revelation of the Savior's grace and the proper arrangement of Christian life. In gathering together the scattered fruits of the Word sown among the peoples, the Church brings about by the power of the Spirit the eschatological fullness when God will be all in all. At the same time, the riches of the nations, illumined by the Gospel, receive from the fullness of Christ. By this wondrous exchange cultures and traditions are made all the richer.

The task of adaptation of the Church in Asia was given a fresh impetus and a sense of urgency by a letter of Paul VI to Asian bishops:

"The propagation of the Christian message must in no way cancel out or lessen these cultural and spiritual values, which constitute a priceless heritage. The Church must make herself in her fullest expression native to your countries, your cultures, your races. . . . Let the Church draw nourishment from the genuine values of venerable Asian religions and cultures."[9]

The letter is not a novelty in the area of adaptation. At most it is a timely application of the principles formulated by Vatican II or an echo of the 1659 instruction of Propaganda Fide to the Vicars Apostolic of China.[10] It is a clarion voice rousing the Asians to assume the task of adaptation. Asia has so much to offer to Christ and his Church. Its ancient cultures tested by the vicissitudes of time, its sacred traditions heavy with age and buttressed on the rock of Asian genius, its social refinements equaled only by the splendor of its religious rituals: from all these the Church can draw nourishment. These she must claim for Christ for whom they yearn and in whom they find their fullness.

The exchange between Christian cult and native culture involves certain adjustments in both. Cultural ingredients will have to pass through the death of purification and critical evaluation. They will have to shed off every claim to finality and assume their proper role as God's prophetic instruments for the revelation of Jesus Christ. When Christians adapted Jewish rituals to their worship, they re-

---

[9]Paul VI, "Letter to the Asian Bishops," *L'Osservatore Romano*, April 21, 1974.
[10]"Instructio Vicariorum Apostolicorum ad Regna Synarum Tonchini et Cocinnae Profiscentium," *Collectanea Sacrae Congregationis de Propaganda Fidei*, I (Rome, 1907).

garded them as types and prophecies of Christian realities, as shadows of Christian truth. Thus Justin Martyr gives the generic title of "prophet" to Old Testament readings at the liturgy of the Word.[11] And the Mass of the Roman rite regards them as prophetic preparations for the New Testament. In its traditional scheme of readings it called the Old Testament *propheta*.[12] This practice indicates the attitude of the Church when she adapts indigenous elements into the liturgy. Christian revelation holds primacy over every human creation. Everything must tend toward it. In practice this can be as simple as finding an indigenous element which can illustrate the message of the liturgy, or it can be as complex and delicate as introducing the reading of the sacred books of non-Christian religions in the liturgy. While the Church in the Philippines might not be confronted by the latter case, in India, which possesses sacred scriptures, the Church is put to the test.[13] To accept them she must conjure up solid theological reasons which satisfy the requirement of faith; to reject them she must be willing to face the consequence of further alienation from the Hindu world.

But contact with indigenous cultures implies certain accommodations also on the part of the Christian liturgy. The history of the Roman rite during its migration to the Franco-Germanic regions is an example of how culture irresistibly modifies what it receives.[14] And perhaps this is the best thing that can happen to the liturgy, if it is to become native to every culture. And since no culture is static, the liturgy will be constantly subjected to modifications. In this sense the incarnation of the Church's worship will be an ongoing process. While its basic content must remain unvaried, its structure, language and symbols will have to bear the mark of each culture. In one culture

[11] *I Apology 67*, 142.

[12] J. Jungmann, *The Mass of the Roman Rite* (New York, 1961): "It is plain that wherever the Old Testament appears in the readings of the fore Mass, it is not for its own sake, nor simply to have some spiritual text for reading, but it is chosen for its prophetic worth and its value as an illustration of the New Testament": 273–74.

[13] D. Amelorpavadass, *Towards Indigenization in the Liturgy*, 51–52.

[14] C. Vogel, *Introduction aux sources de l'histoire du culte chrétien au moyen âge* (Spoleto, 1975): "Pour l'histoire du culte chrétien notre periode est capitale: la liturgue latine qui s'est fixée à cette époque (*Hadrianum* supplémenté par Alcuin vers 801–804; Pontifical romano-germanique vers 950), et qui continue d'être celle de Eglise latine d'Occident, n'est pas purement romaine; elle est mixte, hybride ou, si l'on préfère, romano franque, voire romano-germanique": 43–44.

it may mean adaptation according to *[Sacrosanctum Concilium]* SC 38–39; in another it may mean a radical restructuring of forms, creation of new texts[15] and the use of native signs.

Liturgical pluralism is an incarnational imperative, rather than a concession of Vatican II.[16] The Church must prolong the incarnation of Christ in time and space. This she can realize only through the faith which she proclaims and celebrates. In other words, her liturgy must be embedded in the culture and traditions of the people. Liturgical pluralism is a necessary corollary to the premise of the Church's obligation to be local and native. Where the Church has become indigenous, where the hierarchy and laity come from the ranks of the people, there her liturgy will have to be native. A borrowed rite is an alien rite. There should be no dichotomy between the liturgy and the life of a native Church.

[15]"Pour une liturgie pleinement rénovée, on ne pourra pas se contener de textes traduits à partir d'autres langues. De nouvelles creations seront nécessaires. Il reste que la traduction des textes émanant de la tradition de l'Eglise constitue une excellente discipline et une nécessaire école à la rédaction de textes nouveaux": *Instructions officielles sur les nouveaux rites de la messe, le calendier, les traductions liturgiques* (Paris, 1969) 205.

[16]*GS* 58: "Living in various circumstances during the course of time, the Church, too, has used in her preaching the discoveries of different cultures to spread and explain the message of Christ to all nations, to probe it and more deeply understand it, and to give it better expression in the liturgical celebrations and in the life of the diversified community of the faithful."

Tércio Bretanha Junker

Justo L. González: Mystery and Fiesta Go Together

Justo González (1937–), one of the most prolific writers among Latino theologians, grew up as Protestant (Methodist) in Cuba, where most of his neighbors were Roman Catholic. González attended United Seminary in Cuba, received his M.A. at Yale, and was the youngest person to be awarded a Ph.D. in historical theology at Yale. His diligent participation and support for Hispanic theological education is coupled with tireless labor for the healthy growth of churches in Hispanic communities in the United States. He is the executive director of the Hispanic Theological Initiative and director of the Hispanic Summer Program managed by AETH *(Asociación para la Educación Teologica Hispana).*

A popular Jewish proverb declares: "Memory is the pillar of redemption and forgetfulness is the beginning of death." This concept is relevant for liturgical theology, and González, as a historian of the Church and its theology, is aware that historical memory is one of the most important ingredients of a Christian community's liturgical practice. Historical memory for González is not an "innocent historical perspective" but a "responsible remembrance," which "leads to responsible action." Thus, González is particularly concerned about the identity of the Hispanic community as a pilgrimage people, with its constant struggle of being an ethnic minority immersed in a dominant culture. Undoubtedly, his historical approach and liturgical insights contribute meaning, cultural identity, reclaiming of values, and hope for Hispanic celebrating communities. González describes active participation in the liturgy as "an act of empowerment and liberation."

The text that follows is an expressive contribution to liturgical theology. González' understanding of worship as *fiesta* reflects the
Latino sense of family, joy, interaction, multiplicity, inclusiveness, belonging, and the paradox between catholicity and particularity in
Christian worship. It is significant that the formal and transcendent
concept of the mystery acquires a festive and immanent dimension
among Latino communities. Hispanic worship includes embracing,
movement, dance, rhythm, shouts, and clapping. According to
González, these are issues of "faith and culture, culture and language, of worship and aesthetics." Latino worship is a creative process where "*fiesta* and mystery go together."

FOR FURTHER READING
Mañana: Christian Theology from a Hispanic Perspective. Nashville: Abingdon
Press, 1990; With Catherine G. González. *The Liberating Pulpit.* Nashville:
Abingdon Press, 1994; ¡*Alabadle! Hispanic Christian Worship.* Nashville: Abing-
don Press, 1996; With Catherine G. González. *In Accord: Let Us Worship.* New
York: Friendship Press, 1981.

Justo L. González

Worship as Fiesta[1]

Latino worship is a fiesta. It is a celebration of the mighty deeds of God. It is a get-together of the family of God. It is important to remember this in order to understand some of the features of our worship that sometimes disconcert or even upset those of the dominant culture.

First of all, because worship is a fiesta rather than a performance, it may be planned, but not rehearsed. Oftentimes, Hispanic worship seems chaotic. Indeed, there are some Hispanic pastors and other leaders who are remiss in that they do not even plan the celebration, but simply let it happen. But in most cases the difference between our worship and that of the dominant culture is that we think in terms of planning a party more than rehearsing a performance. Certainly, choirs and bands rehearse; but the service, as such, is never rehearsed. We plan, as one does for a fiesta, in order to make sure that the necessary arrangements have been made. In the case of a fiesta, one arranges for enough food and chairs, for a mariachi or some other kind of music, and for parking. But one cannot actually plan all the details, as one does in a performance, because the success of the fiesta depends on the attitude and participation of those present, not just on the performers. Likewise, in worship, the celebration is the people's fiesta, and therefore the pastor and other worship leaders can plan only up to a point, leaving the rest to the celebrants themselves—and, as many Hispanics would stress, to the guidance of the Holy Spirit.

[1]Excerpted from Justo L. González, from ch. 1, "Hispanic Worship: An Introduction," ¡Alabadle! Hispanic Christian Worship (Nashville: Abingdon Press, 1996) 20–27. Used by permission.

The very word *celebrant* is significant. In traditional ecclesiastical jargon, the "celebrant" is the one who presides. That is tantamount to calling the singers in a fiesta, or the master of ceremonies, the "celebrants." The fact is that in worship all participants are "celebrants," in that they are gathered to celebrate the fiesta of God and God's people. In this respect, Roman Catholic Latino worship has changed drastically since the days before Vatican II. When I was growing up, devout Catholics used to say that they were going to "hear" Mass—*voy a oír misa*. To them, the Mass was a performance—a supernatural performance, but a performance nonetheless—in which the priest and his entourage participated while the rest of the people watched and listened. But after Vatican II all of this changed. Most Hispanic Roman Catholic Masses in this country now reflect the culture of the people, and engage the people in active participation. In order to promote that participation, several Latino Masses have been produced, many of them with direct involvement of the worshipers in the creative process.

Sometimes people in the dominant culture complain that our worship is too emotional, too festive. We reply that all the books about worship state that we must offer God our best music and our best art, and we feel that there is nothing in the world as worthy of celebration as the gospel—the Good News of Jesus Christ. Therefore, we must give God in worship the fullest of our emotions and the liveliest of our celebration.

Furthermore, in our culture the most significant fiestas are connected with a sense of family—of an extended family that includes all sorts of relatives, and whose limits are never clearly defined. This is not a closely knit, tightly defined, and exclusive family, as when we speak of the nuclear family in the dominant culture—a family where one main value is privacy. It is rather a vast assemblage of people who are related in a multiplicity of ways, so that they have a sense of belonging, but not necessarily of excluding others. In this sense, our worship is a family celebration. We gather as God's children, to celebrate the new birth that makes us such, and in a large measure to celebrate having one another as family. At this point, it is important to remember that for many of us, as exiles and wanderers in this land, the extended family that is so important in our culture is no longer a reality. Therefore, the church often takes on this role. We gather to worship and to celebrate, very much as in the old country relatives from all over a valley would gather to celebrate Pancho's baptism, Josefa's wedding, or just being a family. That is one reason why in many of our churches there is a service practically every night. Our people need that sense of family in order to survive in an alien world; they need to celebrate God's future in the midst of an oppressive and alienating present. To those from well-installed positions in the present social order who would call this escapism, we reply that theirs is the true escapism—living and acting as if they could at once claim the gospel and ignore its promised future of love and justice.

A fiesta is characterized by movement and by sensuality. Significantly, this point is made . . . although with different words, by Allan Figueroa Deck when speaking of Catholic piety, and Samuel Solíván when speaking of Pentecostal worship. Often the room or sanctuary is decorated with vivid colors, and filled with the sounds of music and the smells of food. The people move around. They dance. They embrace. They shout. They cry. They laugh. They eat and they drink. Much of this is reflected in our worship.

[Referring to] Pentecostal worship, Dr. Solíván speaks of windows decorated with plastic to make them more colorful. In many churches the walls are decorated with quotations from scripture, with children's art, or with banners. All of these somehow remind us that we are part of this large family that is celebrating its great reunion. When we enter, there is sound—not always soft music—reminding us that this is the fiesta of the people of God. In many of our churches, both Catholic and Protestant, we move to rhythm as we sing—or at least clap our hands to rhythm. In some cases, people seem to be almost dancing to the tunes of hymns, the *coritos*, or some typical rhythm that has been adapted for worship. At times they are actually dancing. In Catholic churches as well as in some others, the smell of incense is part of the celebration.

Our church members tend to be very interactive. We embrace as we arrive; we embrace during the passing of the peace; and we embrace again before we leave. When the time comes for sharing concerns before intercessory prayer, many of us speak about things that in other circles would be considered too private to be discussed in such a large company. In prayer, many lift their hands to heaven. Others cross themselves. Still others sway as if moved by an imperceptible breeze. Some mumble their prayers, producing a hum throughout the congregation. Others cry out in longing or in joy. Sometimes more than one person prays out loud. In many cases, it is impossible to tell all that is going on. But then, the same is true of any good fiesta!

When I visit churches of the majority culture and speak of Hispanic worship, or of the rapid growth of Latino churches, the question often arises of multicultural worship. There is a legitimate concern behind that question, for the goal of Christian worship is that day when "a great multitude that no one can count, from every nation, from all tribes and peoples and languages," will worship together, "standing before the throne and before the Lamb" (Rev 7:9). Thus, the fact that today we find it difficult to worship together across cultural lines should cause us significant disquiet.

There are many issues at stake here—issues of faith and culture, of culture and language, of worship and aesthetics, and of aesthetics and culture—and this is not the place to try to resolve them. But at least there are some hints that Hispanic worship may offer to the Church at large.

The first of these is that we must reevaluate critically much of what we have inherited from the Reformation and, even more, from the Enlightenment. The Reformation quite rightly insisted on the value of worship in the vernacular. But then the Enlightenment led us to a view of worship in which there is no place for that which cannot be clearly understood. The reason for the use of the vernacular, we were told, is that people must understand what is being said and what they are saying in worship. Otherwise, worship becomes gibberish and mumbo jumbo.

There is much truth in that view. Certainly, worship that does not engage the mind fails to engage the entire human being. We must hear the Word of God with at least sufficient understanding that we may know what it is that God requires of us; and we must also hear it with sufficient understanding that we may have at least a glimpse of what it is we are gathered to celebrate.

But there is a grave error in that view, which reduces human nature to the intellectual. There is much we do not understand that is nevertheless of great significance to us. (It is said that Pablo Picasso, upon hearing a man comment that he could not understand one of his paintings, asked, "Sir, what did you have for lunch today?" "Why, steak," said the man. "Did you enjoy it?" asked Picasso. "Certainly," came the reply. To which Picasso then asked, "And, did you understand it?") I do not need to understand Dvořák's Fifth Symphony in order to enjoy it, and I don't have to enjoy Wagner's music to be overcome by it. Yet much Protestant mainline worship seems to be based on the premise that what is significant in worship is what we understand—to which perhaps is added a bit of music we can enjoy. That is why children are so often left out. In a Presbyterian church that I attend occasionally, children are given "worship activities" to entertain them while the adults go about the business of worship. That is also why the uneducated and illiterate are excluded along with the children. There is no mystery left to cut us all down to size, to make us like those little children to whom belongs the kingdom of heaven. We think that we are excluding the children, the uneducated, and the unsophisticated, when in truth we are excluding ourselves—or, we exclude them from our worship, and thereby exclude ourselves from the heavenly banquet.

This is where the Latino worship experience may be able to make a significant contribution to the Church at large. Fiesta and mystery go together. In a fiesta, as in a steak dinner, we are not required to understand everything that goes on. We are not even expected to agree with everything that everyone says. We are simply invited to join the party, to allow ourselves to be carried and defined by it, to make our own contribution, whatever that might be, and above all to celebrate whatever the fiesta is about. In churches representing different Latino subgroups—which are rapidly increasing in numbers—several variants of Spanish are spoken. Sometimes someone even says something that in another's version of Spanish is offensive or even lewd—in which case we are momentarily shocked, then smile and move on. In those churches, not all the music represents our own taste, but we have learned to live and to worship together because, after all, we are family. In Catholic Hispanic churches, the sense of mystery at the Eucharist is heightened rather than lessened. In Latino Pentecostal churches, and in many others, it is not unusual for someone to speak in "tongues." In that case, if there is someone to interpret, it is done: but if there is no such person available, the unintelligible words are still considered part of the worship of God.

It is for all of these reasons that I said at the beginning of this essay that perhaps it is in our very multiplicity—in the impossibility of defining and describing us as a whole—that our greatest contribution to the worship of the Church at large lies. We have learned how to worship together, even though we are not all alike. We have learned how to worship together in congregations in which people come from radically different strata of society, where some speak mostly

English and very little Spanish, while others know mostly Spanish and very little English, and where there are several different variants of Spanish spoken. We have learned to worship and celebrate together even across significant theological lines. We have learned how to do this by combining a spirit of fiesta with a profound sense of mystery. The fiesta makes us all participants, and thus leads to the mystery of transgenerational, transclass, and transcultural communication. The mystery reminds us of the otherness of God, and thus makes it possible for all to celebrate the glory of one another's otherness. In mystery and awe we celebrate the fiesta, until the final veil shall be removed, and in fiesta we shall all worship together the everlasting mystery of God. It is our prayer and our hope that the rest of God's family—including our monolingual English-speaking sisters, brothers and cousins—may share in the same mystery and the same joy!

Laurence Hull Stookey

Harold Dean Trulear: Black Preaching as Microcosm of Christian Worship

Harold Dean Trulear works within a broad sociological framework; he has particularly been interested in sociological factors within the African American community and church. He has written articles on Black ecumenism, Black pastoral theology, Black secular music, Black spirituality, and worship.

Trulear is a Phi Beta Kappa graduate of Morehouse College and earned a master's degree and doctorate at Drew University; his Ph.D. dissertation was "An Analysis of the Formative Roles of Ideational and Social Structure in the Development of Afro-American Religion." From 1990 to 1996 he was dean and professor of church and society at New York Theological Seminary. He has also served on the faculties of Drew University and Eastern Baptist Theological Seminary in addition to having done adjunct teaching and lecturing at a variety of other schools. He has published nearly fifty articles, sermons, and reviews in journals, including *The American Baptist Quarterly, The Journal of Religious Thought,* and *Prism.* Trulear has a particular interest in church music, and a number of his works have appeared in *Black Sacred Music: A Journal of Theomusicology.* He serves on the national boards of InterVarsity Christian Fellowship and Evangelicals for Social Action. Trulear is director of the Partnership for Research on Religion and At-Risk Youth and vice president of Church Collaborative Initiatives at Public/Private Ventures in Philadelphia. He also serves on the ministerial staffs of both Zion Baptist Church and St. Mary's Episcopal Church in Ardmore, Pennsylvania.

In the following article Trulear particularly looks at African American worship (with specific attention to the sermon). He expounds on what is often a neglected matter: the interrelationship of sociological factors (in this instance, the legacy of racism and oppression) in relation to theological content (specifically the paschal mystery). He very helpfully sets the character of preaching in the Afro-American church within the framework of the theological categories of eschatology, revelation, and a rhetorical drama that conveys the reality of the divine drama of redemption. Thus he illustrates and substantiates his thesis that "the black preaching event is a microcosm of the whole of good Christian worship."

FOR FURTHER READING

"Good Religion, Spirituality, and African Americans." *Cross Currents* 46, no. 4 (1996–97); "Theomusicology and Christian Education." *Black Sacred Music: A Journal of Theomusicology* 3, no. 2 (1989); "To Make a Wounded Wholeness: Disability and Liturgy in the African American Context." *Human Disability and the Service of God.* Ed. Nancy Eiseland and Don Saliers. Nashville: Abingdon Press, 1998.

Harold Dean Trulear

The Sacramentality of Preaching[1]

Divine worship is eschatological, revelatory, and dramatic. It declares the ultimacy of God's reign and points to the day of "the fullness of the times; that is, the summing up of all things in the heavens and things upon the earth" (Eph 1:10).

Divine worship reveals the perspective of almighty God from which the devoted are bid to interpret or to reinterpret all the activities of everyday life: eating, sleeping, personal relationships, working, playing. Worship defines being in the world in a different mode from that offered by the world itself.

Divine worship provides the context for the rehearsal of life in the reign of God; it is a call for believers to take their places in the unfolding of eschatological history and to act out life in Christ to the fullest.

These three qualities of worship are ever present and interrelated; each sheds light on the task of preaching. They are also powerfully present in the experience of black preaching and worship, and serve as lenses within that particular experience through which we can view the universality of the Christian witness. My task in this essay is not to examine the totality of black Christian experience and spirituality.[2] Rather, given our focus on the central symbols of worship, we will use the insights of the black Christian tradition and its emphasis on the crucifixion and resurrection to reflect on the task of preaching.[3]

[1]Excerpted from Harold Dean Trulear, "The Sacramentality of Preaching," ch. 30, *The Landscape of Praise: Readings in Liturgical Renewal,* ed. Blair Gilmer Meeks (Valley Forge, Pa: Trinity Press International, 1996) 202–10. Copyright 1996, The Liturgical Conference. Reproduced by permission of Trinity Press International, Harrisburg, Pa.

[2]See Luther E. Smith, Jr., "Spirituality and Social Freedom," *Liturgy: In Spirit and Truth* (Washington, D.C.: Liturgical Conference) 5, no. 3 (1986) 47–51.

[3]Perhaps the volume that deals best with black preaching and its implications for the universal homiletic task is Henry Mitchell's vastly underrated

My own fascination with the relationship between preaching and worship in the black church tradition and in the whole of Christian witness was spawned during a conversation with a graduate student early in my teaching career. Aware of my decision to enter the Baptist ministry after twenty-plus years as an Episcopal layman, she remarked, "I don't see how you could have handled being an Episcopalian." Curious about her remark and still in love with the communion of my youth, I bid her qualify that statement. "Well," she continued, "week after week you use the same prayers, the same mass, the same service. Where is the room for spontaneity? Where is the room for the Holy Ghost?"

My response to her did not consist of a defense of Anglican liturgy. Instead, I found myself thinking about the major role that liturgical order plays in the black free church traditions.[4] Examples of order, symbol and sacrament come quickly to mind. There is liturgical order in the procession of black church choirs, their members often dressed in brightly colored robes, reflecting the joyous nature of life in Christ.[5] There is deep meaning in the symbolic gesture of handshaking, i.e., greeting one another during worship as the radical recognition of mutual personhood under the auspices of God. This eschatological identity stands in stark contrast to the depersonalization inherent in the institutional and interpersonal racism in the world. There is sacramental reality in the preaching event as the preacher declares the gospel with an accompanying ecstasy that assures the congregation of the "real presence" of grace. In short, I found myself excited about the spiritual intuitiveness of a people from whom many of the rites and symbols of the Christian tradition had been withheld but who nevertheless captured the meaning of the

---

The Recovery of Preaching (New York: Harper & Row, 1977). See also H. Beecher Hicks, *Preaching Through a Storm* (Grand Rapids: Zondervan Publishing House, 1987); Gardner C. Taylor, *How Shall They Preach?* (Elgin, Ill.: The Progressive Baptist Publishing House, 1977).

[4]This idea is expanded in the author's "The Lord Will Make a Way, Somehow: Worship and the African-American Story," *Journal of the Interdenominational Theological Center* 13, no. 1 (1985) 87–104.

[5]The late Wendell Whalum, one of the finest church musicians and musicologists to dedicate his talents to black church worship and liturgy, details this and parallel phenomena in "Black Hymnody," in Emmanuel McCall, ed., *Black Church Life-Styles* (Nashville: Abingdon Press, 1986) 83–103.

gospel and connected it to their own rites and symbols, which are faithful to the witness of the tradition.

Subsequent study of and participation in black church worship revealed to me that the black preaching event is a microcosm of the whole of good Christian worship. There is the declaration of eschatological reality, the proffer of the divine perspective, and the invitation to take one's place in the dramatic movement of God in this life. All three of those hinge on understanding the connection between the Easter event, its liturgical expression and contemporary life. In the black church tradition, it is imperative that one see the reality of everyday life mediated through the crucifixion and resurrection of Jesus Christ. Preaching in the black church and in any church gains its authenticity from its ability to relate the sufferings of Christ, as well as the victory of the resurrection, to what's happening now.

ESCHATOLOGY AND MARGINALITY

The preaching event announces a new order; a new reality has come. Eschatological preaching derives its power, in part, from declaring a distinction between the old order and the new, *nomos* and grace, the suffering of this world and the victory of the next. It is a hollow victory that is announced without a recounting of the reality of the battle, i.e., the suffering that is part of and parcel of life in this world. The resurrection has meaning precisely because of the crucifixion.

Black preachers have always taken suffering seriously, since it presents itself as an ever-present reality for our community. Slavery, segregation and discrimination on one hand, depersonalization, miseducation and inequality of opportunity on the other, have created the conditions of marginality that are painful in a world that celebrates the value of belonging. Conformity to the majority opinion is an itch engendered by the powerful to enhance the sale of all sorts of scratching devices designed to make one depend on anything but God to be fully human. Being marginal hurts; it leads to psychological damage, the withholding of goods and services and literal physical danger.

But marginality also begets a sensitivity to suffering that enables the marginal community to understand something of the passion. Jesus' suffering becomes recognizable, as pain wears a neighbor's face and the crucifixion's hammer has a familiar ring. The joy that comes as a result of preaching the gospel—the good news of the kingdom and the eschatological reality ushered in with the resurrection of Christ—is manifest because that reality stands in stark contrast to the reality of current suffering and marginality. The resurrection means "trouble doesn't last always"; it announces that there is an alternative to the predicament of complicity in this world as a determinant of personhood.

Could it be that it is in failing to realize the marginality of the Christian message that we fail to impress its power on the congregation? Could it be that in failing to enable people to see the pain of this life, we also fail to help them see the glory of the next? Could it be that people can't see the power of the resurrection because they have been anesthetized to their own passion and hence are numb to the passion of Christ? Could it be that the Easter they see is more a baptism of Western prosperity than the announcement of a new humanity available in Christ?

The point is not that Blacks own any spiritual superiority but that conversion to a new world rests on dissatisfaction with the old. When the preacher declares, "We're all God's children," the words are radical for those who have constantly been told otherwise. Perhaps this means that the Easter preacher must break open the experiences of his or her community in which the new eschatological identity is being eschewed in favor of idolatry, narcissism and alienation.

PREACHING AS REVELATION
This does not mean that Easter preaching degenerates into a lengthy harangue, listing the sins that so easily beset us. Preaching is more than a moral diatribe. Preaching does not read us the riot act; it does something far more radical. It dares to say that God is watching the world, and then it declares what God sees. God sees and knows the world in which people must live. God knows their suffering, even as God knew the awful passion of Christ. Preaching not only declares that God's eyes are on the world, but in the best of the black tradition, it claims to represent those eyes and to say what they see. In this sense perhaps more than any other, preaching is sacramental, and the preacher herself or himself becomes the symbol of grace in the midst of the congregation.

* * *

If the preacher in the black church can rehearse the struggles of the people, he or she does more than stir up wounds and heartaches. He or she fashions that trouble into a litany in which every sentence of sorrow is punctuated with an exclamation point of God's care. Using the words of familiar songs, the preacher declares, "Jesus knows all about our struggles," or "He knows just how much we can bear." Or heightening the empathy between the passion of Jesus and the trials of the congregation, the preacher recalls the words of the old spiritual

"Nobody knows de trouble I see
Nobody knows but Jesus
Nobody knows de trouble I see
Glory, Hallelujah!"

There it is: the sentence of sorrow punctuated with joy. And joy because Jesus knows; i.e., God sees the difficulty of this life. Sorrow and joy, crucifixion and resurrection—the hearers recognize their own story in the preacher's words.

WATCHERS FOR GOD

The preacher as sacramental presence must not only see; he or she must also offer an interpretation of life. C. L. Franklin, regarded by many as the prince of black preachers until his death in 1984, talks about this interpretive role in the recorded sermon, "Watchman, What of the Night?"

"That cry was an inquiring cry, 'Watchman, What of the Night?' What are the times? What time of history is this? What time of trouble is this? For after all history is God's Big Clock . . . and inasmuch as we cannot see within the next five minutes in our system of time, in God's system of time, in God's clock of history we can't see. We must call out to our prophets as Edom or the Edomites did in those long days of bygone days. Men who can pierce the future. Men who can interpret the future. Men who can see beyond now . . . and inquire of them, 'Watchmen, What of the Night?'"

The preacher as sacramental presence is a listening presence. Therefore, Franklin hears the cry of the people and is in touch with their passion. He even plays their part: "We are blinded by the mystery of history" and the "destiny of time." We are unable to "read the writing" on God's scroll of history:

"Only God can reveal it to us, or reveal it to His men of mystery. And so, as the Edomites did thousands of years ago, with anxiety of the future, with questions of the future, we inquire to the men of vision who walk upon the lofty walls of God's inspiration, 'Watchman, What of the Night?'"

Franklin then performs the role of the watchman, as he reports on the tense state of international affairs. He covers events from the emergence of Sudan as an independent nation to the Hungarians' resistance to communism. The report highlights the struggle of oppressed peoples around the world. These struggles are indicative of the human predicament. The signs of international struggle indicate a seemingly unpredictable future:

"We're living in times that are like the nighttime
We don't know what the morning will bring.
We see oppressed people
Not only abroad
But also in our own lands
Becoming impatient for full citizenship.
Not only in Africa,
Not only in Egypt,
Not only in the Arab world,
Not only in Germany,
Not only in China,
Not only in India,
But we see—
We see Montgomery, Alabama,
We see Florida,
We see other parts of our own land
Impatient for world brotherhood and full citizenship."

He has captured their struggle in his words and therefore has announced that God sees. In relating the community's suffering to global suffering, he shows just how big God's vision is. More succinctly put, the sacramental presence is that of an omniscient God. God not only sees, God acts!

God will win, declares Franklin. We have to wait, but waiting is not passive. Franklin calls for an active waiting: "Just a few more days. A little while to wait, a little while to pray. A little while to sing. A little while to labor, a little while to watch."[6]

[6]Gerald L. Davis, *I Got the Word in Me and I Can Sing It You Know: The Performed African American Sermon* (Philadelphia: Westminster Press, 1985) 59–60.

Resurrection is sure to come. The presence of a seeing, saving God guarantees it.

DRAMA IN BLACK PREACHING

The reality of trouble in this life has been identified, and it has been proclaimed that God is watching the people's passion. The eschatological age has been announced in the declaration of the resurrection. But one task remains. The congregation must now participate in the ritual of worship as the celebration of new life. They must take their places in the drama that moves from crucifixion to resurrection.

Here, the dialogical nature of black preaching becomes a way of inviting participation in the drama. As the sermon rehearses the reality of suffering and passion, the images and examples used evoke participatory responses from the congregation. The difficulty of hard labor is captured in the image of "our foreparents toiling from 'can to can't'" (i.e., "can see," meaning dawn, to "can't see," meaning dusk or night). The pressures of urban life are recited, from "drugs on every street corner" to "nobody knows your name downtown." The reality of employment problems that cut across class lines is called to mind: "We're the last hired and the first fired." Voices from the congregation affirm each proposition. "That's right," "Tell it," "Amen," "Well." People are hearing *their* stories from the pulpit.

How important it is, then, that the Easter preacher knows the congregation's Good Friday stories. The responses may be verbal or overly demonstrative, though one may argue that they ought to be, if there is liberty in Christ. But when people hear their Good Friday story, their own passion narrative, they are bound to respond. A nodding head, a wincing face, a heaving sigh, a knowing glance, may be the roots of response coming to bloom.

The black preacher has other homiletic tools that invite participation in the drama. Such admonitions as "Are you praying with me?" "Can I get a witness?" and "I believe somebody here knows what I'm talking about" are standard invitations to dialogue. More stern phrases such as "You don't hear me," "If you can't say 'Amen,' say 'Ouch'" and "Wish I was in the right church" push a recalcitrant worshiper to witness to the truth, even if it is painful.

As the sermon progresses and the stories of the congregation have been effectively identified with the passion of Christ, the preacher must now proclaim the victory of Christ through the resurrection. That the new order has come has already been announced. But having led the people through their passion and the passion of Christ, the even greater announcement is that the new order has come *to you!* In black preaching, this announcement comes in power as the closing section of a sermon. Sermon closings have long been of great importance to black preachers. The oft-told story of Martin Luther King is that he frequently began developing his closing first and then worked on the rest of the sermon.

As the preacher approaches the closing, the emotional intensity mounts. It is clear that she or he is preparing to describe the word of Easter victory, if only by noting the intensity of the conflict inherent in the passion story. Soon, the preacher indicates that the Holy Spirit's power is manifesting itself, either through the declaration "I feel my help coming on" or through the development of a chanted and more rhythmic style,[7] or even through increasing the volume and animation of voice and body.

While some may view this as theatrical antics, the reality is that all good worship is theatrical or better put, dramatic. When done properly and in awe of the one whose gospel we preach, this move into an intense spiritual state is the same as the priest invoking the presence of Christ in the eucharist. It is the transubstantial moment in which the word is most intensely sacramental. "I feel my help coming on" is a moment in which the word is consecrated in a manner not unlike the elements in the eucharist. The ensuing ecstasy of both preacher and congregation are, then, celebrations of the real presence.

Three formats of sermon closing are traditional in black preaching. All derive their power from the crucifixion-resurrection motif; all involve passion and victory.[8] The first is the preacher's own testimony.

[7]Mervyn Warren calls this "effects style"; see his *Black Preaching: Truth and Soul* (Washington, D.C.: University Press of America, 1977). See also Pearl Williams-Jones, "The Musical Quality of Black Religious Folk Ritual," *Spirit* 1, no. 1 (1977) 21–30; Willis Laurence James, "The Romance of the Negro Folk Cry," *Phylon* 16, no. 19 (1955) 15–30.

[8]The following sermon-closing examples represent a composite of recorded messages from "Black Worship and Religious Identity," a research project undertaken in 1984 with sponsoring grants from the Association of Theological Schools of the United States and Canada and the New Jersey State Historical Commission. These sermon excerpts, preached by Fred LaGarde, William A. Jones, Ernest Lyght, and Ruth Satchell, could have come from any number of preachers who could consider these phrases to be in the public domain. So often do they occur in black preaching that William B. McClain, professor of homiletics and worship at Wesley Theological Seminary in Washington, D.C., considers them part of "The Black Litany."

Sometimes she or he recalls the events of her or his own conversion, often embellished in great figurative language:

"I was on my way to hell
Not fit to live and too mean to die.
When Jesus stepped in
And spoke peace to my dying soul.
He picked me up, turned me 'round
Planted my feet on solid ground."

At other times the testimony is about victory over some trouble in the preacher's life. Financial difficulty, problems securing education or employment, confrontations with racism or a battle with some other "messenger of Satan" will be recalled and the victory affirmed in the words of another popular song:

"Trouble in my way
I have to cry sometime
Lay awake at night
That's alright
Jesus will fix it, after awhile!"

In the second format, the preacher paints a picture of heaven. Whether in the general language of "No more cryin' there, no more dyin' there" or whether made particularly relevant in words such as "no more racism, no more 'Yessuh boss,'" it is clear that the predicament of this life *will* end and that a new order *will* emerge. The implication is, of course, that this new order engenders hope to live in this world.

The third format is a rehearsal of the actual crucifixion and resurrection. Black preachers have gone to untold lengths to portray vividly the events of passion week. Good Friday's heartache is given clear view:

"They put him through the mockery of a trial.
They put a crown of thorns on his head.
They whipped him all night long.
The crowd yelled, 'Crucify him!'
Soldiers laughed at him
Bystanders mocked him
Disciples deserted him
Clouds began to gather

Sky grew dark
Lightning played its zigzag games of tag
And with a loud voice,
Jesus cried and gave up the ghost."

"But," cautions a seasoned preacher, "don't leave him in the grave."

"But early Sunday morning
While the dew was still on the roses
An angel rolled away the stone
And Jesus . . .
My master
Jesus . . .
My redeemer
Jesus . . .
My savior
Jesus . . .
Lily of the valley
Bright and morning star
Jesus . . .
Rose of Sharon
Jesus . . .
Mary's baby
Jesus . . .
The only Son of God
Got up from the grave
Declaring
'All power is given unto Me in heaven and in earth.'"

Worship has come full cycle. The same God whose eschatological order has been proclaimed to be the ultimate reality raises Jesus from the dead. As Jesus is raised from the dead, so too are the hearers, for their stories have been identified with the passion of Christ. Joy comes as the people are raised to new life in Christ in vicarious resurrection through the preacher's rehearsal of the crucifixion-resurrection motif. The celebration is not a shadow or a sham. It is the rehearsal of reality. Christ has been present in the word, identifying with the passion of the hearers and ushering in a new life by the resurrection.

9

How Are Liturgy and Life Related?

One aspect of liturgy may reflect its cosmic and eternal dimensions, in which we join the song of the angels and the "music of the spheres" in praising God. But if liturgy's head is sometimes in the clouds of heaven, its feet are firmly planted in the here and now of human life. Don Saliers will not settle for superficial, "feel-good" worship. We are reminded of the role of lament in authentic worship. Saliers' "Myrtie" joins Kavanagh's "Mrs. Murphy" as representatives of the "unnamed faithful" whose voices liturgical theologians need to hear.

Ruth Duck leads us into a consideration of liturgical language in the context of a theology of baptism that recognizes the inextricable connection between liturgical action and sacramental living. This gifted hymn-writer, whose worship resources are widely used, shares her work as liturgical scholar and theologian in an essay written especially for this volume. The brief excerpt by Ed Phillips is included because it so clearly articulates some of the key considerations in reflections on liturgy and ethics to which liturgical theologians need to attend.

Joyce Ann Zimmerman has written the final article, bringing many of the themes of this volume together. Her post-critical reflections on the paschal mystery provide a far-reaching perspective on which to build future liturgical theologies.

Now it's your turn. You've read and thought about and argued with and revised and amended the concepts included in these pages. What difference will it make to how you design and lead and experience liturgy? How do you understand this "work of, and on behalf of, the people" now? For finally you see, it is not the reform of the liturgy that is crucial but the transformation of our lives as the body of Christ. And in that mission we are "stewards of the mysteries of God" (1 Cor 4:1).

Ruth C. Duck

Don E. Saliers: Humanity at Full Stretch before God

Don E. Saliers (1937–), professor of theology and worship and director of the sacred music program at Emory University in Atlanta, has contributed immeasurably to the field of liturgical theology. His theological reflections on the spirituality and aesthetics of liturgy are complemented by empirical research and dialogue that keep his thinking grounded in the life of congregations. A composer of liturgical music, Saliers is Sunday organist/choirmaster at Emory's Cannon Chapel. He has contributed to the renewal of worship in the United Methodist Church as well as lecturing, preaching, and leading worship throughout North America with Christians of many denominations. He is a past president of the North American Academy of Liturgy and a recipient of its 1992 Berakah Award, recognizing his contributions to the field of liturgical studies.

Saliers' foremost contribution to liturgical studies is his thought concerning how, as we bring our "humanity at full stretch before God" over time, prayer and worship form us in Christian character and transform us through God's self-communication in Christ. In the present chapter Saliers reminds us that Christian liturgy must be hospitable to the whole range of human experience and suffering (pathos); it must lament life's crushing tragedies and evils, give thanks for life's beauty, and express our joy and hope. Yet liturgy does not focus on ephemeral emotion or self-expression but on the glorification of God and the sanctification of human persons and communities. Thus human pathos encounters the divine ethos "in which human energies and passions are transformed in light of the passion of God for the world."

Four characteristic aspects of liturgy "school" Christians in the divine ethos. First, in liturgy we learn the language of gratitude, which can be expressed spontaneously but only adequately developed as communities continually gather around Scripture, font, and table. Second, we discern how to "speak the truth in love"—to listen to the cries of the world and our own hearts and to voice them honestly. Third, liturgy is "a school for remembering who God has promised to be" and thus of cultivating hope that God will transform this world. Finally, our common worship teaches us to join our prayer with that of Jesus Christ, interceding for healing and justice in and out of season.

Saliers' linking of "humanity at full stretch" with the transforming grace of God is an essential voice within ecumenical liturgical studies, lest those who reflect upon and participate in worship be so caught up in its beauty and wonder they ignore the world God loves. It is also a distinctively Wesleyan voice, integrating divine initiative and grace expressed through liturgy and sacraments with authentic human response as part of the process of sanctification.

FOR FURTHER READING

The Soul in Paraphrase: Prayer and the Religious Affections. 1st ed., Seabury Press, 1980; 2nd ed., Akron, Ohio: Order of St. Luke Publications, 1992; *Worship and Spirituality.* 1st. ed., The Westminster Press, 1984; 2nd. ed., Akron, Ohio: Order of St. Luke Publications, 1996; With Hoyt L. Hickman and others. *New Handbook of the Christian Year.* Nashville: Abingdon Press, 1992; *Worship as Theology: Foretaste of Glory Divine.* Nashville: Abingdon Press, 1994; ed. with Nancy L. Eiesland. *Human Disability and the Service of God: Reassessing Religious Practice.* Nashville: Abingdon Press, 1998.

Don E. Saliers

Human Pathos and Divine Ethos[1]

INITIAL SOUNDINGS: LITURGY AND PATHOS

We have all been taught to rethink worship as communal action: response, dialogue, and communion with God. Communal worship is first and last blessing God, praising and giving thanks. Certainly the whole economy of the Christian liturgy is much more than praising, thanking, and blessing, but it is rooted and grounded in these. Such praise and thanksgiving is evident in our eucharistic prayers: "It is right, and a good and joyful thing, always and everywhere to give thanks to you." If only we were to take that in with our lives over time, we could understand ourselves and our world so differently. The language of praise, the language of the vocative in addressing God is *enacted* by human beings in our speaking, listening, singing, eating, and drinking.[2]

When we come to the liturgy on the Lord's Day, "until the day of the Lord," we gather in that *deep pathos of memory* of God with us. Still deeper is the *pathos of hoping* for God's promises yet to be fulfilled. Without remembering that creation is a gift, without remembering that our lives are gifts, without remembering that the whole history of God with the earth points toward the liberation from

[1]Excerpted from Don E. Saliers, "Human Pathos and Divine Ethos," ch. 1, *Worship as Theology: Foretaste of Glory Divine* (Nashville: Abingdon Press, 1994) 25–38. Reprinted by permission.

[2]Like many engaged in recent liturgical studies, I have been deeply influenced by developments in ritual theory and analysis. The best starting point may be found in Ronald L. Grimes, *Beginnings in Ritual Studies* (Washington, D.C.: University Press of America, 1982). The "performative" character of living liturgy is essential to any subsequent theological work on the basis of liturgy.

bondage and death made real in Jesus, we can never begin to grasp the hope that is offered to us in the symbols, words, and the ritual actions of the Christian assembly. Without the desire and yearning for history to be different, memory becomes nostalgia or self-serving.[3] If we are to make any sense at all of God's offer of salvation, we must attend to the pathos of those memories and that hope. Born as response to God—who God is and what God has done—authentic liturgical life lifts up all that is human to the transforming power of communal life animated in the Spirit. The study of liturgy is everywhere and always the study of what real men and women do and suffer in their lives. Liturgy thus enacts that which devotional prayer alone cannot. The assembly of believers, the gathered body, comes out of the pathos of living and struggling, seeking God together with restless hearts. This itself is an intensification of social being before God. The very act of remembering who God is and what God has done confers dignity and honor and deepens the pathos of those who gather. "You have held us worthy to stand before you and [praise] you." Later we must ask how this corporate sense of social being is possible in contemporary American life.

Liturgy is an intentionally gathered community in mutual dialogue with God's self-communication. We are to bring our *pathos* to the time and place, to the book and the table of living memory that is God speaking to us. In every generation, God calls forth a people in their time and circumstance to be a holy people. Therefore, liturgy is the art of acknowledging the Holy One who creates us, who loves us into freedom, and who knows the pathos of our lives.

Let us then consider some initial definitions of liturgy. Think first of the Church gathered, as the ongoing prayer and word of Jesus Christ—and the ongoing self-giving of God in and through Christ's body in the world made alive by the Spirit. Christian liturgy is something prayed *and* something enacted, not something thought about or merely "experienced." Liturgy is a common art of the people of God in which the community brings the depth of emotion of our lives to the ethos of God. In these acts we discover who we are, but also and primarily, we discover who God is in this art. If understood fully, liturgy is doing God's will and work in the world while providing

[3]The contributions of feminist and liberation theologies to a rethinking of what is remembered and how the process of remembering takes place are critical here. The notion of retrieving forgotten or suppressed memories in the tradition, both biblical and liturgical, is restoring crucial dimensions of *anamnesis*.

human beings with a time and a place for recalling who God is and who we are before God, and identifying the world to itself—what it is in God's eyes—the pathos of this terrifying and beautiful world. Therefore the ongoing prayer of Jesus, and the ongoing word and self-giving of Jesus, shapes our existence and brings *us* to expression. Worship that focuses primarily on self-expression fails to be worship in Spirit and in truth.

If this is so, that the art of joining Jesus in his liturgy is God's ongoing work, then the promise of real life is given and received. Here the essential connections between communal worship, devotional prayer, and work are found. The words, the texts, the songs, the actions, and the symbols of the liturgy, *wait* for us, just like the Holy Scriptures wait in each context for a fresh rereading. Symbols without the life experiences of the believers brought to the liturgy can indeed become empty. Individual faith without the symbols of liturgical action can remain blind and isolated. Joseph Gelineau, in *The Liturgy Today and Tomorrow*, reminds us of this connection by observing: "Only if we come to the liturgy without our hopes and fears, without our longings and hungers, will the rite symbolize nothing and remain an indifferent or curious object."[4]

Our pathos, the reality of human life, our daily struggle to make sense of longings, hopes, fears, joys, provides an experiential link. In the language of the Second Vatican Council, "full, active, and conscious participation" in this art depends in the first instance upon our acquaintance with prayer and daily life over the whole range of our humanity. Put another way, participation in the liturgy requires our humanity at full stretch. Let us say that liturgical celebration is that place of convergence where our lives are brought together about the book, the font, and the table of the Lord in which the grace of God becomes audible, visible, palpable, kinetic.[5] In this way the ongoing prayer and work of Christ in the Church must always and everywhere be *both* fully communal and deeply and profoundly personal. This reminds us of the central paradox of the Christian life itself. Christ, in and through the Spirit, prays for the world and for us in and through our prayers in his name. Hence, Christian liturgy both forms us in certain characteristic ways of being human, and brings these things to expression through the arts of worship.

[4]Joseph Gelineau, *The Liturgy Today and Tomorrow* (New York: Paulist Press, 1978).

[5]See Saliers, *Worship as Theology*, ch. 13.

The very act of gathering is a slow, inexorable dance by which we assemble in the name of and by invitation of Jesus. One can see this in the gathering of very ordinary people on an ordinary Sunday morning in a very ordinary church. When we least expect it, on the most "flat EKG" Sunday you can imagine, people gather and we may not have noticed the inexorable dance because it seems so habitual and so unremarkable. Then they make their way to the altar and with those rough hands that know the farmer's art or skill of a carpenter or that have cared for many a person by many a sickbed, stretch out and with trembling receive their own mystery back. Yes, we have gathered, and this dance and song is real. Some traditions go on to sing the question, "Shall we gather at the river?" Suddenly the ordinary gathering becomes itself a metaphor for what is given in the invitation itself. The words and the dance mean *more* than we can speak.

A wonderful story out of my own ministry may help make this point about the pathos we bring. Several years ago, a former student of mine who had a parish in Florida invited me to come down shortly after the Christmas season and spend a day with him. After the Sunday service, he said, "We're going to see Myrtie." So I went with Gary to see Myrtie, driving out to one of those low, one-story buildings surrounded by the parking lot into which you enter and see the wheelchairs. And you smell the smells of a place of old age and dying. Being the Christmas season, there were many in their housecoats with small trinkets pinned here and there, and the Christmas carols softly reverberated on a Wurlitzer somewhere.

Down the hall and to the last of the doors at the end of this long hallway, we came to Myrtie's room. There she was, expecting us. Gary said, "Myrtie, this is Don; Don, this is Myrtie." And Myrtie looked at me and she said, "Oh boy." We sat down and Gary said, "The children made some Christmas gifts for you this morning, Myrtie." She said, "Oh boy." One by one, the small gifts were unwrapped—a Christmas tree ornament, the small Christmas card made up by the children in the Sunday school, a little book, and a small candle. Each one she, with Gary's help, unwrapped with her one good hand. Then some conversation, mostly between Gary and me, and then Gary said, "I've brought the communion." "Oh boy," she said. And the piece of bread and the prayer and her receiving it, saying, "Oh boy"; and the cup and the same. Then a few farewells and out we went down the hall, back past those smells, out the front door, and into the parking lot. But just as I was getting into the car, I glanced up and there she was at the window, her good hand having parted half of the curtain. She stood waving, and I could see her mouth shape, "Oh boy."

A stroke, I learned from Gary, had reduced this remarkable woman to two words. That was her language. But, oh, what a language! In that short sequence of events that day, I was stunned by how the art of God is to take human pathos and give it an ethos for its flourishing—a place and a time. In this case, few gestures and few sounds; but, oh, what music. So I carry it as a living icon. When I'm in a great festival place, I bring Myrtie with me. When I hear great, great singing, I can hear echoing through it the *cantus firmus:* "Oh boy." A kind of hallelujah, Amen.

Now let me put the point in perhaps a less immediate way. Liturgy is the ongoing mutuality of God and the pathos of our human life. The liturgy exists, the classical definitions say, to glorify God and to proclaim the mystery of faith while sanctifying all that is human before God. Glorifying God, giving praise and thanks together, is a way of coming to know God and ourselves. Yet this is precisely how life comes to fullest truth and to the realization of what it is to exist in faith. To discover and to welcome the gift of creatureliness is to perceive the holiness in this divine art. This means that the cry of pain may comingle with our praise and our thanks. These are offered together in solidarity with the whole Church so our daily life is not fully received or understood until it is conjoined with others in the art of praising God.

* * *

Our current American cultural search for intimacy and our experience of so much laceration and fragmentation, so much privatization, so much loneliness stands out in bold relief. The liturgy waits patiently for us to bring this, and to bring it expectantly. No one who hears and sees the litany of human laceration night after night on the eleven o'-clock news should abide Christian liturgy without our cry, our cry on behalf of others, our cry on behalf of this beautiful world so far from God. Not all of us who say the words in the liturgy participate fully or are fully formed, and not every Sunday can we bring it all; there's so much moral pain to bring and much diversion. Jesus' words still sting: "Not everyone who says to me, 'Lord, Lord,' will enter the kingdom" (Matt 7:21). This is the very theological tension we face, the "already" of God's faithful word and the "not yet" of our pathos in time and place.

To remember God with the Scriptures, to remember God with the holy men and women in all times and places, to remember God with the angels and the archangels and all the company of heaven, those loved and lost and now in the communion of saints, means that we seek to be living reminders of these truths.[6] This leads us, as Annie Dillard reminds us, right back into a place far from home. We are taken by the living God to places we do not wish to go. I'd rather have a liturgy that was my language, my values, my self-congratulation, my "feeling good." But God will not have it this way, and certainly not among those of us belonging to this community of memory and witness. We are to nurture the ethos in which the Spirit of God may work to bring our pathos to God's saving mystery.

* * *

ETHOS OF LITURGY: GOD'S SELF-GIVING

To speak of the ethos of authentic Christian liturgy is to speak about the time and place in which human energies and passions are transformed in light of the passion of God for the world. To remember God in prayer and in life requires a continual participation in what the liturgy promises but cannot guarantee. Human affections such as yearning for justice, love of God and neighbor, gratitude, and even anger over injustice and suffering are not alien to the ethos of God. If we are disposed to the paschal mystery celebrated every Lord's day in the gathered community, our daily lives receive a new illumination. Father Godfrey Diekmann, the salty and peripatetic monk from St. John's Abbey, puts the point this way:

"Holiness is not something I get in the morning at Mass and then which throughout the day leaks out of me, grows ever less so that I must recharge myself again the next morning or the next Sunday. Instead, our day, our day's meeting with other people, our work should itself become an unfolding, a development, a deepening renewal of the morning's mystery of love."[7]

We take our human suffering of the world—not only moral pain or individual struggle, but the condition of being human in its wide and wild stretch—before God. In that place and time where God's self-giving is figured in Word and sacrament, and in the embodied healing

[6]See also Henri J. M. Nouwen, *The Living Reminder: Service and Prayer in Memory of Jesus Christ* (New York: The Seabury Press, 1977).

[7]Godfrey Diekmann, *Personal Prayer and the Liturgy* (London: Geoffrey Chapman, 1971) 62.

of becoming a human community there, we are empowered to unfold, as Diekmann observes, "the morning's mystery of love."

Pathos without God's ethos is tragic self-expression; God's ethos without human pathos figured in Jesus is opaque, that is, sovereign but not saving. As Augustine said long ago: "Without God we cannot. Without us, God will not." But we must not confuse the bringing of human desires and longing to the ethos of the divine self-giving in liturgy with experiencing the highs and lows during the actual time of liturgical celebration. We live in a culture that finds it difficult to distinguish between immediacies of feeling and depth of emotion over time. Blatant consumerism obliterates this distinction.[8] This is a cultural problem for worship and the arts ingredient in liturgical celebration. Thus to speak of how modes of prayer form us in deep emotions such as thankfulness and trust in God, does not mean simply "feeling thankful" from time to time. Vital liturgy certainly may produce feeling states, but that is not the criterion for praise and thanksgiving to God.

The ethos of God as the transformative power of liturgy relocates our tendency to look for immediacies of feeling. Over time, authentic liturgy deepens our disposition to perceive the world as God's creation. Thus Christian gratitude is not so much "felt" or "produced" as it is elicited in season and out of season. Joy in the midst of tribulation, or speaking the truth in love, or coming to love as God loves takes time to unfold.

So, too, the matter of remembering God, for who among us can say that in one single instance he or she remembers all that God's grace has conferred? This is the problem with the instantaneous conversion approach and the pragmatic utilitarian spirit that takes a perfectly good religious affection and turns it into a commodity. Flash it on the screen, "feel it now," and everything's OK. No, it is not this way, for God takes the long way with our condition. It is God's passion for us and for the complexly fallen world that makes this so. While we can experience particular liturgical events in the immediacy of its engagement, the set of meanings that illuminate life can only unfold over time. Even immediacy of feeling, however intense, deals with something selected out of the rich and largely inchoate, concealed pattern present to our consciousness.

[8]For further reflection on consumerism's impact on liturgy, see James L. Empereur and Christopher G. Kiesling, *The Liturgy That Does Justice* (Collegeville, Minn.: The Liturgical Press, A Michael Glazier Book, 1990) 231–46.

Consider, for example, the experience at a family reunion. We listen to Uncle Fred tell the old stories, we meet a new relative, and we eat foods often placed on the table in a highly ordered sequence with Grandma's cream fruit salad last because it is the ritual dessert now. Yet we only receive part of the significance of the gathering at the time. We go through an array of meeting, eating, talking, singing, stories, but not until much later, or next year, do we seem to have "taken in" our belonging. The deeper levels of symbolic presence necessarily go beyond immediacy toward shared memories, encoded in the actions becoming ritualized.

With respect to Christian liturgy, the following episode is typical.[9] A parishioner came to the Sunday liturgy vaguely aware of her father's illness. At several points during the rite she drifted into her sense of "a lot of pain in the world." She became very engaged in singing the "Gloria," she reported, and in specific moments in the liturgy. Then she observed, "But again, I think I was thinking about my dad." Later, during the eucharistic prayer she remarked, "I remember thinking about my husband's grandmother who passed away and an aunt of mine." Vivid episodes of consciousness were triggered by participation. But what we could not see in her report is how, over time, the ethos of God took that pain and fused it with the communion of saints.

There is no reason to deny that people have moving immediate experiences in the liturgy—perhaps especially prompted by music. But the transformative power of God's self-giving in and through liturgical action has to do with the shaping of perception, of knowing, and of feeling over time. The true ethos of Christian liturgy is that web of grace through word, sacrament, and song, through eating and drinking together, and being remembered by God, whereby God's saving power in the flesh transforms and transmutes all human pathos. This is what eye has not yet fully seen, nor ear heard. God sees in our life patterns what we cannot yet see. Authentic liturgy lures us by grace into a new pathos, now directed to the passion of God at the heart of the gospel.

[9]This is drawn from interviews conducted by the Georgetown Center for Liturgical Study of fifteen Roman Catholic parishes in the United States in the late 1980s. See Lawrence Madden, ed., *The Awakening Church* (Collegeville, Minn.: The Liturgical Press, 1991).

Robin Knowles Wallace

Ruth C. Duck: Expanding Our Horizons of Liturgical Language

Ruth C. Duck, born in 1947, is one of the first liturgical scholars in the twentieth century to study liturgical language and intentionally expand it to welcome all persons into the baptized community of believers. One of Duck's contributions to liturgical theology is her ability to dialogue across denominational lines. Her academic work has been varied: M.Div. and ordination in the United Church of Christ, master's degree in liturgy from the University of Notre Dame, and doctoral work at the United Methodist-affiliated Boston University. Her work as a teacher and scholar continues at the United Methodist Garrett-Evangelical Theological Seminary in Evanston, Illinois.

Soon after she received her M.Div. degree in 1973, Ruth Duck embarked on work that would bring her to prominence: theological revision of liturgical language as that language extends or inhibits God's grace in Christian community. Issues of justice, both local and global, shape her hymns and worship resources. Duck's love of the Church and her service as pastor in two congregations between her master's and doctoral work keep her work grounded in lived experience. She began her work with practical resources for congregations, editing and writing hymns, prayers, and other worship resources. Her edited works include two early collections of hymns, three books of worship resources, and a co-edited book about trinitarian language. She has also published two collections of original hymns, many commissioned by congregations and worship leaders.

Duck's Th.D. dissertation from Boston University was reshaped for her book, *Gender and the Name of God: The Trinitarian Baptismal Formula.*

284

It is this work on the rootedness of equality in Christian baptism that moved her published work from worship resources to liturgical theology. In this book Duck delves into early Christian baptismal understandings, demonstrates how language shapes and is used to justify behavior, and suggests an alternative baptismal formula grounded in early Christian tradition and revealing the truth of equality in baptism. Subsequent books and essays continue Duck's commitment to liturgical theology and to our relationship to the Holy.

Duck's work is also at home within the framework of feminist liturgical theology. The concerns of feminist liturgical theology for inclusion of women and women's lives in worship, for issues of social justice, for truthfulness and the continuing revelation of God's Spirit, all appear in Duck's work. Her Reformed perspective keeps her in dialogue with Scripture as well, occasionally making her unique in the field of feminist liturgical theology, some of whose scholars are equally apt to look elsewhere for revelation.

The following essay, written for this volume, demonstrates Duck's understanding of sacramental living and baptismal identity in dialogue with the limitations of human language. She reminds us that liturgical language is metaphorical, and she argues for expansion of the metaphorical field of liturgical language. This field may be expanded by drawing on baptismal and eucharistic theology as well as Scripture, tradition, and contemporary experience. Liturgical language is communal language, language of relationship with God and each other. Through the power and inspiration of the Holy Spirit, our language can more clearly express and shape us in our walk of faith. If our language is to express the newness of life promised in Jesus Christ, it needs to express that newness in fresh and inviting ways, in ways that express God's call to justice and mercy, to love and grace.

FOR FURTHER READING
Gender and the Name of God: The Trinitarian Baptismal Formula. New York: The Pilgrim Press, 1991; "Sin, Grace, and Gender in Free-Church Protestant Worship." *Women at Worship: Interpretations of North American Diversity.* Ed. Marjorie Procter-Smith and Janet Walton. Louisville: Westminster/John Knox Press, 1993; *Finding Words for Worship: A Guide for Leaders.* Louisville: Westminster/John Knox Press, 1995; *Circles of Care: Hymns and Songs.* Cleveland: The Pilgrim Press, 1998; *Praising God: The Trinity in Christian Worship.* With Patricia Wilson-Kastner. Louisville: Westminster/John Knox Press, 1999.

Ruth C. Duck

Expansive Language in the Baptized Community[1]

Since the 1970s the issue of "inclusive language"—the question of gender and liturgical language—has challenged the churches. Historically, the language of Christian worship has been replete with masculine images of the human and the divine. In recent decades numerous denominations have made at least modest changes in their worship books and hymnals to be more inclusive of women—either by avoiding gendered language or using both masculine and feminine images. Metaphors related to race and disability have also received some attention. Local churches have experimented with alternative liturgies, often using supplemental and non-official resources published to address their needs. It is no secret that these changes have occasioned painful and heated conflict. The need for continuing serious theological reflection on this matter has also become apparent. The present article articulates a theological basis, grounded in the baptismal covenant, for seeking a richer diversity of metaphors for God.

One fundamental theological question related to liturgical language is whether it has reference in divine reality or whether we are merely projecting our experiences and wishes upon God. A relational theology of baptism helps to answer this question.

The baptismal covenant marks the church's relationship with God in Christ through the Holy Spirit. Traditional Western theologies of the sacraments have focused on categories of substance: baptism washes away original sin, as a substance; Eucharist communicates grace, as a substance. Current understandings of the sacraments em-

[1]Printed with the permission of the author.

286

phasize transformed and transforming relationships with God, neighbor, and the whole creation. As Christian educator Robert Browning and liturgical scholar Roy Reed explain:

"More recent understandings of baptism emphasize the incorporation of the child into Christ's body, in which the child is surrounded by incarnate love from parents, sponsors, and congregation and is strengthened to participate spontaneously in the ministering community. Infant baptism does not wash original sin from the child . . . it brings the child into relationships and actions which can, in fact, save the child from fear, isolation, and a self-centered rather than a God-centered life."[2]

To be baptized is take part in a new constellation of relationships with God, the baptized community, and the world. This is Paul's point in Rom 6:1-5: United in baptism with Christ's dying and rising, we are called to "walk in newness of life": to live in a new and right relationship with God, one another, and the world.

Our sacramental participation in dying and rising with Christ and in life with the triune God enables us to hope that our language in worship says something about God and not just ourselves. The communion with God in Christ that baptism signifies and effects is not only an affirmation of doctrine (as in a creed) or a statement of commitment (as in a contract). Through baptism we share in living relationship with God; we participate in the very life of the Trinity. As the baptized community, when we speak of God, we speak out of this relationship. Because in baptism we enter into this living relationship with God, we have freedom and responsibility to give witness in worship to divine presence in our lives—to attempt to speak the unspeakable.

To speak about God is to speak metaphorically. Our liturgical language describes the infinite and holy God in terms based in earthy human experience: rock, wind, shepherd, mother, father, potter. Such language is metaphorical, because God is both like and unlike such earthly realities and relationships. A metaphor makes meaning by describing one thing in terms of another that is both like and unlike it, stretching "the limits of human thought and perception so that we

[2]Robert L. Browning and Roy A. Reed, *The Sacraments in Religious Education and Liturgy* (Birmingham, Ala.: Religious Education Press, 1985) 6–7. A wholesome understanding of the baptism of those who confess faith for themselves also emphasizes relationship with God in the baptized community.

grasp new meanings."[3] Christian liturgy is full of metaphor. On reflection we realize that, for example, even the name "Christ" is a
metaphor growing out of the anointing of rulers and prophets. Metaphors amplify one another and operate in systems. In the same
breath, we call God a "fortress" and a "very present help in trouble"
(Ps 46:1). As a "very present help" God takes on personal characteristics, but saying "fortress" keeps us from regarding God as literally
human while at the same time bringing out characteristics of strength
and endurance. The most commonly used metaphors, which provide
a field in which to interpret other metaphors, guide our perceiving
and behaving, yet they can become literalized and fail to provoke
new insights. "Father" as a name for the divine is a central metaphor
that points to God's relational nature, yet it can become literalized as
if God were literally male, operating like a patriarchal human father.
Complementing "Father" with maternal, emancipatory metaphors
tends to counteract literalized understandings. Expanded liturgical
language, drawing on diverse imagery from Scripture, tradition, and
contemporary experience, helps familiar metaphors continue to stim-
ulate new insight.

To say that liturgical language is metaphorical is not to deny its
revelatory power through the working of the Spirit. It is to say that
the language of worship reveals the Holy One in a particular way.
Using metaphorical language invites worshiping communities to participate in making meaning as the metaphors interplay with their ongoing relationship with God. Live metaphorical language continues
to provoke new insights that factual, literal, categorical language can
never summarize. In this way, the language of worship both expresses and nurtures our ongoing baptismal relationship with the triune God. For as liturgical theologian Mark Searle wrote, "The role of
liturgical language is not simply to convey supernatural 'facts,' but to
engage us in relationship."[4]

Reflection on the implications of baptism for human relationships
also addresses the question of whether using inclusive language
merely mirrors secular feminism, or whether it is grounded in the life
of faith. In baptism, all are gifted and called to ministry. According to

[3]Ruth C. Duck, *Gender and the Name of God: The Trinitarian Baptismal Formula*
(New York: The Pilgrim Press, 1991) 14; refer to ch. 1 of that book, as well as
to John D. Witvliet, "Metaphor in Liturgical Studies," *Liturgy Digest*, vol. 4/1
(1997) 3–41, for more on liturgical language as metaphor.

[4]Mark Searle, "Liturgy as Metaphor," *Worship* 55 (March 1981) 100.

the ecumenical document *Baptism, Eucharist, and Ministry*, baptism is "liberation into a new humanity in which barriers of division whether of sex or race or social status are transcended."[5] James White has said: "Baptism is the foundation for justice within the church. It is the sacrament of equality."[6] The apostle Paul wrote: "As many of you as were baptized into Christ have clothed yourselves with Christ. There is no longer Jew or Greek, there is no longer slave or free, there is no longer male and female; for all of you are one in Christ Jesus. And if you belong to Christ, then you are Abraham's offspring, heirs according to the promise" (Gal 3:27-29). Baptized into one body, drinking of one Spirit, heirs of the promise, both women and men belong to Christ in mutuality and equality (1 Cor 12:12-13). This baptismal equality is based on God's love signed and sealed in baptism, since "God shows no partiality" (Acts 10:34). Yet this is not a "spiritual" equality alone. Baptismal equality is meant to affect relationships in everyday life so that the powerful do not abuse their power, the comfortable do not withhold food or drink from those who need it, and no one presumes on family background or ethnic status for their standing in the religious community (Luke 3:7-17).

Since some slaveholders in the South glimpsed the revolutionary potential of baptism ("There is no longer slave or free . . . for you are all one in Christ Jesus"), at first they refused to allow the baptism of slaves. Later, six colonies passed laws declaring that baptism would not change the status of slaves.[7] One baptismal ritual asked slaves to affirm that in coming for baptism they were seeking only the "good of their soul" and the blessings of the church, not freedom from their masters.[8] Through such strategies, slaveholders could commend themselves for encouraging slaves to be baptized, while their business in this world continued in its cruel reality. Such views—in which baptism affects only spiritual, otherworldly matters—not only perpetuate injustice, they pervert the theology of baptism. Through the equality given in baptism, the baptized community is to embody relationships

[5]World Council of Churches Faith and Order Commission, *Baptism, Eucharist, and Ministry* (Geneva: World Council of Churches, 1982), section on baptism, par. 2.

[6]James F. White, *Sacraments as God's Self-Giving* (Nashville: Abingdon Press, 1983) 96.

[7]Melva Wilson Costen, *African American Christian Worship* (Nashville: Abingdon Press, 1993) 33.

[8]Ibid.

of justice and respect among all people and thus to live out a new reality and provide a foretaste of God's reign in the world.

The language of our worship may reflect or contradict this new reality in Christ. Constant use of negative images of race and disability contradicts the justice and respect that characterize God's reign. The unbalanced use of masculine imagery for God also reflects the patriarchal realities of this world, not the reign of God. Theologian and hymn writer Brian Wren compares our liturgical naming of God to an art gallery. A few images, particularly Lord, King, and Father, appear on one huge canvas after another, whereas other images such as Mother, Wisdom, and Midwife, also found in Scripture, are hidden away in the storeroom.[9] The small gallery of images that Christians have displayed in worship reflects the social reality of patriarchy— domination of men over women, humans over earth, owners over slaves, and people of one race, culture, or religion over another. This narrow range of images implies that God approves and sustains these unjust social arrangements. What a contrast to the ministry of Jesus, who proclaimed God's love for all and by his actions lifted up women, the poor, children, and others society rejects or devalues. In baptism we are born anew into an alternative reality of love and mutuality beyond all human domination and subordination.

It matters whether liturgical language reflects new life in Christ or whether it reflects unjust social values, for words and imagery are one way that children and adults learn unjust values. Biased language reinforces unjust attitudes and behavior. Language that constantly refers to God in masculine terms (but never or rarely in feminine terms) contributes to the assumption that men are more valuable than women. Of course, language is one of many ways— from media images to unequal employment practices to behavior at home, school, and church—in which church and society devalue and demean women. Language is not all-important, but it matters, because devaluing girls, women, or any human being leads to treating them in unjust, even violent ways.[10] As theologian Letty Russell has said, the church's exclusive use of "masculine imagery makes it diffi-

---

[9]Brian Wren, *What Language Shall I Borrow? God-Talk in Worship: A Male Response to Feminist Theology* (New York: Crossroad, 1989) 113–22. Wren further develops the gallery metaphor in the video *How Shall I Sing to God* (Carol Stream, Ill.: Hope Publishing Co., 1989).

[10]Refer to Wren, *What Language Shall I Borrow*, 59–83; Duck, *Gender and the Name of God*, 31–57, for further discussion of how language influences behavior.

cult for women, for the churches, and for society to see how it is that women and men are equally created in the image of God."[11] The ministry of the baptized community is to love and care for all persons and all creation, to heal and not to harm, to bring justice, not to condone violence by our words or actions. Our language matters, because baptism participates in and rehearses a new way of life.

Baptismal theology also speaks to how language nurtures Christian faith. Some people argue that expanded language is theologically acceptable but pastorally unwise, because changing familiar language undermines Christian faith and worship. This argument recognizes neither the need for lifelong growth in faith as one lives out baptism, nor the communal nature of the baptized community.

The ritual of baptism is not meant to be an isolated event but part of a continuing journey of faith, no matter the age of the persons being baptized. Gayle Carlton Felton has summarized the growing consensus (at least among United Methodists) that baptism is a lifelong process:

"Baptism, then, is not so much event as it is process. Like the Christian life for which it is empowerment and metaphor, baptism is dynamic, not static; a journey, not a destination; a quest, not an acquisition. Baptism is promise, the fulfilling of which requires a lifetime and beyond."[12]

If the baptismal covenant is a lifelong process, then our faith and understanding about God are meant to be dynamic. Familiar words learned since childhood can play an important role in sustaining Christian identity, but continued learning and growth keeps our faith from being static, frozen at the point we were baptized or affirmed the baptismal covenant for ourselves. As a full range of scriptural imagery for God is explored in Christian worship, believers continue on a journey of discovery, coming to know more about the God who also goes beyond all words and knowledge. As the baptismal journey of faith continues, Christians experience God in the midst of their lives, which inspires new ways of witness and service. A new or revised hymn, a new way of thinking about a scriptural passage, or the testimony of another member of the baptized community, local or

[11]Letty M. Russell, "The Credal Basis of the World YWCA and the Practice of God's Hospitality" (unpublished background paper, August 1998) 9.

[12]Gayle Carlton Felton, *This Gift of Water* (Nashville: Abingdon Press, 1992) 178.

global, can awaken new insight and support the unfolding relationship that began, perhaps long ago, in the water of baptism.

The life and witness of the worshiping community are an essential part of this baptismal journey. As Browning and Reed write of the baptismal covenant: "A relational view sees God's grace present in the world and interpersonally in the church in the dynamic of a loving, caring, forgiving, justice-seeking body of Christ."[13] In such a view, the way the church, in word and action, embodies God's love and justice makes a difference in how persons will appropriate faith for themselves. Language that goes beyond bias and patriarchal values more clearly witnesses to the all-encompassing love and justice of God; it more effectively communicates the church's engagement in ministries of justice and reconciliation. Such language removes barriers to the Spirit's work of awakening faith and stimulating growth in love and holiness.

To be baptized into Christ is to belong to one another, rejoicing with those who rejoice and weeping with those who weep (Rom 12:15); Christian faith is communal. Thus, the way churches approach issues of language should be dialogical, giving space to express conflicting views in an atmosphere of compassionate and respectful listening. Those who seek change are often concerned that the church embody God's justice and right-relationship in word and deed, while ministering with those who have been hurt by society's injustices. Those who resist change are often concerned to remain in continuity with the historic faith of the church; they remind us that memory plays an important part in Christian worship as familiar words bring to mind life-changing experiences of faith, community, and worship. If members holding these positions are able to listen well enough to recognize the values others wish to uphold, the way becomes more clear toward contextualized solutions that honor all members while moving toward more expansive language for worship.[14]

Baptism is a lifelong process lived out in community. By expanding language in thoughtful, dialogical, contextualized ways, the baptized

[13]Robert L. Browning and Roy A. Reed, *Models of Confirmation and Baptismal Affirmation* (Birmingham, Ala.: Religious Education Press, 1995) 24.

[14]I experienced this dialogical approach to language while serving on the Hymnal Development Committee of the Christian Church (Disciples of Christ), which produced the *Chalice Hymnal* of 1995. At times there were tears and anger, but in the end we listened and learned from one another and developed a much stronger hymnal because of our honest dialogue.

community supports one another in a continual process of growth and discovery in relationship with one another, with God, and with the world.

Expanding the language of worship invites and nurtures living faith. Some attempts at language revision tend to narrow the scope of imagery by removing familiar masculine images such as "Father," "Lord," and "King," and retaining familiar images such as "Savior" or "Shepherd" that are not necessarily gendered terms. Another approach, sometimes called "expansive language," seeks not so much to eliminate traditional masculine imagery as to place it among a broad range of other metaphors from Scripture, tradition, and faith experience. Drawing forth neglected images from Scripture, tradition, and contemporary experience, we, like the householder of the parable of taking treasures out of storage (Matt 13:51-52), witness to the new reality in Christ. The task is not to remove from the gallery all canvases that portray God as masculine but to exhibit a broader range of images in our worship and life together as churches.

Although it is beyond the scope of this article to explore in detail methods of renewing language, two comments are in order. First, one of the best ways to expand liturgical language is to use imagery for God appropriate to a given liturgical context. For example, David Cunningham uses water imagery in a prayer at baptism, saying we baptize in the name of "the Source, the Wellspring, and the Living Water."[15] The texts for the day can shape our imagery; use of Wisdom imagery makes good sense when Proverbs 8, Matthew 11, or 1 Cor 1:18-25 appears in the Lectionary, while John 15 can inspire imagery of vine and vinegrower. One problem with images such as "Father" and "Lord" is their use as generic terms for God without regard for their meaning in context. At the same time, new or diverse images only enhance worship and support new reality when integrated into the whole of a worship service. When developed over time with care and thought for particular worship contexts, a broader range of imagery supports vital worship and growth in embodying God's new reality.[16]

Second, it is important to note that not only the gender and breadth but also the content of liturgical language matters. Feminist

[15]David Cunningham, *These Three Are One* (Malden, Mass.: Blackwell, 1998) 348.

[16]Refer to Ruth Duck, *Finding Words for Worship* (Louisville: Westminster/John Knox Press, 1995) 33–44, and Patricia Wilson-Kastner, *Imagery for Preaching* (Philadelphia: Fortress Press, 1989), for more on imagery for worship.

liturgical scholar Marjorie Procter-Smith has argued that it is not enough to be "non-sexist," avoiding gendered imagery for God, or even to balance masculine and feminine imagery; the language of worship should be emancipatory, revealing God as "one who cries out for justice" with women and others who are violated and abused.[17] Expansive language attends to metaphors concerning race and disability as well as gender. It is hardly helpful to remove gender references from images that still portray God as a distant potentate who legitimizes unjust human hierarchies. Rather, renewed Christian liturgical language will portray the God of justice and tender love revealed in Jesus Christ and still revealed today through the power of Holy Spirit alive in the world.[18]

Dwight and Linda Vogel speak of "sacramental living"—a way of life based on our baptismal union with Christ in living, dying, and rising.[19] Dwight Vogel has written:

"If we know what it means to live out our baptism, we will know what it means to be disciples of Jesus Christ. Disciples are those who have died and been raised to new life in Jesus Christ, who have been incorporated into Christ's body, who have been sent forth for witness and service. The baptismal covenant celebrates who we are, where we belong, and what we are about."[20]

To live sacramentally is to live out baptism every day in the church and the world as those who belong to God and one another. Expanding our language is one way we can live out the grace, the love, the justice, and the hope of our baptisms and our table communion.

[17]Marjorie Procter-Smith, *In Her Own Rite* (Nashville: Abingdon Press, 1990) 113.

[18]In *Praising God: The Trinity in Christian Worship* (Louisville: Westminster/John Knox Press, 1999) Patricia Wilson-Kastner and I explore approaches to faithful and expansive witness to trinitarian Christian faith.

[19]Dwight W. Vogel and Linda J. Vogel, *Sacramental Living: Falling Stars and Coloring Outside the Lines* (Nashville: Upper Room, 1999).

[20]Dwight W. Vogel, *Food for Pilgrims* (Akron: OSL Publications, 1996) 61.

Dwight W. Vogel and Kimberly Anne Willis

L. Edward Phillips:
Scholarship for Liturgy and Life

L. Edward Phillips works at the intersection of liturgical history, historical theology, and pastoral liturgical theology. His divinity degree is from Candler School of Theology at Emory University, and he completed his M.A. and Ph.D. in liturgical studies at the University of Notre Dame, with doctoral minors in liturgical theology and ethics. He has written numerous articles on both pastoral liturgical theology and the early history of liturgy. His recent research focus is a commentary on the *Apostolic Tradition* of Hippolytus, with translations of the Latin, Coptic, Arabic, and Ethiopic versions, for the *Hermeneia* commentary series, in collaboration with Paul F. Bradshaw and Maxwell Johnson. An ordained elder in The United Methodist Church, he currently teaches historical theology and liturgical studies at Garrett-Evangelical Theological Seminary, where he is dean of the chapel.

Beginning with an insightful quote from Augustine, Phillips sets the stage for exploring the relationship between liturgy and ethics. In the pages preceding the following excerpt he addresses three of many possible relationships: liturgy is a source for ethics, liturgy is an object of ethics, and liturgy itself is an ethic. Having surveyed these relationships, Phillips emphasizes that the most important bond between liturgy and ethics is not predicated on a direct relationship but rather is grounded in a commonality that emphasizes faithful service to God.

FOR FURTHER READING

"Liturgy and Ethics," *Liturgy as Companion*. Ed. Paul F. Bradshaw and Bryan Spinks. London: SPCK, 1994; *The Ritual Kiss in Early Christian Worship*, Alcuin/GROW Liturgical Studies. Bramcote Notts.: Grove Books Limited, 1996; "How Shall We Worship?" and "Whose Worship Is It Anyway?" Ed. Ron Anderson. *Worship Matters*. Vol. 1. Nashville: Discipleship Resources, 1999; "Homosexuality and the Social Principles, Blessing the Incompatible?" *The Loyal Opposition: Resisting the Church on Homosexuality*. Ed. Amy Delong and Tex Sample. Nashville: Abingdon Press, 2000; *In Spirit and Truth: Toward an Understanding of Worship for the Emerging Church*. With Sara Webb Phillips. Nashville: Discipleship Resources, 2000.

296

L. Edward Phillips

Liturgy and Ethics[1]

"To bless God in the churches, brethren, means so to live that each
one's life may give glory to God. To bless God in word and curse
Him in deed is by no means to bless Him in the churches. Almost all
bless Him with their tongues, but not all by their works. But those
whose conduct is inconsistent with their profession cause God to be
blasphemed."[2] [Augustine]

* * *

1. The relationship between liturgy and ethics is not always obvious. . . . [T]he connection must be demonstrated. Historically, this is
what the Church refers to as catechesis. Theologians in the fourth
century recognized this when they lectured newly initiated Christians on the meaning of the rites they had just experienced. Participation in the rites themselves did not sufficiently communicate their
full meaning; this meaning had to be explained through mystagogy.[3]
Despite the insistence of some liturgical theologians and ritologists
that liturgy "forms" ethical behavior, without proper catechesis
liturgy will not be sufficient as an agent of ethical formation, as the
overwhelming testimony of church history bears witness. Wealthy

[1]Excerpted from L. Edward Phillips, ch. 5, "Liturgy and Ethics," *Liturgy and
Dialogue: Essays in Memory of Ronald Jasper*, ed. Paul Bradshaw and Bryan
Spinks (Collegeville, Minn.: The Liturgical Press, A Pueblo Book, 1993) 99–101.
Reprinted by permission.
    [2]*St. Augustine on the Psalms*, trans. S. Hegbin and F. Corrigan, Ancient
Christian Writers 29 (Newman Press, Westminster, Md., 1960) 252.
    [3]See Edward Yarnold, *The Awe-Inspiring Rites of Initiation* (Slough: St. Paul
Publications, 1971).

Christians all too easily can participate in the Eucharist with poor Christians and not understand the justice issues inherent in this act. Christians can pray "give us this day our daily bread," and not understand the limits this places on the consumption of food resources. As noted above, ritual is inherently ambiguous, and perhaps it is most ambiguous to those who participate in it regularly. Therefore, today, as in the fourth century, the ethical relevance of liturgy must be periodically explained in order for worshiping Christians to make the connection.

2. This leads to a second observation: in any discussion of liturgy and ethics, a distinction must be made between their primary functions and the reflection upon these functions. As regards liturgy, this is the distinction between worship as *theologia prima* (first-order theology) and *theologia secunda* (second-order reflection). As regards ethics, this is the distinction between right action and the systematic evaluation of what constitutes right action (using deontological or consequentialist reasoning, for example). That is to say, a distinction must be made between liturgy *per se* and liturgical theology, as well as between right action and ethical theology or philosophy. Therefore, the discussion of the relationship of liturgy and ethics must include a discussion of their relationship to theology: *lex orandi, lex credendi, lex bene operandi.*[4] These three go together in the life of the Church and each maintains its own particular function. It is pointless to try to rank their importance as if one could some how supersede the others.[5] To use an analogy, there is no reason to argue which is more important to the human body, the heart, the liver, or the lungs. Without all three in reasonably good working order, the whole human body will suffer. Likewise, liturgy, theology, and ethics have a vital relationship, and no one can be neglected without affecting the others.

3. A problem with many approaches to liturgy and ethics is the tendency towards reductionism on the liturgy side: only those aspects which are ethically relevant appear to count. This ignores the gratuitous element of worship. Yet, as Willimon has stated, "We do not worship God in order to become better people. Christians worship God simply because we are God's beloved ones. Christian wor-

---

[4]See Teresa Berger, "Lex orandi–lex credendi–lex agendi: Auf dem Weg zu einer ökumenisch konsensfähigen Verhältnisbestimmung von Liturgie, Theologie, Ethik," *Archiv für Liturgiewissenschaft* 27 (1985) 425–32.

[5]See the critique by Vigen Guroian, "Seeing Worship as Ethics," *Incarnate Love: Essays in Orthodox Ethics* (Univ. of Notre Dame Press, 1987) 51-52.

ship is an intrinsic activity."[6] This suggests that any discussion of the relationship between liturgy and ethics must acknowledge the ways in which they are *not* related. The quotation from Augustine with which we began is relevant here. Augustine recognized that it is entirely possible for a worshiper formally to bless God with words in church while living a life that does not bear witness to the gospel. For Augustine, this turned the blessing uttered in church into blasphemy. Augustine does not suggest that the blessing in church forms the ethical life; rather, the ethical life authenticates the blessing in church. Yet, this does not lead to the opposite conclusion that an ethical life without liturgy is sufficient. Augustine does not call for the ethical life to the neglect of worship, for the blessing in church indeed has its essential place.

This observation certainly does not deny there are ethical dimensions to liturgy, since liturgy involves human beings who are called to ethical living. Likewise, there are liturgical dimensions to ethics, since ethics is not merely our duty, but our delight—our thankful response to God.[7] Nevertheless, I suggest that the most important relationship between liturgy and ethics is not direct or causal, but is to be found on a higher level in their common goal, the faithful service of God. Because they have a common goal, a critical principle may be formulated: sound liturgical practice will never subvert Christian ethics, nor will proper Christian ethics denigrate liturgy, because each is necessary for God to be well served. This is why it is important to recognize the degree to which liturgy and ethics are *not* related; by keeping them distinct we may give each the proper attention it deserves.

At the heart of the consideration of liturgy and ethics from Augustine to the present is the longing for deeper human faithfulness to God. We may examine the ways we pray or believe or act to find clues for some formula that will produce faithfulness, holiness, and sanctification. But, finally, we must acknowledge that there is no formula. The work of sanctification belongs to God, and how God accomplishes this work will always be a mystery, out of our control, and beyond our complete understanding.

---

[6]William Willimon, *The Service of God: How Worship and Ethics Are Related* (Nashville: Abingdon Press, 1983) 37.
[7]See Geoffrey Wainwright, "Eucharist and/as Ethics," *Worship* 62 (1988) 128.

Dwight W. Vogel

Joyce Ann Zimmerman: Interpreter of the Paschal Mystery in Liturgy and Life

Joyce Ann Zimmerman (1945–) professed perpetual vows as a Sister of the Precious Blood in 1970 and completed her undergraduate degree in secondary education from the University of Dayton. Her passion for learning and scholarship over the next two decades is reflected in the academic programs she completed. She has master's degrees in philosophy (Athenaeum of Ohio, 1973), theology: liturgical studies (St. John's University, 1981), and theology (University of Ottawa, 1982). She was awarded a Ph.D. in theology from the University of Ottawa in 1987 and received S.T.L. (1983) and S.T.D. (1987) degrees from St. Paul University, Ottawa, Ontario, Canada. Her work as a liturgical theologian incorporates her academic work in these related fields into a coherent whole marked by careful scholarship and lifelong learning in both the academy and the Church.

Zimmerman was introduced to the thought of Paul Ricoeur by John Van Den Hengel in her doctoral studies. Although Ricoeur is a prolific writer, he seldom writes a systematic work on a particular subject, especially in areas related to liturgy. Zimmerman has made herself acquainted with the breadth and depth of Ricoeur's thought. She is not content with using insights from a particular article or chapter in isolation but is always careful to place each aspect in the context of his total work. Zimmerman finds dialectics to be a key to understanding Ricoeur (for example, meaning is a dialectic between linguistic structure and life structure). Using his philosophical hermeneutic as a foundation, she has creatively developed a comprehensive framework for a liturgical hermeneutic that includes both critical and post-critical methods.

Her major contribution to liturgical theology is her insistence that liturgy and Christian living involve a common structural dynamic and the same referent, namely, the paschal mystery. It is not only printed liturgical texts but the celebration of the liturgy itself as a "text" in its own right that is her concern. Meaning includes not only the sense of a text (the surface structure of what is said) but the reference uncovered in the depth-meaning of the language used, which points to "extra-linguistic reality." Liturgical texts contain meaning that have salvific implications for living. Interpreting a liturgical text provides insight into the meaning of our lives.

Zimmerman is not alone in using post-critical methods in liturgical theology. For example, she points to Lawrence A. Hoffman, Kevin W. Irwin, David N. Power, and Louis-Marie Chauvet as other liturgical theologians who also borrow from and reflect that methodology. Yet I find her appropriation particularly self-conscious, consistent, and coherent.

The article that follows, written especially to conclude this volume, is representative of her work, although it is also a contribution to the liturgical theology of material not found elsewhere. In it you will discover her dynamic understanding of the paschal mystery, which reaches out to embrace components that have always been implicit in it but have not been consciously recognized and labeled as such. In this article themes that have been articulated and developed by other writers in this volume come together in a dynamic and coherent whole. Here is an understanding that can serve us well as liturgical theology moves into the twenty-first century.

FOR FURTHER READING

Liturgy and Hermeneutics. Collegeville, Minn.: The Liturgical Press, 1999; *Liturgy as Living Faith: A Liturgical Spirituality*. London and Toronto: Associated Univ. Presses, 1993; *Liturgy as Language of Faith: A Liturgical Methodology in the Mode of Paul Ricoeur's Textual Hermeneutics*. Latham, N.Y. and London: Univ. Press of America, 1988; "Language and Human Experience," *The New Dictionary of Sacramental Worship*. Ed. Peter E. Fink. 644–51. Collegeville, Minn.: The Liturgical Press, 1990; "Theology of the Liturgical Assembly: Saints, Relics and Rites," *Liturgy* 14 (1998) 45–59.

Joyce Ann Zimmerman

Paschal Mystery—Whose Mystery?
A Post-Critical Methodological Reinterpretation

Sacrosanctum concilium (The Constitution on the Sacred Liturgy of Vatican II; hereafter, *SC*) sets out a tall order for liturgy from the very outset of the document. Paragraph 2 states that in liturgy is redemption accomplished and "it is through the liturgy, especially, that the faithful are enabled to express in their lives and manifest to others the mystery of Christ and the real nature of the true Church." These few words—in one sweeping statement—explicitly connect liturgy to redemption, the mystery of Christ, and Church. These three realities have been the object of countless hours of research, study, reflection, prayer, sermons, publications, and discussions for the past two millennia and—at least in the patristic era—have been even directly connected to the work of liturgy. But this alone would not account for the startling breadth of *SC* 2 and why it might particularly catch our attention today. What is new—or a challenge to be recovered—is the concern that redemption, Christ's mystery, and Church are to be expressed in our Christian living and witnessed to others as an essential component of our discipleship.

Several implications and many questions arise. First, liturgy is hardly something we "attend" as passive spectators (much less is it something optional for the serious Christian); nor is liturgy the source for a deposit of graces that we tap. The council fathers implied that we are *active participants* with Christ in working out our redemption, and this takes place preeminently in liturgy. How so? No small question! Second, if paschal mystery is *Christ's* life, passion, death, resurrection, ascension, sending of the Spirit, and promised Second

302

Coming (cf. *SC* 5), how is it that it is *our* mystery as well? How do we bridge the gulf between the historical Jesus and our own participation today in the mystery? From Christian Scriptures (see Romans 6) on through mystagogy, patristic homilies, and reiterated in *SC* 6, the Church has always taught that our baptism plunges us into the mystery of Christ. How so? No small question! Third, does not the initial passage from *SC* that we quoted above imply that the real nature of the Church is only manifested in those who live the paschal mystery? The very identity of the Church itself cannot be separated from Christ's redemptive act. Being members of the Church means that we are necessarily inserted into the ongoing unfolding of redemption.

So far we have ferreted out implications and raised questions from a basic requirement for being Christian: being grafted onto Christ. There is nothing new here *per se*. For centuries this has been asserted and confirmed. However, today as never before we have methodological tools at hand that permit us to delve deeper and ask other questions. Until recently scholarship and pastoral approaches have consistently "asserted" and "described" the relationship of Jesus Christ's redeeming actions and our participation in it.[1] Given our post-modern penchant for scientific analysis, *assertion* and *description* of our participation in Christ's mystery is not enough. We are given to asking the further question, why is this so? As soon as we ask the "why" question, we have stretched the limits of the traditional historical-critical methods and push ourselves to take advantage of the methodological tools of the post-critical methods.[2] Far from merely an academic endeavor, moving into this new methodological direction offers us fresh insight into how we might existentially grasp our own participation in the paschal mystery.

[1] For two recent examples of such approaches, see my column, "Liturgy Notes," *Liturgical Ministry* 8 (Spring 1999) 102–108, for a perusal of paschal mystery in early tradition; and Jeffrey M. Kemper's "Liturgy Notes," *Liturgical Ministry* 8 (Winter 1999) 46–51 for the notion of paschal mystery in Vatican II.

[2] The so called "critical methods" address historical and authorial questions such as the origin of texts, historical contexts, redactions, etc. The newer and developing "post-critical" methods address textual issues that derive largely from contemporary developments (in communications and social sciences, for example), study a text *qua* text, and set aside questions of authorship or textual development. For an overview of critical and post-critical methods, see my *Liturgy and Hermeneutics*, American Essays in Liturgy series (Collegeville, Minn.: The Liturgical Press, 1999). In ch. 5 I review contemporary liturgists who are working with post-critical methods.

This brief chapter cannot address all the post-critical methodological possibilities for exploring the question "How do we participate in the paschal mystery in liturgy and live it in our lives?" Instead, in order to support the tradition that maintains our active participation, we offer a few brief methodological considerations (part 1) and then use them to explore how the dialectics of liturgical time and narrativity deliver a framework for a reinterpretation of the paschal mystery in terms of our participation (part 2). We draw on French philosopher Paul Ricoeur's post-critical method using a dialectical and structural approach to texts as a guide for our reflection. The chief problems we address—and the one that leads us to use time and narrativity as heuristic tools—are "How do we participate in a historical event that is past and not yet come?" and "How do we *live* this mystery today?" In order for Christ's mystery to be a driving force in our Christian living—and, indeed, that from which we interpret all of our Christian existence—we must show how both the past (life, passion, death, resurrection, ascension, sending of the Spirit) and the future (Second Coming) are recoverable in the present for living, and this is what we *enact* and celebrate in liturgy.[3]

1. METHODOLOGICAL CONSIDERATIONS

Paul Ricoeur is an existential phenomenologist who has published copiously on the notions of time and narrativity.[4] Our first methodological task is to apply his general notion of time to the specific domain of liturgy. Second, since Ricoeur asserts that "speculation on time is an inconclusive rumination to which narrative activity alone can respond,"[5] our next methodological consideration must account

[3]In my earlier descriptions of the breadth of paschal mystery I made no temporal distinctions (see my *Liturgy as Language of Faith: A Liturgical Spirituality* [Scranton, Pa.: Univ. of Scranton Press/London and Toronto: Associated Univ. Presses, 1993] 52), although I have always been concerned with how *we* participate in the paschal mystery (see *Liturgy as Language of Faith*, chs. 4 and 5). I use "enact" quite pointedly here. We sometimes hear that liturgy "re-enacts" the paschal mystery (or the Lord's Supper), language that speaks more of "copy" than "creative imitation" of the Christ event.

[4]See, especially, his three-volume *Time and Narrative*, trans. Kathleen McLaughlin and David Pellauer (Chicago and London: The Univ. of Chicago Press, 1984, 1985, 1988).

[5]Ricoeur, *Time and Narrative*, vol. 1, 6. See also p. 52: " . . . my basic hypothesis [is] that between the activity of narrating a story and the temporal character of human existence there exists a correlation that is not merely accidental but that presents a transcultural form of necessity."

for a narrative[6] quality about liturgy that permits us to use Ricoeur's research to better understand paschal mystery, liturgy, and life.

Time and Liturgy[7]

Ricoeur draws on Augustine's meditation on time as laid out in Book 11 of his *Confessions* as a springboard for his own reflection on time. Placed in the larger context of the relation of time to eternity, Augustine is piqued by the passage of time (duration) and its measurement. To summarize[8] for our purpose: Augustine grapples with the issue of past, present, and future and concludes that neither past nor future are (the past has passed out of the present and is no more, and the future is not yet), but only the present is. Nonetheless, all three—past, present, and future—"exist in the soul [mind]." Hence Augustine speaks of time in terms of memory (past), attention (present; also, "sight" or "attending to"), and expectation (future).

[6]In common language use, "narrative" frequently means "fictional." Fictional narrative is a large part of Ricoeur's analysis (it occupies vol. 2 of *Time and Narrative*) but not the only part; Ricoeur also addresses historical narrative (in vol. 3). Neither of these two uses of "narrative" fits liturgy as such; nevertheless, it is fruitful to see how certain narrative qualities do fit liturgy and help us delve deeper into the mystery.

[7]For a different, pastoral approach to the notion of time see my "Making Sense of Time," *Assembly* 22 (November 1966) 736–37, 742. The reader will see how my more methodological and specialized development here is at the heart of the pastoral remarks.

[8]Ricoeur draws on Augustine's material on time in the *Confessions* (Book 11, 14:17–28:37) and Aristotle's material on *muthos* (emplotment) and *mimesis* (imitative activity) from *Poetics* (covered in the next section). It is impossible for me to do justice to Ricoeur's rich exposé of this material in the short space of this brief chapter. I can only draw on key points that directly help to develop my own thesis that features of narrative structure can help us understand liturgical time and broaden our appreciation for paschal mystery. So, with respect to time, another important reflection by Augustine is on the being and nonbeing of time, one that we do not address here. The reader is encouraged to turn to the original texts to flesh out these brief remarks and further substantiate our position.

Additionally, I wish to note that I am applying Ricoeur's *method* to the field of liturgy; needless to say, this is an application that Ricoeur himself does not make. I also wish to point out that there is a parallel between the work in this chapter on liturgy, time, and narrative and my previous work (see *Liturgy as Language of Faith* and *Liturgy as Living Faith*); specifically, I draw the reader's attention to the parallels between participation, distanciation, and appropriation in the domain of discourse and text theory and $mimesis_1$, $mimesis_2$, and $mimesis_3$ in the domain of narrative literature.

And further, since past and future do not exist as such—but since they exist in the soul or mind as memory and expectation—he speaks of a "present of things past, the present of things present, and a present of things future."[9]

Having concluded this much, Augustine next enters into a lengthy discussion of the measurement, extension, or duration of time (chapters 21 to 28).[10] Using one of his clear examples: in chapter 38 he speaks of repeating a psalm. When he begins, the whole of the psalm is in the future; then, as he says the words, some of the psalm still remains in the future while some has passed into the past. Time is measured as it "passes" through (21:27) the present from the future to the past until, in the recitation, all the future has been consumed and is now past, which has increased (27:36). In this measurement of time the present is a single instant, a point, a moment through which the future is relegated to the past.

It is here that Ricoeur picks up Augustine's analysis and moves it further. Referring to Augustine's example of reciting a psalm, Ricoeur contends that the "theme of this entire paragraph [chapter 38] is the dialectic of expectation, memory, and attention, each considered no longer in isolation but in interaction with one another. It is thus no longer a question of either impression-images or anticipatory images but of an *action*."[11] Our minds are actively creating the presence of the past, present, and future.

One point Ricoeur wishes to make clear is that Augustine's discussion moves time out of the realm of chronology; exactly at the point where it seems Augustine has abolished time (because it exists only as a point through which future passes into the past), he has opened up a deeper temporality. Now the "measurement of time owes noth-

<hr>

[9]Augustine, *Confessions*, 11, 20:26.

[10]Again, Augustine's interest is the relation of time and eternity (which we do not go into here), but his discussion of the measurement of time sheds further light on his threefold present (the importance of which cannot be stressed enough for our purpose).

[11]Ricoeur, *Time and Narrative*, vol. 1, 20; italics added. One critical key for understanding Ricoeur rightly is that his method is thoroughly *dialectical* ("interaction with one another"). Different from Hegelian dialectics whereby the tension of the opposing poles is resolved by means of a synthesis, Ricoeur's use of dialectic does not involve a synthesis but keeps the opposing poles in creative tension such that neither pole is ever eliminated (see n. 44, p. 37 in my *Liturgy and Hermeneutics*). Indeed, it is precisely the creative tension that is his "synthesis," a creative tension that produces something new.

ing to that of external motion."[12] Instead, "the mind itself [is] the fixed element . . . [and] the important verb is no longer 'to pass' (*transire*) but 'to remain' (*manet*)."[13] The present is always in a dialectical relationship with both past and future.

This reflection has enormous consequences for understanding liturgical time and paschal mystery in a new light. Above, we referred to the mystery of Christ, namely, the life, passion, death, resurrection, ascension, sending of the Spirit, and Second Coming of Christ. In fact, this introduces a problem of time. With respect to Christ's mystery itself, we have both past and future events. Additionally, we ourselves live in the present—between the life, passion, death, resurrection, ascension, and sending of the Spirit, on the one hand, and the Second Coming, on the other hand. Drawing on our analysis above, we can now say that our present of the present includes the present of the past and the present of the future. In other words, our memory of the past of Christ's mystery is not a mere "recall," but a remembering *action*, which is the present of the past. Similarly, our expectation of the Second Coming is an *action* that is the present of the future. By our present holding in dialectical relationship both the past and the future, we can say that our celebration of the paschal mystery in liturgy is an event wholly and completely here and now. Liturgical time is the dialectic of our present with the past and future of Christ's mystery.[14]

Let us set aside this reflection for the moment, and attend to the second methodological consideration, narrative, since for Ricoeur narrative and time are inextricably related. In the reinterpretation of paschal mystery in the second part of the chapter, we revisit this dialectical notion of time with respect to liturgy.

---

[12]Ricoeur, *Time and Narrative*, vol. 1, 18.

[13]Ibid.

[14]In my *Liturgy as Living Faith,* I described the paschal mystery as a dialectic of soteriology and eschatology. This parallels in a textual domain what I have outlined in a temporal domain. Particularly the last chapter of that volume extends this dialectic. From our temporal viewpoint, we might also describe liturgical time as the dialectic between *chronos* and *kairos*, between past and future, between daily and weekly rhythms of liturgy, or between Ordinary Time and festal time.

I also wish to alert the reader that I am making a distinction between "Christ's mystery" and "paschal mystery," a distinction that becomes clear in the final remarks of the chapter.

Narrative and Liturgy

Narrative might be simply defined as any literary work that is "distinguished by two characteristics: the presence of a story and a storyteller."[15] At first glance, it would seem that liturgy hardly qualifies to fit the category "narrative," especially if "story" is taken to mean reciting the unfolding of an event (either fictional or real). It would appear that there is no single "story line" in the liturgical text[16] nor single storyteller. This needs further examination, and turning to Ricoeur's borrowing from Aristotle's theory of mimesis and emplotment helps uncover liturgy as a kind of narrative activity.

Mimesis is the imitation of action, and emplotment is the organization of action in a narrative: "Imitating or representing is a mimetic activity inasmuch as it produces something, namely, the organization of events by emplotment."[17] The author of the mimetic activity is the narrator of the story.[18] Setting aside the question of whether the story is true or not, what we have for narrative—in its simplest description—is someone (the author of the mimesis as storyteller) organizing the events of the action into a whole.

Ricoeur refers to a threefold mimesis, which he distinguishes typographically by means of subscripts. $Mimesis_1$ is a "prefiguring" that implies the author of the narrative already has some understanding of the events of the narrative action. In $mimesis_2$ the author "configures" the various events of the action into a narrative. $Mimesis_3$ is a "reader" activity in which the reader (or hearer of the story) fills in from his or her own life experience "holes" in the story[19] and by so doing engages his or her own life experiences. Simply put, in mimesis we have an action consisting of events (or episodes), an organizing (or emplotment) of the action, and a receptivity of the action in a

---

[15] Robert Scholes and Robert Kellogg, *The Nature of Narrative* (London: Oxford; New York: Oxford Univ. Press, 1966) 4; Ricoeur follows Scholes and Kellogg on this. In this technical context "story" does not necessarily mean fiction but a "telling."

[16]"Text" here is taken in the broad extension of meaning both a written text (as, for example, that contained in a service or ritual book) and celebration. For further reading, see my *Liturgy as Language of Faith: A Liturgical Methodology in the Mode of Paul Ricoeur's Textual Hermeneutics* (Lanham, N.Y., London: Univ. Press of America, 1988), especially pp. 25–33 and 61–69; also, my *Liturgy and Hermeneutics*, 14–20.

[17]Ricoeur, *Time and Narrative*, vol.1, 34. On p. 45 Ricoeur notes that "mimesis" is not a copy, but a *creative* imitation.

[18]Ibid., 36.

[19]Ibid., 77.

new context by a reader. Ricoeur maintains, moreover, that the configuring activity of mimesis$_2$ is a *mediating* activity between the two other sides of the narrative.[20] Mimesis$_2$ is integrative in that it mediates between the individual events and the story as a whole and it brings together disparate factors (for example, agents, goals, interactions).[21] A third way in which mimesis$_2$ is integrating is, perhaps, the most important for our purposes and deals with the temporal dimensions of the narrative.

Mimesis$_2$, in its configuring activity, has two temporal dimensions, one chronological and the other not. The chronological dimension involves the various events of the story itself. The second temporal dimension is a configuring one in which the events are grasped as a whole story. In other words, a story is more than a succession of chronological events; it is the configuring of those events so that the reader "follows" the story to its ending.

This threefold mimesis does not emerge chronologically in our human reckoning of time. Nor do mimesis$_1$, mimesis$_2$, and mimesis$_3$ stand as isolated moments but rather function in dialectical relationships with each other. This means that the mediating, configuring task of mimesis$_2$ always stands in creative tension with both mimesis$_1$ and mimesis$_3$. And so the refiguring proper to mimesis$_3$ is never really severed from the prefigured action-events of mimesis$_1$. The configuring of the events into a plot is never severed from the action the plot imitates, nor is it ever severed from the receptivity of the action in the lives of the readers. The dialectic enables emplotment to mediate action and receptivity.

With respect to liturgy, let us propose that the prefigured actions being imitated (mimesis) are none other than the events of Jesus' life, passion, death, resurrection, ascension, sending of the Spirit, and promised Second Coming that have been configured into a liturgical text (emplotment). In terms of an actual liturgical celebration, mimesis$_1$ could be taken as our (the worshiping community's) initial grasp (prefiguring) of the action imitated by liturgy (our own grasp of Christ's mystery through our heretofore Christian living), mimesis$_2$ would be our configuring of those events in the actual liturgical celebration, and mimesis$_3$ would be our "receiving" the events by a refiguring of our lives in greater conformity to Christ's mystery.

[20]Ibid., 53.
[21]Ibid., 65–66.

This narrative approach directly addresses the recurring challenge of the relationship of liturgy and life. As Ricoeur remarks, "narrative has its full meaning when it is restored to the time of action and of suffering in mimesis₃."[22] Liturgy, then, from the purview of narrative theory, has its fullest meaning only when the emplotment of action that liturgy celebrates actually refigures the lives of those who celebrate. In such a way is Christ's mystery *our* mystery.

2. A POST-CRITICAL METHODOLOGICAL REINTERPRETATION OF PASCHAL MYSTERY

Our remarks on time enable us to account for both the past and future dimensions of Christ's mystery as mediated by the present. Our remarks on narrativity enable us to account for Christ's mystery and our living of it as mediated by the liturgical celebration. Let us flesh out how these two reflections point to a reinterpretation of paschal mystery.

First, our remarks suggest that both the historical and eschatological dimensions of Christ's mystery are in dialectical relationship with our present experience. With a slightly different twist to "realized" and "future" eschatology, our dialectical approach puts forward the argument that Christ's Second Coming is already as much present to us as is Christ's life, passion, death, resurrection, and sending of the Spirit. This, because we *mediate* in the present both the past and the future. Our *expectation* of Christ's Second Coming *already* figures in our experience of Christ's mystery. In a word, Christ's mystery is a *whole*, and we already enjoy the "ending."

Second, following the first point, to the *anamnesis* of liturgy we must add *expectation* if we are to integrate the *whole* mystery of Christ. Or, to put it a better way, since the present of the future is also in the present of our present, we might say that *anamnesis* is both a remembering "back" to actual historical events and a remembering "forward" to that which is yet to take place.[23] Others have asserted

---

[22] Ricoeur, *Time and Narrative*, vol. 1, 70; "suffering" here means "acted upon."

[23] There is no consistency in the various service books about the inclusion of the Second Coming or not in the *anamnesis* of our Eucharistic Prayers or Great Thanksgivings. For example, in the present Roman Missal, only Eucharistic Prayers 3 and 4, the Eucharistic Prayer of Reconciliation 1, and the Eucharistic Prayer for Masses for Various Needs and Occasions include the Second Coming in the *anamnesis*. In *The Book of Common Prayer*, Eucharistic Prayers C and D of Rite 2 mention the Second Coming, as does the Great Thanksgiving

that the Second Coming is part of the *anamnesis*;[24] our post-critical methodology enables us to show a *sine qua non* dialectical relationship between the past and the future of Christ's mystery such that mention of the Second Coming *must be included* in every *anamnesis*.

Third, we are not passive "receivers" of the grace of redemption, but *actively participate* in its unfolding. This suggests an initial grasp of Christ's mystery (cf. *SC* 9, where the council fathers mention a call "to faith and to conversion"); essential for faith and conversion is sacred Scripture (especially the Gospels) and the Church's preaching activity. The configuring activity (mimesis$_2$) of liturgy presupposes a "full, conscious, and active" participation (see *SC* 14) that is more than singing and postures at liturgy itself; it means we engage ourselves in an ongoing immersion in many ways of grasping Christ's mystery (prefiguring mimesis$_1$; for example, praying, *lectio divina*, preaching). Accordingly, in very concrete ways does everything we do redound to and flow from liturgy (see *SC* 10). Moreover, the configuring activity of the liturgical celebration (mimesis$_2$) offers new possibilities for our Christian living (mimesis$_3$), which, in turn, becomes the new prefiguration of Christ's mystery. There is a kind of circularity here, yes, but each time we pass through the three moments of mimesis there is always a gain in our depth-immersion in Christ's mystery. His mystery is never exhausted but always promises greater richness for living.

Finally, our remarks suggest that the celebration of liturgy does more than change us or "affect" our lives (although it does do that). The liturgical event itself is a mediating configuring of the whole of Christ's mystery (on its one side) and our refiguring of it in our daily living (on its other side). This rescues liturgy from a ritual that simply unfolds in chronological time (although it does do that) and opens it up to a point in time that mediates Christ's mystery and our lived Christian experience. As such, a reinterpretation of paschal mystery

---

for "An Order for Celebrating the Holy Eucharist"; Rite 1 omits mention of the Second Coming. *The United Methodist Hymnal* includes the Second Coming in Word and Table Services 1 and 2, and the *Lutheran Book of Worship* includes the Second Coming in the anamnesis of the Holy Communion service.

[24]For example, David Power draws explicit attention to the inclusion of the Second Coming in the *anamnesis*; see David N. Power, O.M.I., "The Anamnesis: Remembering, We Offer," *New Eucharistic Prayers: An Ecumenical Study of Their Development and Structure,* ed. Frank C. Senn (New York and Mahwah: Paulist Press, 1987) 146–68.

cannot simply describe it as Christ's mystery alone but must include in the very notion of paschal mystery *our own living of it*. Paschal mystery in its very meaning has to do with us as well as with Jesus Christ. Consequently, it is less accurate to speak of the relationship of liturgy *and* life and more accurate to say that liturgy *is* life (or Christian living). The paschal mystery has an extension beyond Christ's mystery that includes our own selves and our living of his mystery.

We finally come to a startling and new reinterpretation of the paschal mystery: it is not coextensive simply with Christ's mystery but the very meaning of paschal mystery includes our own engagement in it. Thus, the paschal mystery is the life, passion, death, resurrection, ascension, sending of the Spirit, and Second Coming of Jesus the Christ *and our refiguring of those events in our daily living*. The qualifying distinction between Christ's mystery and the paschal mystery is *our Christian living*.

Wherefore, whose mystery? Both Christ's and ours, when we live that into which we have been plunged by the waters of baptism. This surely gives fresh, concrete meaning to St. Paul's cry, "I have been crucified with Christ; and it is no longer I who live, but it is Christ who lives in me" (Gal 2:19b-20a; *NRSV*).

Alphabetical Index of Primary Contributors

Chronological Index of Primary Contributions

Index of Selected Themes

CPSIA information can be obtained at www.ICGtesting.com
Printed in the USA
BVOW04s1547190913

331493BV00003B/628/P

9 780814 661789